HARDPRESS.NET

ISBN: 9781314784299

Published by:
HardPress Publishing
8345 NW 66TH ST #2561
MIAMI FL 33166-2626

Email: info@hardpress.net
Web: http://www.hardpress.net

JOZSEF KOVAGO was born in Hungary in 1913. A graduate of Budapest University, he also attended the Military Academy and served as an officer in the Hungarian Army. When the Germans occupied Hungary, he joined the resistance movement against the Nazis, became one of its leaders, and was subsequently arrested by the Gestapo in November. 1944. Elected Mayor of Budapest in 1945, he served in this post until 1947, when the Communist coup brought to an end the short-lived Hungarian experiment in democracy. Since his flight from Hungary after the Revolution, Mr. Kovago has participated in the meetings of the International Federation of the Cities of the World and was one of the chief witnesses before the United Nations Special Committee on the Problems of Hungary. Now a resident of Wilmington, Delaware, he is Vice-Chairman of the Assembly of Captive European Nations.

You Are All Alone

By JOZSEF KOVAGO

Frederick A. Praeger
Publishers
New York

BOOKS THAT MATTER

Published in the United States of America in 1959
by Frederick A. Praeger, Inc., Publishers
15 West 47th Street, New York 36, N.Y.

Library of Congress catalog card number: 59-15541
Printed in the United States of America

To my wife

Acknowledgments

It is most fitting that I should express my sincere thanks to Mr. A. Felix Du Pont Jr., and Mr. Pierre Du Pont III, whose magnanimous help through the Institute of Fiscal and Political Education made it possible for me to undertake the writing of this book. I would also like to acknowledge the understanding help given me by Mr. Harry G. Marquis, director of the Institute of Fiscal and Political Education.

I would like to express my thanks to the officers and staff members of the International Rescue Committee as well as to those of the Free Europe Committee and to all my many Hungarian and American friends who, with sympathy and affection, urged me on with my work. In this long list of friends, which space does not permit me to enumerate, I would like to mention two: Mr. Paul L. McConomy for his valuable advice in editing the English text and Dr. John Farago, an old friend of mine, on whose advice I relied continuously during the writing, translating, and editing of my book.

Last, but not least, I would like to express my thanks to the American community, where I found a new home and where the spirit of friendship and freedom from fear created the necessary atmosphere for a new life and for creative work.

September, 1959
Wilmington, Delaware

JOZSEF KOVAGO.

PART I · IN THE SHADOW OF DEATH

"Brightest in dungeons, Liberty! Thou art . . ."
—Byron

1 • THE HOUSE OF SECRETS OPENS UP

The sun streamed brilliantly through the conference room windows of the sprawling plant near Budapest. It was Wednesday, May 24, 1950. My engineer colleagues and I were seated at a long table, perspiring freely in spite of our short-sleeved shirts, for it was an exceptionally warm day. I was glad that I was wearing my thin summer suit.

Someone called the presiding Chief Engineer outside. We continued with our discussion. Soon the Chief Engineer returned and stopped at the door. "Kovago," he said, "would you please come out for a second, someone is looking for you."

I got up automatically. For a second I glanced at the face of the Chief Engineer. He seemed unusually pale. But I became conscious of this only by the time I had left the room and was in the corridor. Four men surrounded me, a fifth one closed the door and put his back to it. Three of the four began to circle around me. It looked as if they were crazy. The fourth one explained to me in low tones that they wanted to ask me a few questions. The whole thing appeared to be a silly, childish joke. All five, however, seemed excited and took the procedure very seriously. In a daze and automatically, I took a few steps forward. They continued circling around me. Then I stopped. "What's wrong with you? What the hell do you want? Why are you so excited?" I demanded querulously.

"Just keep quiet," one of them whispered in my ear.

"There's nothing to it," another whispered.

"It is just a brief interrogation. Don't make any commotion, please," the third one whispered. Meanwhile, they kept circling around me in such a manner that they pushed me gently forward with their shoulders. I had to move whether I liked it or not.

"You are the ones who create a commotion," I exclaimed in a loud voice and reached into my back pocket for my cigarette case. At that point a hand grabbed mine, and I felt the barrels of two pistols shoved against my ribs. A threatening voice whispered, "Don't try to put up a fight or we'll shoot you like a dog." At last I understood. I suddenly realized that these were members of the AVO, the dreaded secret police. I had feared this moment for years. A cold shiver raced along my spine, but I tried to put up a bold front.

"Do you mind if I smoke?" I asked my captors, for want of something better to say. My hand was freed, but the guns remained pressed against my ribs. The fifth man was still guarding the door to the conference room to make sure no one was coming out. The corridor was deserted. I was hoping that someone might come out of one of the drafting halls and see me. Perhaps I could give some sort of a signal. I decided to play for time. Reaching into my back pocket with a leisurely gesture, I pulled out my cigarette case. The suspicious glare of four pairs of eyes followed every move I made. With a cheerful expression I opened the case and offered them cigarettes after I had taken one myself.

"Won't you have one?" I asked. "There's no point in getting excited about all this. I understand the whole thing. You are here to take me to Number 60 Andrassy Avenue." I tried to keep my voice steady. Somehow I felt no fear; on the contrary, I thought the whole situation was rather funny. They did not take my cigarettes, but one of them replied in a friendlier tone: "Now you see . . . you're an intelligent man . . . our duty is to accompany you in."

But another one, with a devilish grin on his face, added, "It is just one of those short interrogations."

"Of course," I replied sarcastically while I searched for

matches. Then I remembered they were in the pocket of my jacket. "Wait a moment," I began and stopped again. "I have to go back for my jacket for I don't have a match."

"We'll give you some matches, but you can't go back for your jacket," a surly voice informed me.

Once again the circle tightened. They stood so close to me that I could hardly move my hands. "You don't really think that I am going to leave without my jacket?" I exclaimed, displaying anger for lack of a better plan. Their excitement was infectious. My face and my voice must have expressed this, for they started hushing me up immediately.

"Just stand still . . . everything is all right . . . no commotion, please . . . the comrade will go back for your jacket. . . ." In the meantime their eyes kept darting about nervously for fear someone would come into the corridor.

The man at the door spoke up in a gruff voice: "I'll get the jacket."

"You see, it's all right," the one who seemed to be in charge told me. "Just smoke and don't worry. We'll get your jacket for you. But no commotion, please." And once again they started shoving me forward.

"Well, let's go," I suggested and started walking. "It's you who create the commotion," I explained to the man in charge. "Why on earth are you so excited? Don't you see that I'm going?"

A sharp look by the chief was enough to stop the circling by the agents. Two of them moved to my sides and two advanced from behind. Each had a hand in his pocket, holding a gun. The one on my right whispered to me: "You know, of course, that we can shoot well from our pockets, too."

"I believe you," I answered hastily, and I did, for they looked like men with exactly that type of background.

In order to leave the building we had to go down a staircase and through a hall. I was hoping that we would encounter people there, maybe even someone who knew me, who would realize that I was being arrested. Unfortunately, my chances were slim. This plant was not my regular place of work, although I was an occasional visitor.

It seemed to be the regular practice of the AVO to arrest people away from their homes or their place of work so they could vanish without an immediate trace.

The man in charge started a conversation.

"What do they manufacture in this building?" he inquired.

"This is the experimental machine-tool plant," I replied. "Don't you want to look it over? There are many interesting things to see."

"Perhaps on some other occasion," he answered.

One of them added with a sarcastic smile on his face: "Maybe when we bring you back."

"Fine," I agreed. As we walked along the hall, two men who were strangers to me passed by. I kept staring at them, hoping they would understand the situation, but they hardly noticed us. When we arrived outside, a beautiful limousine awaited us. I had to get in the back with an AVO man sitting on each side of me. The man in charge was on my right. I reached for a cigarette again, only to be told by the man on the left not to put my cigarette case into my back pocket. When the car reached the gates of the plant, a sixth person was waiting for us. Every detail seemed to be prearranged, for the car could leave without any of the customary security procedures. The driver stepped on the gas, and we sped toward the center of Budapest.

Hundreds of thoughts crossed my mind. One in particular seemed to bother me more than the others: "What's going to happen to the milk?" I used to take home a liter of milk for my little daughter every day. Near our own plant there was a farm where one could buy very good milk. A full bottle was in my briefcase which I had left in the conference room. Strangely enough, this thought angered me more than anything else. I knew that milk was not available in the city. The poor child would have to do without it now. "The milk will go sour," I blurted out angrily.

The AVO men looked at each other with suspicious surprise. They immediately became more hostile and wondered what it meant. "What milk are you talking about?" the chief inquired.

"The bottle which I take home to my little daughter every day," I explained.

He smiled and answered that some way or another the milk would find its way to my home. We drove on in silence. Rays of sunshine were dancing in the streets of Budapest. I saw the passersby on Andrassy Avenue. Suddenly a thought occurred to me, painfully, like the stab of a dagger: "Maybe I'll never see it again."

Finally reaching its destination, the car entered a drive at the side entrance where so many good Hungarian patriots had disappeared, never to be seen again. I was taken up to a room and handed over to a new set of guards. They roughly ordered me to turn against the wall. I was slow in understanding. A strong kick by one of them and a push made clear to me what it was all about.

"You dirty Fascist dog," a guard yelled at me. Soon I was blindfolded and taken downstairs. I tried to count the steps for awhile, but we turned around and around and came to some other steps. I lost count. The air was cold and damp. We must have been in a basement. Dead silence everywhere. We stopped. I heard the guards whispering to someone. Finally, I was pushed in somewhere and felt a door pressed against my back.

"Take off the blindfold and your clothes!" a whispering voice commanded. I could see very little except that I was in the corner of a semidark basement, and that a heavy iron door was pushing me against the wall.

"Take off your things! Come on, let's go!" I heard an impatient voice order. I took my jacket off. A hand grabbed it from me. "Come on, faster!" I heard the voice again. The speaker was an enormous man who looked like a paid assassin. Somewhere from a nearby room I could hear the hushed tones of conversation. I had to remove all my clothes. I was trembling from the cold. The guard searched through every piece of clothing carefully and removed the contents of the pockets. Then he searched my body. He checked everywhere. It was a disgusting and humiliating experience. Then I was permitted to put my things on again. By that time, however, my shoes were without laces, and my pockets were completely empty. Without saying a word, two guards grabbed me and took me through the dark corridors of the basement. In one place water was seeping in a flood and I had to jump over it. In this corridor, guards were placed every ten yards wearing warm-up suits and rubber-soled shoes. They stepped from one cell door to another and, clicking open the tiny peepholes, checked them.

The door of a cell swung open, and I was pushed in. It was a tiny hole without the benefit of a window. All the light came from a single bulb. There were two wooden bunks about 12 inches apart. Nothing else. All the walls were dripping wet. The cement floor showed marks of water seepage. It certainly wasn't a health resort! For the time being, however, this was to be my home. It was a strange, silent place. Even the guards spoke in whispers as they scurried about in their rubber-soled shoes.

Suddenly I felt completely exhausted. My eyes closed automatically. This has always been my reaction to severe nervous strain. Lying down on the wooden bunk, I fell asleep in no time.

2 • I MEET THE RAT

I awoke suddenly. An AVO man was shaking me. I heard another one whisper: "Hey, we didn't bring you here to sleep. This isn't a nursing home." I stood up.

"Let's go," said the guard who had shaken me awake. In front of the door I had to stop and be blindfolded once again. It occurred to me that the last time I played such games was when I was a little boy. All this whispering and blindfolding had a childish quality to it. Grabbing my arm, the guard led me roughly along the corridor. In one place I stumbled. Then I stepped into some water. This must be the little stream I passed on the way here, I mused. They are taking me back to the same place they brought me from. We climbed stairs, around and around, and went through doors. Then I was told to stop. The pleasant summer air felt nice and warm. The blindfold was removed from my eyes. We stood in a corridor, and I saw stairs covered with thick red carpet. We started out without a word along corridors with padded doors. A door opened and I was led through another door guarded by two armed soldiers. I found myself in a large study overlooking the street. The room was filled with beautiful, heavy furniture. The only disturbing impression was that every piece of furniture, although of fine quality, was of a different period. The display included furniture of the Empire period, Louis XIV, and even some late Victorian pieces. It was obvious that they had been stolen by the AVO from wealthy private homes. Oriental rugs covered the floor. For all its appearance it could have been the study of some *nouveau riche* banker. The only clues to the character of the place were the pictures of Stalin, Beria and Rakosi. So this was the way the AVO headquarters looked from the inside!

From the top of a cabinet, the well-known statue of Stalin smiled benevolently at the visitor. Now I was the one at whom he smiled. Behind the enormous desk stood a small thin-faced man. He must have been around thirty-two years old, and had an evil look in his eyes. His pose was nonchalant, with one foot on a chair behind the desk. His hands were playing with a letter opener.

"How do you do," I greeted him politely.

"So we got Mr. Kovago at last," he replied sociably, overemphasizing the "Mr." His dark glittering eyes were peering into mine. We started the sort of duel we used to play at as children: "Let's see which one can outstare the other without blinking an eye." It lasted for quite a while. I was becoming afraid that I couldn't keep from blinking any longer when one of his eyes blinked slightly. Then he sat down. Gazing at the daggerlike letter opener, he started to speak in a monotonous tone.

"Many people come to this building thinking that they are strong. Many have tried to resist confession. We break them down. Even your famous Cardinal, Joseph Mindszenty, broke down. Laszlo Rajk, the imperialist agent, also toed the mark and confessed. Here everyone has to confess. We have inherited thirty years of experience from the Soviet Union. We can make everyone talk. We have the methods and the know-how."

I wasn't paying attention to his words so much as I was trying to get a clue to his personality. I remembered how as children we used to give names of animals to unknown persons. That's it—I'll call him "The Rat," I thought. That suits him best.

"Our methods are such," he continued, "that they make a man want to speak up. They make a whimpering baby out of even the strongest man."

I was listening with an expression of rapt attention on my face. I wondered if he would get drunk on his own oratory and continue endlessly. This often happens to novice speakers. Next to me, a big comfortable easy chair stood invitingly. After a few moments' hesitation, I sat down in it quietly. The Rat looked up. His face became contorted.

"You dirty Fascist, you bum! Stand against the wall. Put your hands up," he shouted. Like a summer shower I heard the flood of abuse and insults. I stood against the wall with my hands raised. He pressed me close to it. It was an unpleasant, humiliating position. It reminded me of some punishment as a child. He left me thus. Soon I felt sweat dripping from my forehead. Each time one of my arms moved he started shouting. Then he left the room and summoned the guard to replace him. This man stood behind me prodding me with shouts and kicks. After a long, long time the Rat came back and dismissed the guard.

"Turn around," he ordered me in a cold voice. "Step forward, right in front of me. You, too, will confess." Then he started playing with the articles which had been removed from my pockets. He took pictures out of my wallet. They were photos of my wife, my daughter, and my mother.

"Do you love your wife very much?" he inquired somewhat casually.

"Yes," I replied calmly.

"Then be careful that no harm should befall her. How old is your daughter?"

"Two-and-a-half years old."

"It's hard to part from her, isn't it? Especially forever," he continued sarcastically. He lit a cigarette. "Do you like to smoke?" he inquired.

"Yes."

"How many do you smoke a day?"

"About forty to fifty."

"This is a habit you'll give up," he smiled sarcastically. "You won't get a single cigarette here until you make a confession." Once again I saw his hands playing with the objects on the desk. I saw objects there which must have been brought from my apartment; in fact, some of the items were from our country home. He played with them without saying a word. Then he picked up a book which looked familiar. Of course, I realized, that is my horoscope. Three years earlier my friends had compiled it for me. It consisted of sixty typed pages. I regarded most of it as foolishness. It had been put away in one of the wardrobes, and now I saw it in his hands.

Turning the pages, he started reading in an even, monotonous tone: "A career which will skyrocket . . . his death will not be devoid of violence . . . beware of water. . . ." He stared at me silently, expecting a reaction.

"So probably we will hang you, or maybe it will be an accidental drowning," he added with sarcasm. Meanwhile he must have pressed a bell, for suddenly a guard showed up behind me.

"Take him away, Comrade," the Rat commanded. Once again he stood up, putting his foot on a chair. He stared at me from behind the desk with a cold smile.

The guard grabbed me and ordered in a whisper, "Pressure." I learned this expression as part of the lingo. It meant that I was supposed to get started fast. This guard handed me over to another one. Again we went through the luxurious corridor, then I was blindfolded and led farther on. We descended many flights of stairs. The cool air and the dampness revealed that we were in the basement again. I was taken back to my cell.

A few minutes later the door opened. A gigantic guard stood in front of me. Without uttering a word he pointed at the floor. It was exactly as a man shoves the food to a no-good dog. A metal plate stood there, filled with what passed for food. Next to it there was a slice of bread. I ate. It tasted good; in fact, I could have eaten more of it. Then I decided to take a nap and lay down on the wooden bunk.

In a few seconds the door opened, and the giant guard stepped in. "If you ever dare to lie down again before the retirement hour, I'll break every bone in your body, you filthy Fascist," I heard him whispering in a hoarse voice. A few hours passed by, and then the little peephole in the door opened.

"Bedtime," a red-haired guard whispered. I lay down and formed a pillow with my hands, for the wooden plank was very hard.

Immediately the guard stepped in and bawled me out. I was not to dare to put my hands under my head or under my body. They always had to be visible. I was forbidden to turn against the wall while sleeping. I fell asleep again. It seemed as though I had hardly slept when I was awakened with a shake. Soon I found myself marching sleepily with the guard. Up we went to the Rat's office. He stood behind the desk again, this time assuming a Napoleonic pose. Again he preached a sermon to me about how everybody here has to confess all sins committed against the regime, or else. . . . I was listening with feigned courtesy and sympathy. Finally he stopped and informed me that my interrogation was to start. I could sit down.

"Look here, Kovago," he said in a confidential tone, "we can start our work now. Everything depends on how sincere you are and how you adjust to the State Security Authority."

"Pardon me, but I can't quite understand what you mean by adjusting to the State Security Authority," I said in a polite tone.

He looked at me for a while before he spoke. "Look, Kovago, don't try to fool with me, or you will feel the ruthless fist of the Proletarian Dictatorship. We know all about you."

In a monotonous tone he began a catalogue of personal items: "You are a mechanical engineer; thirty-seven years old; before and during the war you were a professional officer; twice during the war you fought the Soviet Union; you were decorated at the front; during the last years of the war you served in the Army Engineering Corps as a major; in 1944 you were one of the chief organizers of the Anti-Nazi Resistance Movement; you were captured and almost hanged, but your friends freed you; you were a close associate of the head of the Smallholders Party, Endre Bajcsy-Zsilinszky, who was executed by the Nazis; you were a member of the Smallholders Party, and in 1945 your party put you in the position of deputy-mayor; then they appointed you Mayor of Budapest."

"Pardon my interruption," I said, "they did not appoint me. I was elected for five years as the Mayor of Budapest."

"Against the wall," he yelled threateningly, "raise your hands and squat." I had to stay in this position until I began to tremble. Then he permitted me to sit down in the chair. "Every time you interrupt that is what will happen to you," he explained.

"Pardon my remark, but this way it's impossible to make a frank confession," I said with indignation.

"What do you mean, it's impossible to make a frank confession?" he inquired in an unfriendly voice but with obvious curiosity.

"Well, you see," I explained deliberately, "I thought it my duty to point out factual errors when they occurred."

This made the Rat smile. It certainly did not improve his appearance. His evil features became more pronounced.

"Look, Kovago, you're trying to be smart again. What difference does it make whether you were appointed or elected. It's all a formality in any case."

"No, it's not, for the election of 1945 was a free one. I became mayor as a result of that."

"And the youngest mayor in Europe," he added sarcastically.

"Yes, I believe that I was the youngest head of a large capital like Budapest."

"And you're very proud of it, aren't you?"

"It was a great honor," I answered.

The Rat scrutinized me. "The time will come when you will regret it," he added, "but that's enough. Now keep your mouth shut." He continued with my biography.

"As mayor you worked against the Soviet Union and the Communists. You visited Vienna, Paris, London, and Berne. You tried to get loans for reconstruction from the West for Budapest. That's how you tried to sell the Hungarian People's Democracy down the river to the capitalist imperialists. Naturally, the anti-Communist press glorified you, claiming that you started the reconstruction of Budapest. We know, however, that it wasn't you who did it but the Communist Party. You and your like would much rather have sabotaged the effort. As a patron of the churches you naturally tried to build churches and vestries."

Suddenly, like a magician, he pulled out a photograph. "Here you can see Mayor Kovago with Cardinal Mindszenty, of currency smuggling fame, as they consecrated the chapel of Rokus Hospital," he smirked.

I wasn't surprised by the picture, for that was how it happened. In fact, the newspapers at that time had reported it in detail. However, the way the Rat was holding the photograph, it almost looked as if he had discovered some sinister secret.

"Then during your mayorality you were constantly with imperialist agents. Look at all the pictures—with the British Minister and his deputy, with the American Minister, with the head of the United States Military Mission, with the head of the British Military Mission, with military attachés, journalists, all of them infamous imperialist agents. Naturally they are all friends of Kovago. Then we have the friendships with the conspirators." He started to enumerate those members of my party with whom I was on friendly terms. Most of them had been convicted in the course of the so-called conspiracy trials. The Rat emphasized my friendship with the former Minister of Reconstruction.

"We have plenty against you, Kovago. Think it over. You might as well get ready to confess all your subversive activities. We know everything, and you know your fate." With this he picked up the horoscope once again and started reading, "A career which will skyrocket . . . his death will not be devoid of violence . . . beware of water." I saw his red eyes piercing through my expression. His hand rested on the bell. A guard entered and took me away.

I was exhausted. It must have been near dawn. The guard did not bother to blindfold me. He led me through ghostly, silent corridors. There was an armed guard at every turn. Then the door to the cellar swung open, and we started down the spiral staircase. We passed the guards in warm-up clothes who kept peering first into one cell and then into another. My guard whispered something to another one working near my cell. I was handed over, and as we went into the cell I was informed that I was not permitted to sleep. I could sit down on the edge of my bunk, but I wasn't to dare to close my eyes.

The instant I sat down my eyes closed. A few seconds later the face of the guard appeared at the door. In quiet whispers, abuses and swearing were hurled at me. This was kept up all through the next day. Every so often my head nodded or my eyes closed for a moment. Without delay the guard appeared. Once in a while he came in unexpectedly and poured cold water on me. I was chilled to the marrow. I trembled from exhaustion. I saw different faces appearing at the cell door, some with brown hair, others reddish or blonde.

"Pull yourself together," a red-faced one came and told me in a whisper, "if they see you can't take it they won't let you sleep for a week." Then he glanced through the door of the cell to make sure no one was around. He went out, and when he returned he brought me a piece of bread.

"Remember, I didn't give it to you," he warned me. "If by any chance another guard asks where you got it, tell him you saved it from your regular ration."

Apparently there are people with hearts even in this silent crypt, I comforted myself. I kept staring at the walls of the cell. Dampness and water drew grotesque figures on them. Suddenly these lines seemed to come alive. Look there, that's my wife, she wants me to be strong and—wait, that's my little daughter playing with her dog. I can even hear her laughter. Then new images came crowding into my memory, all showing on the walls of the cell like movies on a screen. All this was somewhat terrifying. I really felt as if I was in a crypt, being buried alive. The sinister guards with their whispering, the silent cellar with the haunting shadows of past crimes filled me with terror. "Here one wants to speak up." I remembered the words of the Rat. That's it. Apparently nerves give out very fast, but I must hold on. The real battle will start now. Before I realized it the day was over, and a gruff voice informed me it was bedtime. I lay down, but had slept only a few hours when I was shaken awake once more and taken upstairs. Once again I was face to face with the Rat. I could see he was better rested than I.

"Well, Kovago, I must say you look somewhat worn out," he commented. "Why don't you get some sleep? This way you won't be able to hold your own in the duel. Your wits won't be much help to you, Kovago. What's the use of polishing your keen intelligence? You must be the loser. Try to get some sleep."

"Yes indeed, how right Aristotle was—eight hours work, eight hours sleep, eight hours amusement," I interrupted.

"In this place one only gets one of those eight-hour programs," I heard myself saying.

"Which one?" the Rat inquired.

"The amusement," I answered, and tried to assume a composed look and a friendly smile. The Rat smiled too. I knew now that he liked it when I joked.

"Now sit down, please. I don't want to see you tire yourself. But then we have other means: standing erect for days, no food whatsoever, then the beatings. Some of our comrades are real experts in this art."

I felt my stomach turn over with fear and disgust but did not show any emotion.

The Rat changed his tone and started to talk to me in a

friendly voice. He seemed interested in the Resistance Movement. It was obvious that he knew the subject well, but was anxious to get some supplementary information from me. This was one thing I was glad to do without hesitation. Most of the persons in that movement were by now either in the graveyard or had escaped from Hungary and were living in the free world. The Rat seemed to have exact information as to how we had organized an anti-Nazi Resistance Movement in the army back in 1944. Our aim was to get Hungary out of the Nazi alliance and to go over to the Allies' side. We also hoped to save Budapest from destruction by preventing the city from becoming a battlefield. On November 23, 1944, however, the Nazis arrested the Resistance leaders. In a few weeks time a court martial had condemned to death Endre Bajcsy-Zsilinszky, the political leader of the movement, as well as the three military leaders, General Janos Kiss, Colonel Jeno Nagy and Colonel Vilmos Tartsay. A few others were sentenced to life.

"Tell me something, Kovago, the Resistance Movement was anti-Communist, wasn't it?" the Rat asked me.

"The Resistance Movement was anti-Nazi," I replied. "In fact, the Communist Party promised to participate in it."

This was followed by a lecture. The Rat explained to me in great detail that the real resistance to Nazism was by the Communist Party, and that middle-of-the-road parties and the soldiers' parties were just playing games. This was diametrically opposed to the truth, but I didn't bother to argue.

He summoned a secretary and dictated a memorandum to her. It included a "confession" by me to the effect that I was a member of the Resistance Movement which seemingly was anti-Nazi but in reality was an organization formed to spearhead the fight against Communism. Every second sentence was Communist propaganda. It claimed that the leaders of the Resistance Movement "maintained connections with agents of Western imperialism, connections which Kovago continued to develop after the war."

By the time the "confession" was finished, it must have been near dawn again. I was half dead from exhaustion. The Rat pushed the papers in front of me and asked me to sign them. I refused.

"All right, you'll sign them tomorrow," he informed me angrily. "Up against the wall, you swine!" I heard the shower of abuse again. When he stopped, a wonderful feeling of fatigue came over me, and I fell asleep standing up. Half asleep, I could still hear his monotonous, sinister voice reading, "A career which will skyrocket . . . his death will not be devoid of violence . . . beware of water." I awoke in the arms of a guard who was carrying me down to the cell. By then night and day had merged into one.

The Rat kept bringing me back to his office. It was obvious that he was trying to break down my morale, and put the fragments of my past life into a jigsaw puzzle which would prove that all I had ever done was in preparation to serve Western imperialists, to start secret conspiracies in order to overthrow the People's Democracy. Interrogation followed interrogation, and the only comical part of all this effort was that he insisted on tracing back the beginning of my sinister scheming and planning to a date so early that no one in Hungary could have dreamed that there could ever be a People's Democracy. Back in those years, about 1944, probably not even Stalin saw this clearly.

3 • DOWN AND ALMOST OUT

The only break in the routine of my constant interrogation was that, once in a while, I was put into a small room and ordered to write my biography.

Unfortunately, the Rat rejected every new edition of my effort, saying, "It's not detailed enough." Thus I recorded my whole life about eight times, over and over again. Needless to say, constant fatigue, as well as loss of control over my nerves, made certain lapses inevitable. There was always a name, a date, or an event which may have been different from those in the previous editions. These errors supplied the Rat with excellent ammunition. I was more and more handicapped in the duel. As each day passed, I was more worn out and exhausted. He was rested and worked with the assistance of a full staff.

It was about a week before the Rat started to hint what they were aiming at. Apparently they were getting ready for a major show trial. Their plan seemed to be to prove that our whole army was honeycombed with traitorous pro-Western elements, and that these persons were almost without exception identical with the members of the former anti-Nazi Resistance Movement. They wanted to expose Resistance members as constantly active in espionage and sabotage, and preparing for a major armed insurrection against the regime. The regime had already arrested seven generals. I was needed as the political figurehead for this trial. I understood more and more clearly what the charges were that I should get ready to defend myself against. There was one good reason why this was most essential. I would loathe to become a defendant in the same group as these Communist generals. If they should convict me with them, it would destroy my reputation as an honorable human being and an honest politician.

Meanwhile, physical complications arose. Perhaps as a result of my nerves or the dirty rags in the cell, large and painful infections appeared all over my skin. My body was swelling in many places. Soon the walls of the cell came alive. I had visions. I saw my daughter coming. That's it. That's her little haircut. There's her stubby little nose . . . . And over there I saw my wife. Look, my mother is coming and she keeps staring at me with tears pouring from her eyes.

"Why are you looking at the wall, you dirty Fascist?" a voice whispered to me. When I gave no answer, the guard entered the cell and ordered me to keep my eyes on one particular spot. I was not supposed to look around.

So it was day after day. My nerves came close to the breaking point, and I started to understand the psychology of Communist mock trials. A person in such a condition will admit virtually anything they want him to. He becomes eager to talk. He is ready to speak in detail about things in his life he was not even conscious of before. He is ready to make accusations against his friends and acquaintances, thus supplying the material with which the AVO spins its spider web. After a certain amount of juggling, the secret police can use these fragments of factual information, distorting them and setting up a charge. That's how an innocent social discussion with a British Embassy consul can become a charge of espionage, or a conference with two men at the plant a conspiracy for major sabotage, and so forth.

After the procedure is completed, the unfortunate victim has no more resistance left to argue. He is ready to sign almost anything. This was the method they used in my interrogation. The Rat made a point of rereading the same part of my horoscope in an eerie tone. Once in a while he added a few remarks.

"Look, Kovago, you know anyway that you will be hanged. Why don't you make a clear slate, and I'll see to it that you get better food and more of it, too. We'll also give you an extra blanket. Perhaps you'll get some clean clothes. In any case, those boils on your neck and your body are no good. That means a lot of unnecessary suffering, Kovago. Think it over and confess."

"But, sir, I'm ready to confess," I said haltingly. "I told you that as Mayor of Budapest I was anxious to build a close liaison between the capital and the West. I wanted to get a loan from the Western nations, and I am a fanatical believer in Western ideologies. I believe in Western democracy. Why don't you convict me for those things?"

"Stop that gibbering," he barked. "What we want to know are the details of the military conspiracy which you were preparing."

"As far as the Adorjan-Kakukk[1] organization is concerned—"

"Leave that conspiracy alone!" he interrupted. "That's only of minor importance. What we want you to confess is how you conspired with the Chief of Staff, General Solyom[2], and the other traitorous generals. We want to know everything about the military conspiracy you were preparing, and all your other crimes as well."

And so it went. One day, I suddenly remembered that the day after I resigned as mayor, the roof of the most important church in Budapest, the Bazilika, caught fire. "This could be a good hunch," I assured myself. "It's impossible not to make a confession in this place. Why don't I try to take some initiative in directing the line this interrogation is taking?"

[1] This was a conspiracy plan of former Smallholders Party politicians. For two years they talked about ways and means of overthrowing Communism. The Communist secret police discovered these men and they were arrested.

[2] Laszlo Solyom was a career officer in the Hungarian Army prior to World War II. After the war he became police chief of Budapest and soon joined the Communist Party. Returning to the army, he rose to become a four-star general. As a Communist army general, he was arrested by the secret police on a charge of conspiring against the regime with pro-Tito tendencies.

Next time they took me up to the Rat I started out by saying, "Please, sir, there is something of importance which I just remembered. It's a crime I forgot to confess up to now."

"Well, at last!" he reacted with a smile of satisfaction.

"Well, sir, I wanted to put the Bazilika on fire in the summer of 1947."

"So that's it. What was your motive?"

"I felt that it would create a sensation, and in a way would be the end of the Communist system. You took over political control, by and large, in the summer of 1947, Under these circumstances, to set the most important church on fire would have been a major achievement."

"But you failed, didn't you?" he asked sarcastically. "You see, we, the secret security organization, are present everywhere. We put out the fire in time."

"Yes, sir, but even so there was a fire there," I answered.

The Rat seemed to like this very much. Then I gave details, plenty of them. How it was, and why. Afterwards I was sent back to my cell. That day the Rat even forgot his usual ritual of ending the interrogation by reading my horoscope. They let me sleep. It was wonderful. If one is as exhausted as I was, even sleeping on a prison bunk is heavenly. The boils on my neck, my waist, and my back were painful. New ones had started on my arms, too. Even so I slept like a log. The next day they shook me awake and led me up to the Rat again.

"Stand up against the wall, you dirty Fascist." This was the introduction to the interrogation. "Put your hands up." I was left there for two hours. The Rat realized that the fire in the church was a stupid hoax. Then he got down to business. "Look, Kovago, you have been taking it pretty well up to now, but enough is enough. Tell me, do you love your wife very much?"

"I told you before that I did," I said, beginning to worry.

"All right, take him away." They led me back to the cell. I was unable to sleep the whole night. A woman was crying in the neighboring cell. For the first few hours I listened, full of anxiety. Had those gangsters brought in my wife, too, and was she the one they were torturing in the neighboring cell? I strained to hear with all my nerves on edge. Everything in me was taut, ready to break. My forehead was covered with sweat. I made up my mind to sign the confession, which claimed that I was the political leader of the military conspiracy by General Solyom and his assistants. I would wait just a little while, then I would bang upon my cell door and demand that they lead me up to the Rat to sign the confession. I started for the door when the woman's screaming became loud again. This time I could hear a few words of utter despair and pain. That was the moment when I realized that it was not my wife. I became incensed with fury against the Rat. What a dirty trick! I sat back on my bunk and waited. My nerves were ready to collapse.

The following night I was taken up to the Rat once again. When I entered his room, two spotlights were shining in my eyes and I heard the Rat's voice. "Well, Kovago, how did it feel to listen to your wife's screaming? It isn't too good, is it?"

"No, it's not," I said.

"Well, then, will you sign the confession or not?"

"Look, sir, I would like to sign the confession for it is terrible to listen to my wife's screaming, but I have still decided against it."

"You mean you won't sign it."

"No, I will not."

"Are you sure you won't sign it?"

"Yes, sir, I am. You can do anything to me. You can keep my wife here, you can drag my child here. Under this barbaric system I know you can do anything to us. Even then I will not sign the confession, because I am not willing to be put in the same category with General Solyom and the other Communists."

"You filthy scum! Take him away," the Rat snarled.

For the next few days I had new interrogators. They kept grilling me about espionage for Tito's Yugoslavia, for Great Britain, and for the United States. The basis for these alleged treasonous activities were my meetings and conferences with their diplomats. For three days, almost without rest, I was interrogated by different men. On the fourth day the beatings began.

They had a special technique for this. After the Rat handed me over to an AVO interrogator, I was handed over to a new one each day. I called these interrogators subtenants. It was with the fifth subtenant that we reached the point where they took me into a well-padded room. The subtenant, laughing sarcastically, left me there. Soon two thugs arrived, and started beating me all over with rubber truncheons. The only variation in the merciless beatings was the kicking I got in between. I tried to keep my courage up, and kept repeating to myself that I must withstand the beatings. If I broke down now, then the beatings would continue endlessly. That would be disastrous, for I would go to pieces. Even if, through God's mercy, I could survive all that, I would only get out of the prison a cripple. Therefore, I had to stand it. In about an hour they gave up. I fainted a few times. They poured cold water on me to bring me back to consciousness. Then I was carried back to my cell.

The physical pain was almost unbearable, but even worse was the complete annihilation of all the human dignity that I had built up throughout my life.

I ached all over, especially around my kidneys. Quite a few of my boils broke open. I needed a doctor badly. Even more than that I desired the caress of a cool, feminine hand, the lovely hand of my wife. All I had, however, were the walls of the cell—dirty white walls, prison guards who looked like murderers, and the shadow of death. There is no way out of this alive, I muttered bitterly. These gangsters will finish me off. With those thoughts I fell into a troubled sleep.

The next day I faced the Rat once again. "Well, Kovago, what's happened to you? You look very bad. You'll die if you go on like this."

"That may be so," I answered in a strange voice, for I had

difficulty in talking. My lips were swollen from the beatings. "However, my nerves feel fine. I was beaten and that is very restful under these circumstances." Through the swollen features of my face I forced a smile. I could see that the Rat was flabbergasted.

"You idiot! Do you know how you look?" he asked. His face was somber. What I saw was not an expression of sympathy, but rather a certain amount of desperation alternating with a feeling of loathing.

"Sit down," he said. "We will continue with the interrogation." But he seemed unable to start. He got up. "I can't do this. You smell terrible because of that blood and pus. Your clothing and your neck are covered with it. I can't bear looking at you. Why don't you put yourself into shape? Why don't you wash?"

"You know very well that I can't wash myself," I replied weakly. "I am not allowed to. You must realize that I, too, would like to get rid of this pus and dirt. In any case, sooner or later, I'm bound to get some serious infection and die."

"Wait a minute," he said and walked out of the room, leaving the door ajar. I saw him summon a guard and whisper something to him. The guard left and the Rat returned to me.

"Come with me," he said. He took me through the corridor and into a room which looked like a doctor's office. "Do you know anything about medicines?" he asked.

"I know something," I answered.

"Could you bandage yourself?"

"Yes, I could." I looked around—cotton, alcohol, gauze—all there. I took off my filthy jacket and the pieces of rag serving as a shirt. I washed and dressed my wounds. Suddenly I spotted a jar labeled "penicillin." That was what I needed. I spread it thickly all over, and bandaged myself.

"Put some more on," the Rat suggested. "Don't spare that goddamned gauze or medicine."

I glanced into the mirror. I certainly looked terrible. I must have aged twenty years. My features were drawn and distorted. My eyes shone feverishly, and there were black circles under them. My nose had become very long. I looked a sight. With my ten-day-old beard I looked like a murderer. But I could understand why even the Rat hated to look at me. There was only one chance and that was to die.

After the Rat had accompanied me to his room, he spoke again, "Look, Kovago, your life's in our hands."

"But not for long," I interrupted him, trying to force a smile on my face.

"What do you mean?" he inquired.

"Soon I'll die and go somewhere where, according to the priests, there is no AVO."

"Look, Kovago, don't get fresh or I'll put you against the wall again and make you squat or have you beaten. Stop this nonsense once and for all. You have a sense of humor, but enough is enough. You have to sign the confession."

"But you know that the confession is not true."

"Keep your mouth shut! It's all true, that's how it happened. Sign it!"

"I won't sign it!"

"Won't you? Look Kovago, we have dozens of ways to liquidate you. We can let you rot to pieces here, or we can take you out near the border and shoot you there. Or else we can release you from here, and then immediately and accidentally a car will run over you. One thing is sure—you won't get out of here alive. Will you please understand that, once and for all. On the other hand, if you sign this confession I guarantee that you'll stay alive."

"But, sir, my horoscope says that I'll be drowned. That is something that cannot be changed. I'm a fatalist."

"You fool! Take him away!" he shouted in anger. They led me down to the cell.

An hour later, it must have been about 3:00 A.M., they

brought me upstairs again. "Stand against the wall and raise your arms," one of my tormentors commanded.

People kept coming and going. I heard chairs being pushed around. There must have been many in the room. It seemed like a decisive moment, for when I heard the voice of the Rat it was shrill and full of tension. "Now you will make a full confession." He started to read the confession.

I interrupted him: "No, it's not true."

He continued.

"No, it's not true," I interrupted again.

Suddenly a new voice, unknown to me, interrupted. "Stop it, Comrade." This voice was firm and commanding. The Rat stopped immediately. Then I heard the new voice addressing me, "Look here, we have factual evidence that what the Comrade just read is true. You were the political leader of this conspiracy." He paused, letting the words sink in. "It was either you or Mrs. Endre Bajcsy-Zsilinszky." This name was pronounced slowly and distinctly. "Think it over. If it is not you, then it is the widow of Bajcsy-Zsilinszky. Think it over carefully."

My heart beating faster, I became enraged. These gangsters were trying to force me to send the widow of Bajcsy-Zsilinszky to prison. "It was neither she nor I!" I shouted. "There is a whole world between us and those generals. They are Communists and we are not and never will be."

"Enough!" the voice said, but now it wasn't as assured as before. Again I heard stirring in the room. It sounded as if people were leaving. I remained standing against the wall with my arms raised. Once in a while my legs gave in. "This is terrible, I can't take it any more. What's the good of it? I can't escape from here anyway. Come to think of it, what difference will it make whether I am hanged as the political leader of the Solyom conspiracy or on some other charge. All my friends, and tens of thousands of other Hungarian patriots, will know that not a word of this is true." My head was full of such thoughts. Tears rolled down my cheeks. My whole body ached. Something must have gone wrong with my nerves.

Suddenly I heard the voice of the Rat speaking to me almost in a friendly tone, "Look, Kovago, give it up. That happens to everybody. It has happened to you now too. You must sign this confession and trust us that perhaps we'll be merciful with your life."

My nerves snapped suddenly. In a rage, I turned around and jumped at his throat. The Rat made a fast retreat and pressed a bell behind the desk. I was panting. Two guards grabbed my arms and held me.

"Stop, you crazy fool! Don't lose your head!" one of them shouted.

All strength had left me by now. I did not even feel the kicks of the guards as they dragged me down to my cell. I knew that a terrible reprisal was in store for me, but I no longer cared. But the AVO is unpredictable, and a few hours later the door of the cell opened. Instead of the usual tormentors, a doctor entered. He glanced sharply at me. When I started to speak, he said: "Keep your mouth shut and take your jacket and shirt off." He left without saying another word and came back with a guard.

I was taken back to the same medical room as before. The doctor took me under his care. My wounds were dressed and bandaged. My pain had diminished by the time I returned to my cell. A wonderful, happy feeling came over me.

"Perhaps it is possible. Life is so beautiful. Perhaps I can survive all this—maybe even with honor. It would be wonderful. God give me just a little more strength and resistance."

I kept staring at the dirty walls. Again I seemed to see the features of my wife. Slender and delicate, but with immense inner strength, she had always detested weakness. Surely she would not wish me to give in—now or ever! The fight would have to go on! It seemed as if I heard her voice warning me: "Be strong, don't surrender!"

No, I couldn't surrender. I was down and they were counting, but it wasn't ten yet! I slowly and shakily got to my feet once again, to await the inevitable next, and possibly final, round.

4 • A NEW CELLAR AND A NEW STYLE

One day the guards came again. Without explanation they blindfolded and handcuffed me and took me away. Now they'll finish me off, I told myself, terror-stricken.

They placed me in a car, and, after a short trip, we arrived at our destination. It was another prison, but it offered quite a contrast to the deadly silence of the previous one. I heard the guards yelling and cursing. They all shouted and kicked at me. There is no doubt that this is the end, I thought. I was pushed into a cell. The cement floor was flooded with water almost up to my ankles. The cell was rank and moldy. I heard shouts and screams in the corridor, the moans of tortured people and yelling guards.

"You son of a bitch, you stinking, you damn," a sharp female voice screamed. "All you can do is swear. You don't like working."

I could hear the sound of a scuffle, then the woman's voice again. "All you know how to do is to beat and torture people. You hate honest work. You're worse than streetwalkers."

Her voice was suddenly muffled, as if someone had stuffed a rag into her mouth. I could hear the noise of the fight as they overpowered her. She emitted wailing sounds like a tortured cat. From another cell I could hear another woman crying hysterically. Then somebody started kicking at the door. It sounded like a gun booming.

A guard shouted, "Which one is it? For God's sake, why

do they bring women down here?" By this time the whole cellar was in an uproar. All the prisoners were kicking and beating the doors, creating pandemonium. Guards ran up and down the corridors, confused and excited. Suddenly a pistol shot rang out. The prisoners yelled louder. I trembled. I felt sick, and cold sweat broke out on my forehead. I was filled with terror. Without thinking, I started running up and down my cell, then I joined the others in the tumult. I pushed against the door and beat on it until my fists ached. I swore and kicked; it felt good to let off steam.

Slowly it became quieter. The corridors were soon silent, and I could hear the guards pacing up and down the hall. There were many of them by this time. Apparently all the prisoners were as worn out as I. My fear returned with the silence. I felt instinctively that they were coming for me—several of them. This must mean the end, at last it's all over, I thought, almost with relief. I could hear the key turn in the cell door. The door swung open, and a young man was pushed in. The door closed behind him. My new cellmate stood with his back to the door. With a grin he introduced himself.

"My name is Geza. This was fun, wasn't it?"

I would never have believed that the sight of another human being could bring me such joy. I was happy at the wonderful prospect of no longer being alone. The atmosphere of the cell changed. My former feeling of terror gave way to curiosity. We made friends and told each other our stories. He, too, was an engineer. He had been arrested because his wife had become intimate with an important Communist, and she was getting a divorce. They wanted to involve him in the "Solyom Affair" too. I tried to comfort him by telling him he would soon be released. Since he had been arrested after I was, he could tell me the latest news of the outside world.

I learned about the increase of international tension, and that the Hungarian question was scheduled to be discussed during the next session of the United Nations General Assembly.

We discussed and analyzed world events. We agreed that the coming years would be decisive ones. The United States would have to force a showdown with the U.S.S.R. before the latter broke the atomic monopoly. This left a two-year leeway at the most.

Geza told me that he was a member of the Communist Party. He felt that the ideologies of the Western world were impotent, and that the United States had no definite foreign policy. He believed that the Soviet Union had more imagination and initiative, and that the West consulted too long and acted too late. He felt that the next decade or two would see the Soviet Union getting in front, and that as the Soviet Union succeeded, its methods would become milder. It would adopt much from the West. For these reasons Geza felt that every intelligent person should become a Communist even though he knew that the theories of both Marx and Lenin were outdated.

We spent about two weeks together. I tried to convince Geza that his viewpoint was corrupt and immoral. He laughed at this.

"You are not even practical," I exclaimed, "for your reasoning is faulty. There's no question in my mind that the West will emerge as the winner from this great struggle. Look at the Marshall Plan, the Truman Doctrine, NATO, and the airlift to Berlin."

He only answered that he felt every intelligent Hungarian should join the Communist Party, and then the situation would be different. I was shocked at his materialistic and Machiavellian thinking.

"I hope your philosophy doesn't characterize the thinking of your generation," I told him.

"Actually, it doesn't," he answered with a cynical smile. "Most of them think differently, but believe me, this will become a Communist country, and everybody will join them."

"All right, Geza, I'll question you about that some other time, perhaps when we are both free again."

"That'll be a long time from now," he answered. "In fact they may even hang you in the meantime."

"Thanks," I said wryly.

"I'm only being objective," he retorted. "Don't be frightened, you do have a chance in spite of the fact that you're the type they hate the most. They can't afford the luxury of letting fanatic pro-Westerners survive. Try to understand and be practical."

There was something attractive about his personality. He was helpful and a good partner; in fact, his actions belied his cynical ideas. We discussed literature and art. He loved Shakespeare. He entertained both of us many times by reciting Hamlet's "To be, or not to be. . . ."

Two weeks passed, and they took him away as suddenly as they had brought him. I learned that he and all the other defendants in the Solyom case had been taken away. I was left alone. Each day I pasted a small pellet of bread on the wall to mark the passage of time. It seemed certain that I had succeeded in staying out of the "Solyom Affair."

After a short time, a new series of interrogations began. Again I had to face the Rat. He didn't refer to my outburst at the last meeting. He reverted to the political line I had originally suggested to him. He tried to get data for a charge that, as mayor of Budapest and a member of the Smallholders Party, I had tried to rebuild Budapest with Western capital. He wanted to show that I had tried to flood Hungary with Western capital and to tie the country culturally, and by every other possible means, to the West. I was willing to help him set up such charges. I even supplied material for additional accusations.

I requested that I be given the bound volumes of the *Budapest Gazette* for further research and study. Within three days my request was granted.

I read through my own speeches, and relived the past. It was strange to follow the sometimes naïve utterances of that well-meaning, earnest young man I used to be.

These were strange séances. The Rat sat at his desk, and, at a small table next to him, I buried my head in these articles. These sessions were at night, and from time to time, I could hear sounds of life from the street. Whatever I confessed was reassembled and distorted by the Rat. He translated my words into AVO lingo. Slowly, a new charge was built up.

Meanwhile, my health had deteriorated. Apparently, one of the beatings I had received had caused minor bleeding of the kidneys. I felt weak, and one morning when I tested my strength in the cell, I realized how worn out I was. I knew that under the circumstances strength was the most important thing for me. I felt degraded. One night a guard peered in. He didn't look as fierce as most of them. He entered the cell.

"Are you the one who used to be mayor? Too bad, because you're finished."

"I guess that's true. Every honest Hungarian must meet the same fate."

"My, my," he murmured, and left the cell. He looked around carefully and then returned. He seemed to be ill at ease, but began to talk. "Actually it's a great pity, many people liked you."

With that he left. I was excited and full of hope. Perhaps this guard would take a message to my wife—just a few words to the effect that I was alive. I was eager for him to come again.

In about half an hour he returned, opened the door quietly, and put in two pieces of bread. I gestured to him to come in. He entered.

"You are an honest Hungarian patriot," I told him. "So am I. Would you do me the kindness of notifying my wife that I am alive?"

He looked at me in horror. "I can't possibly do that! I

would end up by being locked up next to you. Don't ask me such a thing," he warned and left. I was alone again with my disappointment and two big chunks of bread. They made a magnificent feast. I mustered my courage to present my request to a second guard. It didn't work. My only success was that I had to stand for half a day as punishment. Apparently, ninety-five per cent of the guards were enthusiastic Communists, and the remaining five per cent were too frightened to do anything.

One evening the Rat summoned me, his face beaming. "Kovago, this is it. The iron fist of the Communist world is annihilating your Western friends," he informed me triumphantly. "The Americans are retreating and are taking a thorough beating. We are advancing victoriously. I won't tell you where. All I will tell you is that soon the Communists will control a whole continent, and this is only the first step."

I stared at the Rat as he enthusiastically explained his dreams of conquering the world. "You're all through, Kovago, do you understand? One gesture from the great Stalin will mean the end of England and of the United States. Yes, America too. We don't want a world war," he added, sobering up suddenly, "but if there is no other way, and the United States tries to stop us, we'll wipe them out! You see, Kovago, your speculation was mistaken. It would have been better to have believed the Communists."

"I understand you tried to start a secret correspondence from here," he continued, laughing at me sarcastically. "Don't waste your time. Our comrades are loyal." With this he dismissed me.

I wasn't interrogated again for quite a while, and I didn't see the Rat for weeks. My calendar of bread pellets on the wall showed that thirty-five days had passed so far. One day the guard discovered it, and I was badly beaten.

My kidneys were again acting up. I wasn't permitted to use

the toilet when I wanted to. Many of the guards took special pleasure in forbidding the use of the toilet when it was needed. The results were disastrous and humiliating.

I was haunted by fears that the Rat was telling the truth, and that the Communists had really scored a major victory somewhere. My nerves seemed to have given out completely. I had visions, and feelings of wild regret over things of the past, and mistakes I had made, came back to disturb me. It was like purgatory.

I began debates with myself and with God. What can one do in a cell, caged like an animal? Hunger is no longer the worst of it. I dreamed of sunshine and fresh air. I desired freedom like a trapped beast. I wanted to see someone, even the Rat.

Once a day, usually in the evening, a guard inquired if anyone wanted to see the doctor or talk to an official. I was a seasoned veteran by this time, and I knew that to ask for medical attention was a sure way of not getting it. I knew this well, but I tried this means of getting out of the cell. I even asked to be interrogated again. Probably that is a psychosis which occurs with every prisoner at certain stages in the process of psychological atomization. Other prisoners were probably living under the same animal-like conditions. I learned from the guard that some of them had been there for eight months.

The hygienic conditions of the cellar were horrible. Once every two weeks we were taken to have a bath. About twenty people shared the same water. The condition of the toilet was unbelievable. Filth, human dirt, and foul odors were everywhere. The tiny windows of the cells opened on the corridors. It was depressing and hopeless. Once in a while I asked myself: Will I go crazy in here? What will be the end of all this? The difference between day and night had disappeared. I was in a constant daze. More and more frequently I had hallucinations. Usually, I heard the Rat reading my horoscope, "A career which will skyrocket . . . his death will not be devoid of violence . . . beware of water."

I no longer dared to ask for drinking water. No. No. I won't drink it, it's probably poisoned, and I'll die. Or perhaps they'll hang me. Yes, they'll hang me for sure. That's what they told me. It's horrible.

By the end of the second month, I was beating the walls with my fists. Once in a while, I mustered all my strength and hurled myself against the steel door. I shouted and yelled at the top of my voice. They came in and poured cold water on me. I heard myself shouting, "Take me away. Take me anywhere. Just get me out of here. I can't stand it any longer."

5 · HIGH HOPES AND A LETDOWN

The next night I was awakened from a nightmarish dream with the order to get going. I was glad for any change. I wanted to see another human being, no matter who he was. The Rat stood behind his desk, apparently in a somber mood.

"You may leave, Comrade"—he said to the guard, and immediately began to attack me. "What's the idea of acting up? Why did you beat the walls? It doesn't help you. Await your fate with patience. What do you want?"

"I remembered," I began, "that as mayor I compiled a budget for the capital which had a defect—"

"Can't you forget all that baloney? You seem to be anxious to be convicted as a politician, as a follower of 'democracy,'" he emphasized. "You will be convicted as a spy, do you understand?" He paced up and down the room. There were dark rings under his eyes. The self-satisfied, smug look which he had worn before had disappeared. Obviously, he was concerned and worried.

I cannot remember word-for-word the substance of his harangue, but it was something like this: "It's hopeless for you to wait for Western help. You can't hope for a Western victory. There won't be any. We'll still find a way to defeat them."

The word "still" rang in my ears. My heart was filled with hope. It seemed that the earlier confidence of the Rat was shaken. He soon sent me back to my cell with the guard, but his last sentence gave me enough food for thought to last for days.

Later in the week, there was commotion and confusion in

the prison. Cell door after cell door banged open, and I could hear the curt order, "Get going!" It looked as if we were to be transferred to another place. I knew by then that there was no point in becoming frightened. When I had been brought down here, I had been sure it was my last journey. Nothing had happened. Every place had its own atmosphere. Soon my cell door opened.

"Get moving!" a guard barked. I was blindfolded and handcuffed. We went up the stairs, and then the blindfold was removed.

"Don't wave, give a signal or speak," the AVO man in civilian clothes whispered in my ear. I immediately recognized the voice. This man had escorted me before. We traveled through the city in a beautiful and luxurious limousine. I was told to hide my handcuffed wrists. Two men sat close to me. The streets were full of traffic.

Once in a while, when we stopped at a red light, I had a chance to look around. It was a beautiful fall day in the city. It was quite an Indian summer, I told myself with regret and longing. Seeing the city, however, gave me new strength. I was a part of that beautiful city also. The car drove close to my former apartment. Perhaps my wife and child will walk by, I thought longingly! They usually spent hours walking. The playground was full of children. My daughter wasn't there. The car drove on. At one intersection we had to wait for some time. I saw the supervisor of the streetcars whom I knew well by sight. For a second his eyes fell on me, but he glanced away quickly. He hadn't recognized me.

The car neared Conti Street. My terror returned, for the Conti Street prison was the traditional place for spies. Very few who go in ever come out alive. As the car entered the gates, I was immediately blindfolded. In the prison I was led downward to the cellar where I heard loud voices and swearing. I had the feeling of being in a hangman's place. There were savage guards and tiny cells. My heart beat loudly. I was given a small pail of pea soup, which I finished in no time. It was just enough to arouse my appetite. My stomach demanded more. No seconds in this place, I told myself. I might as well accept the situation. The door opened and a big dark guard, who looked like a former wrestler, spat into my cell.

"You Fascist conspirator," he shouted and continued with curses. "You are in bad shape, indeed. This way you won't last long enough to be hanged."

"Sure I will," I retorted. "The rope will be cheaper, for you won't need such a thick one."

He seemed to enjoy my joke, and told me to go out with my pail and get another helping of soup. There was another prisoner with his pail standing against the wall. This was most unusual, for the etiquette of my previous prisons prohibited prisoners from seeing each other. Our pails were filled again. In the meantime, the swearing and cursing continued. What an unusual place, and what a contrast! Anyway, the second pail of soup made me optimistic. Perhaps it wouldn't be as bad as I had first thought.

After I had returned to my cell, the door opened again. A tall, thin, and cross-eyed guard entered. I stood up and was about to greet him, when, to my amazement, he slugged me across the mouth with a championlike swing, and I fell back across the bunk. His eyes were full of joy. There was something childlike in his happy smile.

"Next time I enter, you'd better get up faster," he said and left. It was indeed an interesting place. The contradictions in its character would be worth analyzing, I told myself, feeling my aching jaw. I had to admit that the guard had swung much better than I had expected.

I was soon taken for interrogation. I wondered what it would be like. I no longer predicted anything—neither good nor bad. I had decided that my past experience was not rich enough to be able to forecast future developments. I was taken into a small room. A tall, dark-eyed man stood behind the desk. He must have been around thirty. He waited until the guard had gone and then addressed me: "Sit down, please."

I saw a magazine in his hand. The cover consisted of a full-page caricature of me. He kept gazing first at the caricature and then at me. Then he smiled.

"Those artists certainly have a way of catching the important features. Even in your present worn-out state I can see the similarity to this drawing. All of your characteristics are here," he told me.

"I don't remember that picture," I commented. I was nervous, waiting for him to get through the preliminaries.

"I have others, too," he answered, "and clippings. I have been studying you thoroughly since I learned I was to take over your case. Have a cigarette?"

"Thanks."

"Now look here, I want you to forget everything you have confessed up to the present. All this here," he said, and pointed at the notes which contained the minutes of my interrogations with the Rat. "Tell me everything frankly. I am interested in the truth."

The words tumbled from my mouth without any regard for caution or discretion: "The truth is that all my life has been a struggle against dictatorships. I am not a Communist. I believe in Western democracy. That is what I have been fighting for politically—that my country should become a part of the Western world. I request that you convict me as a politician who does not believe in your form of government, but don't ask me to confess to espionage and conspiracies which I have never committed."

"But you did partake in at least one or two conspiracies. Here, for example, is a report on the Adorjan conspiracy for which thirty-five men were convicted. According to witnesses, you were their leader. Still, you were not convicted in that case, for. . . ."

"For they had decided to keep me for something bigger," I interrupted him.

"That's right, let's presume that's true," he said with a smile. "That doesn't alter the fact, however, that you participated in the conspiracies."

"If the witnesses told the truth. . . ."

"Wait a minute," he interrupted me. He leafed through another pile of documents, and read one of them: "Kovago's opinion is that partisan action causes unnecessary bloodshed. Revolution is practical only if the political situation changes, and assistance can be expected from a nearby country such as Austria or Yugoslavia. As long as such a possibility does not exist, that is, as long as the Russians remain in Austria, and Yugoslavia is not definitely anti-Soviet, such action should not be initiated. Because of this, Kovago has warned the members of the conspiracy to give up their plans for the present and preserve their strength for a more propitious time."

"Well, what do you think of that?" he inquired, looking at me in a friendly way.

"Assuming this is true," I said, "could someone be convicted for that?"

Without answering my question, he continued reading: "According to Kovago, everyone who undertakes such action, is a hero. He feels, however, that this is not the age for heroism but rather for political resistance."

After a pause, he continued: "You're a strange person. In 1944, under the Nazis, you claimed just the opposite. Then you seemed to have believed that political resistance was no longer adequate, and that Hungarians should show their anti-Nazi sentiments in military conspiracies."

I felt that the whole interrogation had a human quality to it. This man offered me cigarettes and fought me with objective, logical arguments. His behavior was somewhat friendly.

"The reason I'm telling you all this is to show you that I am well prepared, and I know the material well. Are you able to continue the discussion? If you're tired, I'll have you taken back to your cell."

"No thanks," I said. I was tired and apprehensive but still happy that I could talk to an intelligent person, someone who didn't radiate hatred like the Rat and the guards. The cigarette by itself was a wonderful treat. I felt a different man, as if I had again become a human being and had some significance.

"Let's discuss something else," he said with a sweeping motion. "You're not a Communist, in fact you hate Communism."

"Excuse me, but I never use the expression 'hate'. I simply regard Communism as something that doesn't answer the problems of our age."

"That's quite a strong statement," he replied. "Hundreds of millions of people all over the world have chosen this philosophy because it is the most progressive one."

"And in no time at all," I interrupted, "a personal dictatorship has developed out of it, illustrating the obvious fact that it is a bankrupt ideology."

"Those are strong arguments. Let's have a cigarette. So you feel that in its present form Communism can exist only as a personal dictatorship?"

"Yes."

"You can't imagine any other development? That's interesting—for in the past, you could foresee another type of development, a brand of Communism which would be accepted and recognized by the Western world."

This was an extremely dangerous discussion, and I did not dare answer his last comment, for I didn't want to enter into a discussion of Titoism. I decided that the whole discussion could be merely a clever trap.

"The only reason I mention this is to get your reaction. I am interested to know whether a solution would be possible in which democratic thinking, middle-of-the-road men like you could also find their places in building a socialist country," he began again.

The discussion dragged on. I was careful, and tried not to go too deep. Meanwhile, his cigarettes were disappearing one after another. Finally he said, "We have four cigarettes left, two are yours and two are mine. When we have finished these you can return to your cell."

"May I ask for another blanket for the night? I am very cold."

"When were you arrested?"

"In May."

"Then why did you have on such a thin suit? By now you really must be cold."

"That's true. At the time, somehow, I didn't expect to be arrested."

"Did you before?" he asked with a laugh.

"Yes, I did. They were always after me. Even when I was living in the country, an AVO man rented the house next to mine."

"That's possible. You were a constant irritant in many ways. I'm not surprised. Well, I don't have much influence on what happens in the cellar, and the fewer requests you make the better off you will be. We can talk more freely," he added, and winked at me. "What do you know about what is happening in the world?" he inquired suddenly.

"Nothing at all. I have only held discussions with the rats. There are plenty in the cellar."

"They may not have told you too much about the war in Korea," he said with a laugh. "Correct?"

"That's true," I acknowledged.

"It's an interesting situation. Tomorrow I'll tell you about it. Don't get excited, because it's not over yet."

I couldn't remember what he said afterwards for the news of the Korean War had so excited me. I was anxious to get back to my cell to think about it. My strained nerves began to foster many fantastic ideas. Apparently the Communists had initiated military action in Korea. If the Western Powers used clever strategy, they would not only accept the challenge, but would also start action in another place such as Austria or Yugoslavia.

Soon after I had returned to my cell, the "Wrestler" entered carrying a blanket on his arm. "You see there was no point in getting excited. You already have an extra blanket." We grinned at each other in a friendly manner.

My interrogations took place during the daytime. "Daddy Longlegs," as I called my interrogator, seemed to be a fine person. He began talking to me in a friendly manner, and in a few words gave me an account of the Korean situation. He made no secret of the fact that the American counterattack was energetic and rapid. He also hinted that the Chinese position in the conflict was not yet clear.

On the third day, he told me it was time for us to settle down to the work of preparing the court charges.

"It's inevitable that charges be made," he said, "so let's try to formulate them according to my ideas."

This was the theme we developed. Back in 1945, I met with friends with whom I was close from the anti-Nazi Resistance times. Our aim was to discuss possible ways of resistance to the inroads of Communism. We were anxious to have the non-Communist parties secure victory in the coming elections, since we felt political resistance should continue until the Soviet troops were withdrawn from Hungary. Then our country would once again be able to take its place among the free nations of Europe. This was the same ideal which had guided me all through my political career. The document which I prepared with Daddy Longlegs detailed my activities along these lines. As a matter of fact, all my political activities were anti-Communist, and could be interpreted in that light.

We compiled the material for the court trial. It was, by and large, acceptable to me, with the exception of only a few distorted sentences. It did include a charge that I had volunteered to be an agent for the Western Powers, but otherwise it was made up of my political beliefs and actions, for which I was to be convicted from the Communist point of view.

After about a week, Daddy Longlegs informed me: "Tomorrow I will present this material to my superiors. If it is accepted, I will not feel that I helped to convict someone on false charges."

"I understand," I replied. "I will always be grateful to you for that."

"It will be all right," he said.

The next day I didn't see him. On the third morning we had an interview.

"There's a chance," he explained, "that some modifications of the charges will be made, but there is also a chance that it will be accepted as it is. You see, there are people even in the AVO who try to work for justice. Tomorrow you'll be transferred to the Marko Street prison, and soon you'll stand trial. Don't be frightened. I know that any change disturbs you. You will see me there. I hope you won't claim that I used force to get this confession."

"No, you can be sure of that."

"Here's another cigarette." He tried to encourage me by saying that in the next prison I would be better off. I would receive books, cigarettes, and might even see my wife.

I asked him if by any chance he could take out a message to my wife.

"That I can't do," he said. "Write a letter to her, and if I get permission from my superiors, I'll be glad to take it to her."

I scribbled a few lines, trembling with excitement.

"Here, you can read it," I told him.

"No, I won't," he replied. "Just put it into an envelope. My superiors will read it." (My wife never received this note.)

Somehow I had come to like Daddy Longlegs. I sensed that he, too, was moved. I stood up, knowing that in a few seconds I would be leaving. I wondered if I could shake hands with him. Finally I did so and added, "God bless you." He shook my hand firmly.

"There is no God," he answered with a smile, "but remember, there are honest Communists in the world." The guard came and led me away.

In the evening, handcuffed once more, I was taken away in a car. Apparently, Daddy Longlegs had told the truth, and they were taking me to Marko Street prison. In a short time, however, I was horrified to realize that I was instead being taken back to the headquarters of the AVO. I was taken back to the same cell where I had started my agony. Again I was in the silent crypt with the sinister whispers.

"Don't lean against the wall," one of them whispered.

"Face front!" another ordered.

Days passed by. I felt that Daddy Longlegs was the worst gangster of all. He had lied in a most convincing manner. What a fool I had been to trust him even for a moment. My nerves began to go to pieces again.

After ten days a new interrogator took me in hand. He had cold piercing eyes, and cursed and shouted at me without interruption. For a whole night I had to recite the charges which the Rat had originally tried to force me to confess. At dawn the interrogator was the one who had fallen asleep. He awoke and cursed me again. I had to continue my recitation until seven in the morning. I was not permitted to sleep. I became bitter and hopeless. The feeling of death came over me again.

In the evening I was taken up to the Rat's office again. The corridors were swarming with people. A guard told me that I was going to the State Attorney. I saw many other prisoners, including Paul Almos. A door opened and "Daddy Longlegs" entered. He looked around carefully before closing the door. Then he began shouting at the top of his voice for the sake of appearances. He came close and whispered to me, "Things didn't work out as I had hoped. I won't be in charge of you for the trial. Please don't worry, however, things will work out somehow."

"Can't you help me at all?" I asked like a frightened child.

"Not now," he answered sadly. "Perhaps later on." He yelled at me once again and left. In a few minutes the guard took me to another room. There was the Rat with the same sarcastic smile on his face. A stenographer and another AVO man were with him.

"Enough fooling around, Kovago," he began. "Here's the confession. Sign it! Then you go to the State Attorney. You have only one word to remember and that's the word 'yes'. Remember, if you say yes," he said laughing, "you'll go to a better place and stand trial soon. It will mean the end of your cellar life. If you don't say yes, the whole business will begin again. You wouldn't like that, would you?"

"No, I don't think I would," I replied.

"Well then, sign the confession," and he handed me a pen.

"May I read it first?"

"Don't start fooling around again. It contains only what you have confessed before. We can make some changes later on." I glanced at it. It was an idiotic story in AVO lingo, which stated that I was a believer in bourgeois dictatorship and had tried to annihilate proletarian democracy. To that end, it continued, I had organized conspiracies.

"Look, Kovago," the Rat interrupted my reading, "instead of wasting your time reading, why not have a cigarette? The comrade will oblige you by reading it to you."

"I don't quite understand," I said, "am I going to the State Attorney's office now?"

"Kovago . . . Kovago," the Rat laughed, "you're still living in the past. We won't take you anywhere. The State Attorney will come here to interrogate you. His office is only three rooms from here. Afterwards, of course, you will still be our guest. We are not as stupid as the Nazis, whose system prescribed that the investigating agency had to hand over the prisoner to the State Attorney. That way you had a chance to withdraw and deny everything. Here we follow through on the matter to its conclusion. We'll even be present at the court trial. In fact, we're the ones who decide the sentence. The court is a mere formality. You see, the Dictatorship of the Proletariat makes things much simpler. Do you want another cigarette? Go ahead, Comrade, read it to him."

I hardly heard what he read, for I was thinking over this brazen show of gangsterism.

"Here, sign it!" I was told. And I signed it.

"Now everything is in order," said the Rat with satisfaction. "Now they'll take you to meet the State Attorney. A few of our comrades will be present. You'll be asked a few questions, and he'll read this confession to you again. Then he'll inform you that you are under arrest, but of course you already know that," the Rat's assistant added with a laugh. They all laughed and seemed to be thoroughly enjoying the situation. I was not. Everything happened just as the Rat had described it. The only difference was that when I met the State Attorney, I denied the charges. "I have not done anything illegal," I said futilely.

He looked at me with cold eyes, like someone who didn't understand and replied, "Your signature is here, you have confessed everything. Are you willing to repeat it in your own words?"

There was a dead silence in the room. Three AVO men

stared at me silent as statues. The silence seemed to last for an eternity.

"Yes," I finally heard myself answering in a tone without hope.

"Sign this statement informing you of your arrest, and the charges made. Now you may leave."

That same night I was transferred to the Marko Street prison.

6 • PRISON FOR LIFE

The new prison was a fantastic change; it seemed almost like paradise on earth, for instead of the animal-like cage, I was taken into a beautiful large cell. There were two beds in it, complete with mattresses, sheets, blankets, and pillows. I could not get over the sight of the pillows. It was almost six months since my arrest, and I had not slept in a bed since. There were big windows and the autumn sunshine streamed through them. This made the room bright and cheerful. I could hardly believe my eyes.

The guard addressed me courteously: "If you need anything, just let me know please; that's why we're here. Are you hungry?"

"As a matter of fact, I am," I replied.

"We will serve food within ten minutes," he promised. With this he left. I sat wondering in my cell. Then the door opened again. An impressive-looking gentleman entered. He wore military trousers with a red stripe, indicating his high rank. His jacket, however, was civilian. I could hardly get over all this. What's it all about? I wondered. Such an honor. This must be the prison commander. I rose and greeted him.

"Good day, sir."

"Good day to you," he answered in a friendly tone. "How do you feel?"

"I feel much better now, thanks," I replied. "But I am anxious to get a lawyer and to see my wife."

"Oh, we'll see to that. You will see your wife. You'll get a lawyer, so just don't worry. The best thing for you to do would be to take a sunbath once in a while. Apparently you did not have much sunshine for quite a while. Perhaps you should make up for it."

"Oh, thank you very much, I didn't realize that sunbathing was allowed."

"Please make yourself entirely at home. We are very anxious that our visitors should enjoy their stay. It's not up to us to decide whether somebody is guilty or not. Very probably you weren't brought here without good reason. However, this will be clarified in court. How about putting this bed here in the sunshine? Why not take your things off and lie down for a while?"

"Thanks, General," I said gratefully.

"I'm not a general," he replied with a modest smile.

"Thank you, Colonel," I tried.

"That's okay," he answered in an embarrassed tone. "What else can we help you with?"

I noticed a box of cigarettes in his hands. "I would like to smoke if I may."

"To smoke? Of course. Help yourself, please. It appears to me that you have not smoked for some time."

"That's correct, sir."

"Why don't we give you about five cigarettes per day for the time being?" he suggested.

"Thank you, Colonel, it really is very kind of you."

"Don't mention it," he replied.

For the next few days I lived a life of luxury. The food was fit for a gourmet. Only the choicest foods were served, including *Wienerschnitzel*, vegetables, and salad, followed by a luxurious cake. Fantastic. I could hardly believe that any of this was true. All these wonderful tastes, and the sunshine. I felt like crying for joy. Life can really be beautiful. Even in a prison cell.

One day the Rat showed up. He handed me the charges all written up. All I had to do was to learn them by heart for the court.

"Look, Kovago," he explained to me, "now everything depends on how you behave in court. Whatever is written down here is unimportant. Whatever the judge says at the trial is equally unimportant. You know well that we, the AVO, are the real power in Hungary, and we can do with you what we want. The judge may say that he sentences you to death. Don't worry, your fate is in our hands. If you play along and learn your role well, you may have hope."

"But, sir, my horoscope."

"Can't you forget about that damn horoscope? You make me nervous! Don't you understand, it was only a trick which we used during the interrogation?" he asked me in surprise. "You're a smart man. Let's not play games with each other. You read this over carefully and learn it by heart. What you see here is the truth. This you must believe. That's the way you have to talk. You are a good speaker, Kovago. You'll have to speak convincingly," he concluded.

With this the Rat left. I threw the four typed pages down upon the table without even looking at them. Half an hour later the guard came in and addressed me with great deference:

"Pardon me, sir, but you have to memorize this."

"All right, all right, I will. But I don't want to read it now."

"Please, don't excite yourself, but this must be learned." With that he left.

Shortly afterward, the same man came in whom I had originally addressed as a general, then as colonel. He was apparently in charge of all the guards and took great pride in his refined manner of speaking.

"You will have to read this, sir. Of course, if you don't want to do it now, you may do it later. Perhaps you would enjoy more cigarettes? Or could we serve you black coffee?

Or anything else? Do you feel that the food could stand some improvements? But please, read this, for you must realize that you have to know everything that is in here. The person in charge of your case made me promise that I follow this through."

I felt like an innocent maiden, who, dragged by force into a house of prostitution, sees that there is no escape. I took the paper in my hand and started reading it.

It was full of ridiculous charges. I felt happy that the whole thing bore such an air of unreality. It was so comical that I knew that if a fair-minded lawyer ever saw it, he would laugh.

Now at last I learned who were my associates in this trial. Besides Paul Almos, Bela Zsedenyi, Bela Padanyi-Gulyas, and Geza Rubletzky, there were many other friends, most of whom were either safely in the free world or dead. I was supposed to have been the leader of this gang, this conspiracy, which we were alleged to have been engaged in since 1945, working toward the overthrow of the Communist system. According to the charges, I concentrated all my political activities in building a stronger pro-Western relationship. I really enjoyed reading some parts of this accusation.

The day before the trial my prison-guard supervisor came in and decided that my suit was not good enough for a court appearance. In no time a guard appeared, bringing in four different suits to choose from.

"Please help yourself," the "general" said to me.

I selected grey trousers and a dark blue jacket which fitted fairly well. The general, too, was satisfied with my selection. The suit was pressed, and they even gave me a clean shirt. In the morning the barber came to cut my hair and shave me. The suit felt nice and warm. In new clothes and clean linen I felt more like a gentleman.

On November 23, 1950, my great day came. I was in a good mood and even had put on a few pounds. Thinking back to that day, I am convinced that the Rat was more excited than

I was. We were taken into the courtroom and faced the five-member court. The trial was closed to the public. Every prisoner had two guards. In the room, the Rat with a few other AVO men acted as an audience. We were not supposed to speak a word to our lawyers. In fact, up to that moment I never even knew I had a lawyer.

The Rat was right. The whole court proceeding was merely an empty formality. It really did not matter what we said or what was said to us. I was the number one defendant, and following me were Paul Almos, Bela Zsedenyi, Bela Padanyi-Gulas and Geza Rubletzky. This was good company—they were men I was always proud to be associated with.

They took our personal data, and then we had to step up in front of the judge one after the other to recite the text which we had memorized. I felt like an actor in a second-rate theater. As the number one defendant I was the first to start the procedure. When I got to the second paragraph and acted as though I might have forgotten some words and was trying to replace them with others, I turned around to see the Rat look very nervous. To him the court trial meant his career. The AVO rule was that the prisoner had to be presented in court, knowing his lesson without fail. I thought: why not give the Rat a few moments of anxiety. Then, on second thought, I remembered the warning that if I didn't act properly I would be beaten half to death and dragged back down to the cellar. I also remembered the promise that immediately after the court trial I could see my wife again.

Well, let's try to get it over with, I decided. After all, I have his word that they will not hang me, and that I'll get into a nice prison and even be permitted to work there. I'll be able to see my wife regularly and correspond with her.

Spurred by this motivation I told the idiotic yarn, feeling as though I were reciting a badly written detective story. Whenever I got stuck, the judge obliged by helping me out. Often he coached me with the very words I was supposed to say. This was the infamous Judge Olty, who had convicted Cardinal Mindszenty. Originally, he started as a Nazi and later became a fanatic Communist. Then he asked me a few questions which, according to the warning of the Rat, I was not supposed to answer. However, when I heard one question I could not remain still.

"What were the espionage data which you supplied to the representative of the Western Powers?" Judge Olty asked.

"The data concerning the temperature of the mineral waters on the Margaret Island, and the possibilities of building health resorts there," I could not resist answering. "In addition to these data I also gave information concerning the spa in the district of Taban. Here I included all the temperatures of the waters and even the details as to the type of hotel which I would permit the Western imperialists to build."

"I see, I see," Olty replied. "These are obviously very important items of information. A grave matter. I'm sure that there were other data too, but this will suffice for us at this time."

The next defendant was Paul Almos. He, too, recited the lesson like a good student.

"I was born into an aristocratic family and have been involved in espionage since early childhood," he said in the singsong of a student's recitation.

One really might have thought that it was a bad theatrical performance. So primitive, but the audience in the court listened with horror to the sinister crimes of the defendants. And so it went, until old Bela Zsedenyi, once the speaker of Parliament and for a time head of the state, stepped up.

"I am completely innocent and not guilty of anything," he said defiantly.

Judge Olty immediately tried to convince him.

"But look here, Zsedenyi, here is your signed confession."

"I signed that under pressure," he said courageously. "They threatened my family and beat me up. I'm an old man and I broke down."

We were impressed by the old gentleman and by his stubbornness. Judge Olty spoke again.

"Well, it's not really important that you confess all this now. Actually, we could send you back for further interrogation. But as a matter of fact, you have already signed this one." With this he turned to the next defendant:

Bela Padanyi-Gulyas, a former member of Parliament and a member of the Smallholders Party, had to confess that whenever he went abroad, he met with spies. Back in Hungary he used to meet the British Minister under the guise of participating in hunting parties. Instead of hunting game he informed the diplomat of the Hungarian military situation.

Perhaps I should here mention that Padanyi-Gulyas had always specialized in foreign affairs and knew next to nothing about things military.

Finally, it was the turn of the last defendant, Geza Rubletzky. His crime was that he had written a novel.

Judge Olty read excerpts from the manuscript. "Hungary consists of a hundred thousand guards and ten million prisoners." After this introduction, there were a few not too complimentary remarks about the Soviet Union and its role. All this made me realize that Rubletzky had at last found himself, and as a good Hungarian patriot had written down the things that somebody had to write down.

Then the State Attorney spoke. He was the infamous Alapi. He called us gangsters, all fit to be hanged. We had betrayed our country to Western diplomats. We were all old-fashioned gentlemen, and none of us was content with petty crimes. Our crimes were worse. As to the importance of the data which we gave away, everything was important. Whether it was the location of the Maria Theresa Barracks or secrets of state, it was espionage just the same. He was a typical State Attorney. By the time he had finished, we were finished too. Intermission followed.

The guards offered us cigarettes but speaking was forbidden. The Rat called me over and admonished me.

"Kovago, you hesitated again, and you said things that you were not supposed to say. Why did you garble all that about the espionage? You see all the trouble you caused with those temperatures. Do you realize how important these are? Now they will really condemn you to death," he snarled.

"Well, it's all the same to me, whether I'm sentenced to death or not. I couldn't even see my wife; I've had enough of this. I don't care if I do die," I said defiantly.

"You shouldn't take it like this," he tried to soothe me.

"I want to speak up, using the right of the last word," I said, angry now.

"No, no, Kovago, you don't have to speak. You are a good speaker, so you shouldn't speak," he pleaded seriously. "I will speak with Olty. Don't lose your head, I told you not to worry. Perhaps you will get only ten to fifteen years, maybe a life sentence. What difference does it make? Even if they sentence you to death, don't worry, for we will appeal. Do you understand? And after the trial is over, say, in about two hours, you will meet your wife. Of course, this depends on whether you keep your mouth shut or not."

We went back to the courtroom. They gave me a cigarette. I crossed my legs, and, since speaking was forbidden, I tried blowing smoke rings with amazing success. One followed the other. In a few minutes it looked like a spiral. The guards looked at me with amazement. Then suddenly the door opened and with the draft, my masterpiece disappeared.

The trial continued. Now our lawyers spoke up. I didn't even know who they were until an old lawyer, who sat on the right, arose. He explained that he was my lawyer, but there was nothing he could say for me, except that I had a wife and a child, and the court should have mercy.

Still, I fared better than Bela Zsedenyi, whose lawyer exclaimed: "All this trouble began for my client because he is so stubborn; even here in court, he denies everything. This client of mine, who claims to be a university professor, is obviously a primitive and ignorant man." He was confused and started stuttering.

Judge Olty saved him by saying: "Thank you, Comrade, please don't bother to continue. We all know what you wanted to say. Thank you very much."

The lawyer sat down. For a long time afterward whenever we wanted to pull the leg of old Zsedenyi, we used to tell him: "You see Uncle Bela, even your lawyer said that you are an idiot and ignorant. At least our lawyers did not tell us that." Old Zsedenyi always became angry at this.

Then came the exciting moment when sentences were pronounced: "Life imprisonment; life imprisonment; life imprisonment; fifteen years; fifteen years." This was the fate of the five defendants.

I felt relieved. The State Attorney rose. He asked for the death sentence. They asked me if I wanted to appeal.

"No, no thanks," I replied, remembering the Rat's warning. The trial was over. I had ten cigarettes, a piece of apple pie, as well as a good book saved in my cell. I hoped they would take me back there, or perhaps I'd meet my wife immediately. Oh God, that would be just wonderful, I thought.

Unfortunately, life is full of frustrated hopes. This was one of them. They put us immediately into the Black Maria, and we were taken out of Budapest, to the country. Soon we saw the ancient walls of the enormous prison in Vac. What a shame about the saved-up cigarettes and apple pie!

In no time they tore off our clothing, and we had to put on dirty, worn prison uniforms. The sweat of many prisoners had soaked through the rough uniforms. One of the boots I got was size ten and a half; the other one was size thirteen. We were thrown into one big cell.

The others had also been promised that they would meet their families immediately after the trial. All we could do was laugh bitterly that we had believed, even for a minute, the words of the AVO men.

7 • DOBERDO

The size of the cell was 10 by 6 feet. Its furnishings consisted of the following: one dirty pail; one enamel basin; three straw sacks, dirty and old, the contents of which had not been changed in years.

In addition, the cell had a fairly large window with bars admitting a little light. Sometimes even sunshine trickled in, as if by mistake. The window opened on a small courtyard. This yard divided the wing of the cell from the other parts of the prison compound. Our wing served for the detention of dangerous political prisoners. They called it the "Private Cell Section." These cells were somewhat small for five people, but after many trials and much loneliness, the company of humans felt good. One gained a sense of belonging, for the cell still meant a community.

We, all actors of the same sad show, were together. This was an exclusive, small company. Bela ZSEDENYI, first President of Hungary after World War II, Paul ALMOS, retired general of the army, Bela PADANYI-GULYAS, experienced diplomat and a leading personality of the Smallholders Party, and Geza RUBLETZKY, writer and former member of parliament.

Within a few days, the initial joy of meeting one another evaporated. We stared at each other, wearing the terrible prison garb, and our hearts were filled with bitterness. Once in a while we would climb up and look out the window. Usually this happened when the monotonous sound of footsteps indicated that the other prisoners were out walking. Round and round they went in the small courtyard. Sometimes we could hear the yelling or cursing of a guard.

"Keep your head down, you swine! Don't you dare to look up! Keep about three yards behind that other gangster!"

These must be real criminals, we figured. After all, if they were political prisoners, we would recognize them. All of them, however, were ugly, worn individuals with haggard faces, all looking alike. Once Almos kept looking for a longer time.

"Why, look," he exclaimed, "who is that if not NN, and that one over there is BB . . . unbelievable."

"Your eyes must be cheating," we answered him. But then we all climbed up and convinced ourselves that many of our political friends were walking in this group of dirty bums—former cabinet members, secretaries of state, and leading personalities of non-Communist political parties.

Suddenly the door behind us opened quietly. We turned around and saw two guards.

"Listen here," one of them said. "This is the strictest part of the prison. Any breach of discipline will be ruthlessly punished. If you look out that window once more, we'll put you on disciplinary. In any case, we have special instructions concerning you."

When they left, we looked at each other and laughed. None of us took them too seriously. We had heard things like this before. We knew that once a man has been convicted, he really doesn't care about minor details.

One day they took Rubletzky out. He did not return. We tried to figure out the mystery. Where had they taken him? A week later a prisoner who was on the cleaning detail whispered through the cell door that Rubletzy had been returned. We were quite excited. We knew that they must have taken him away for some really important reason. Maybe our court trial was just a hoax and there would be a change in our situation, after all. It was impossible to believe that we might spend the rest of our lives in this horrible little cell, eating that garbage for food.

There was a single pipe running through the cell. This was obviously meant to give the illusion of heating in wintertime. One day we heard knocking on the pipe. Complete silence was an iron rule in the building. Even inside the cells we could only talk in whispers, so we could hear the knocks well. The prisoners were exchanging messages in the prisoners' code. This one was simple. The letter "A" was one knock, the letter "B" two, and so forth. It took many knocks to write down the letters toward the end of the alphabet. Sending and receiving such dispatches took hours. We decided to start listening. For two days we did nothing but listen. On the second day we heard a message from Rubletzky. He was sending it to us. One of us watched at the door, two listened for the message. The others tried to put the incoherent fragments into comprehensible words and sentences. "IN NUMBER 60[1] . . . WAR . . . FOUR . . . BRING . . . BACK. . . ." This was all we could get in two days. On the third day the door opened, and the dreaded secret police entered the cell. We were lost. . . . They took us to the commander of the prison.

"I knew for sure you would try to organize a conspiracy even here. Well, now you'll learn about Doberdo."[2]

On the following day we were marching with the guards, carrying our towels and eating utensils. When we passed the prisoners' cleaning squad, they looked at us sadly. I couldn't quite understand what this was all about. I remembered from my army days that even a colonel could sentence one, at the most, to two weeks solitary. Well, it can't be more here either. And that's something one can survive.

---

[1] Number 60 Andrassy Ut was the dreaded address of the Communist secret police in Budapest.

[2] During World War I, Doberdo was the scene of the bloodiest battles between the Italian and Austro-Hungarian armies.

In the meantime, we arrived at an ancient section of the prison known as Doberdo. It was in a basement with enormously wide corridors. It was actually built into a hillside. In these dark corridors had walked students in the time of Queen Maria Theresa. The building was originally erected for the use of young nobles who were candidates for the Queen's bodyguard.

Our steps echoed in the basement. Deadly silence everywhere. At the end of the corridor an enormous guard was sitting in an easy chair, playing with his keys. Our guard handed us over to him. He got up slowly and sleepily. I decided to call him the Big Bullock.

"What is your profession?" he inquired quietly and sleepily. "An engineer . . . and a mayor as well . . . your mother," he added, beginning to shout, and slapped me in the face so hard that I fell.

My eating utensils were rolling all over the floor. Meanwhile, he was beating up the others. They were not surprised at the unusual procedure and did not fall. Therefore, he beat them until they dropped on the floor. A glow of satisfaction spread over his face. I hoped that he was done with his daily work. That same evening I discovered that unfortunately he was willing to exceed his norm.

They put us in solitary cells, each with a hard bunk and a thin blanket. It was a tiny hole, and there wasn't space to move around. The glass in the windows was broken, and a cold December wind blew in, freezing one to the bone. After two days I felt that this was unbearable. Luckily, a man can stand more than he thinks he can. It lasted for six long weeks.

On an average, we were beaten up twice a day. The first time was in the morning (they always found some sort of excuse), and then in the afternoon when they took us for our walk. During our walks they always picked on Almos. He imagined that there was something wrong with his eyes, and that he was going blind. Therefore, while walking, he used to try to test how well he could see by rolling his eyes around and winking. To the guards this was nothing but using his eyes to transmit signals, and so he had to be beaten up. Whenever the Big Bullock got tired, the Gipsy took over.

He was a small man with a rubbery body, who liked to use his truncheon and pizzle.

One day, late in the afternoon, we were taken for a walk. It was dark when we returned to our cells. Somebody whispered, "It's Christmas." We bowed our heads sadly. It was Christmas Eve, the time of brotherly love. The Big Bullock outdid himself by giving us an extra beating. Then he addressed us:

"Well, you dirty Fascists, the law of love is dead. The new law is hatred. We hate the class enemy, and all of you are in that category. . . ."

The days dragged by slowly. One day we saw snowflakes through the broken window. The nights were terribly cold. I counted the days in a morbid mood. On the twentieth day, they transferred us to another cell where there were straw mattresses. The thin layer of worn straw certainly felt good.

We often heard the rattle of chains in the corridors and the mournful cries of prisoners. They were getting extra punishments. We were terrified, and we understood now why they called this place Doberdo. On the battlefield with that name, during World War I, eighty per cent of the soldiers had died.

In my effort to keep my mind off the unbearable cold and hunger, I tried the most fantastic mental exercises. First I went through trigonometry, solving one equation after the other. Some of the more difficult ones kept me occupied for three days at a time. After a while, however, mathematics became too abstract to compete with hunger and cold.

The next obvious thing was to play chess with myself. It took quite a while before I could make a few moves from each side. Although an uncle of mine had insisted at one time that I should take up chess seriously, I had never become a good chess player. So after the first few moves, everything became confused, and I suspected that my two imaginary partners were peeking into each other's thoughts. Nevertheless, chess helped me to pass away time—particularly the most unbearable hours, between morning and noon.

At noon they would open the door for a minute and put our bowls on the floor of the cell. The guards had a beautiful German shepherd dog named Rexi, who made a habit of walking through the corridors and licking every bowl clean. It seemed that even the guards in the death camp had some love left in their hearts—at least they loved dogs. One evening, about ten o'clock, I overheard a conversation from the guards' room across the corridor. The Gipsy was talking to someone: "Hello . . . yes . . . but Comrade . . . yes, sir. . . ."

He came out shouting for the cleaning squad. "You put Rexi out in the courtyard right away."

"But sir, that's impossible. It's cruelly cold outside."

"Keep your trap shut."

"What about her two-weeks-old puppies?"

"Put them out too."

"But sir, they're sure to die there."

"Shut up, for God's sake. We have to put them out whether they die or not. Understand? It's an order."

"I would have much preferred an order to kill off those dirty Fascists, but this time it was a different order."

"Get going, or else I'll kill you too."

This little incident gave me some insight into the iron discipline of the organization. Later on we learned that both puppies had died that same night.

Finally, the miserable six weeks were over. We were taken back to our wretched "homes." All of us except Rubletzky, for he had been sentenced to three months of solitary. We never saw him again. He contracted double pneumonia, then tuberculosis; two years later he died.

Back in our cells we were happy again. It almost seemed like a homecoming after the horrors of Doberdo. Routine cell life began once more. We tried to figure out a way of obtaining books, paper, and pencils. We tried the cleaning squad, but it was hopeless. To pass the time, we tried to entertain each other with stories of our former lives. But soon we tired of this, too. We heard the shouting and cursing of guards, and the monotonous steps of prisoners as they walked the yard, round and round, time and again.

Would it last forever—living in this dirty, filthy place, hungry and frozen, walking round and round the yard for ten or fifteen minutes, our one contact with nature? But against all reason, the hope that all this would end one day gave us strength to face every new and miserable day.

Our morale was getting worse. We began arguing and fighting. We hungered for some information about the outside world. We concentrated all our energies on trying to get it.

If only one of us could get into the hospital! Finally we decided that Almos should contract stomach cramps; then he'd get into the hospital. We tried, but to no avail. He went to the hospital and returned without any news.

A fortnight later we tried again, and this time he established some contacts, and returned with some choice morsels of information. So it went for months. Even the guards got used to the idea that Almos's stomach had to be pumped out every once in a while. After the tenth time he rebelled and declared that he had had enough. From now on somebody else had better get his stomach pumped out. We tried to convince him otherwise, but it was no use. All three of us dreaded the rubber tube. Finally Bela Padanyi-Gulyas volunteered to have one of his teeth pulled. It worked. This channel proved to be even better than the hospital. Thereupon Almos decided to sacrifice a tooth, too. One of my teeth was loose, and the others decided that it should be pulled; a sheer waste, for I couldn't get any news.

We became seasoned prisoners. We didn't talk about the past anymore, but we had terrible dreams, and one of them kept repeating in a pattern. The prisoner would get out and see his loved ones again, but then would have to return to prison.

We were constantly afraid of getting extra punishments or being sent back to Doberdo. Even our interrogators returned, and once in a while we had to face them. They tried to force us to confess, and to denounce our friends or acquaintances. Often we felt like committing suicide.

The dubious comforts of the cell were made worse by the swarms of bedbugs. Some days we killed as many as two hundred. The walls were covered with their bloody corpses, and they had a terrible stench.

8 • THE MONOCLE OF UNCLE BELA

Even prison life has minor variations. One day two guards and a prison trustee entered our cell. They were carrying small machines and some thread. In a rather friendly manner the guards explained that from now on we would have work to do. Then they began showing us how to handle the primitive machines. One ran the machine by hand, winding the thread on the spool. All four of us tried it.

Uncle Bela had trouble with his eyes. He used to wear glasses, but when he was arrested, they were taken away and never returned. Could he get them back, he inquired. The guard promised that he would. But even after ten days the glasses weren't returned. The three of us began working, happy for the change, but soon we became discouraged. This type of primitive slave work alone couldn't save our morale.

I approached Bela one day with a suggestion: "Look, Bela, you speak English. Why don't you start giving us lessons?"

"It's not so easy," he answered. "My knowledge isn't enough to enable me to teach you without text, paper, or pencil. There are certain words that I don't even recall how to spell or pronounce. My grammar also is rather spotty. If I had a textbook I'd be happy to teach you, but. . . ."

"Never mind, Bela. Remember that our life today is a race with the AVO. They want to drive us into mental collapse, they want us to go crazy and lose our abilities. If we start studying English now and learn, say, ten to twenty words per day, then in the terrible race between life and death, between us and the AVO, it will seem as though we are coming out on top."

After some hesitation, Bela, whom we called the Young Bela, to make it simpler, agreed to give us lessons.

So the strange English class began, with Young Bela pronouncing a word, after which I repeated it about twenty times. Another word would follow, then a little grammar. Very often we got into trouble with the guards over our language lessons. But if Young Bela decided to do something he would go through with it, no matter what the obstacles were. We made excuses and tried to bluff the guards, and accepted our punishments. In spite of all this, we kept on studying.

While the English words flew, we kept on spinning in the crowded cell. Every so often the guards tried to have us organize a work competition, but we always declined. Unfortunately, that would be impossible, we explained, especially for the old one, for his monocle is still missing.

"What is a monocle?"

"His glasses, which are deposited in the stockroom. If the old man could get them back, he'd work wonderfully."

The guard promised to bring the old man's monocle, and four days later, four guards appeared. "Is this the man?" they inquired.

"Yes sir, yes indeed," old Bela replied. "Now I can work much better."

"Wait a minute," one of them spoke. "These aren't eyeglasses, there's just one piece of glass."

"Yes sir, but you see, that's what a monocle is, for only one of my eyes is bad."

"Well, put it on then," he ordered.

"Say, that's something," they uttered in amazement, as Old Bela put on his monocle. "Doggone it," one of them exclaimed and looked at the others. The old man had to stand while all four walked around looking at him. "How come it doesn't fall out?"

"Well, I got used to it," Old Bela answered.

"I still can't see how you can work with this glass," the guard repeated. "When you spin the wheel it will fall out."

"No sir, it won't," the old man answered indignantly.

"Well, let's seen then, start working."

So the old man sat down to the primitive craft, and started spinning like a child. He looked like a turn-of-the-century dandy who had been imprisoned by mistake. It reminded me of all the caricatures the Communists used to draw of *l'ancien régime.* The guards were rolling with laughter, thoroughly enjoying the performance. For two weeks after that our cell was a center of interest. Almost every guard in the prison came to see the old man wearing his monocle, and spinning the wheel.

9 • STRANGE EVENTS

Days, weeks, and months lost their significance. All that was left was thinking in seasons. The spring was the season of political hopes; the summer, that of the bedbugs; the fall, dying hopes; and winter meant grim cold and pangs of hunger. We learned how illnesses took care of themselves, that compared to wounds of the spirit physical pain is unimportant. We learned about fear, creeping into one's nerves, and the enormous effort needed to hush it away.

Often we suffered attacks of starvation. We felt like climbing up the walls and eating every piece of wood. We tried to control ourselves, but we could see our faces growing thin, and the deepening circles beneath our eyes. We hated to look at each other, because we felt so old, ugly, and dirty.

During the spring of 1952, we obtained news from some of the other prisoners, during the routine walk, about the deportations from Budapest. Many persons who were regarded by the regime as unreliable were given but a few hours to pack their belongings, so that they could be evacuated to an unknown provincial location. Except for a small bag, they had to leave behind all their things to be taken away by the regime.

We were apprehensive lest some of our friends fall victim to these cruel deportations. We learned, too, that the whole Western world protested to the regime against these procedures. We were so excited that we even forgot about the necessary precautions when trying to procure information from other prisoners. Soon Young Bela and I were caught and taken to Doberdo.

The Gipsy greeted us as old friends and gave us special treatment. His rest home was not as full as usual, but the guests were specially selected.

One evening the Gipsy came, and with a sense of humor informed me: "Pick up your junk, and let's go. You're being taken away, either to be hanged or to be freed."

They took me up to the prison commander. It was past midnight and most unusual. After nine at night there was hardly a stir in the house. The prison commander glanced at me and said to the two guards, "This is the one. You can take him, Comrades."

My eyes were blindfolded, and I was manacled. They led me down some stairs and put me into the prison van. My heart was pounding as it did when I went out on my first date. I knew something important was about to happen.

When we got out of the van, they removed my blindfold. I recognized one of the infamous Budapest prisons. They put me in a cell and gave me food which was decent but not enough. With my bones sticking out of my thin body, I could hardly sleep on the hard prison cot. The next morning I was taken out for interrogation. The questions seemed very unusual. They were about men and institutions which ceased to exist long ago. I couldn't possibly figure out what they were after. Their questions puzzled me.

"Tell me, whom in the Smallholders Party did you regard as the man built-in by the Communists?"

I mentioned a few names as a guess.

"Let's presume," the AVO man said, "that you are correct. But tell me about G, who was a member of Parliament. With whom in the Communist Party did he maintain contacts?"

"How on earth could I know that?" I was on the verge of blurting out, when I remembered some small incidents. This Representative G, once, when I was Mayor, used the telephone in my office to reach Gabor Peter, the infamous boss of the AVO. On yet another occasion I heard him talk over the phone with Kadar, Deputy Secretary General of the Communist Party. I remembered that Representative G fled the country a long time ago; the other two are respected and dreaded still in the Communist Party. So why shouldn't I tell him all this, I figured, and mention both names?

Suddenly my interrogator became excited. "Will you please repeat all this?" he requested.

I obeyed.

"Wait a minute," he said and reached for the phone. After dialing an extension, I heard him say, "Comrade, there's something very important . . . yes . . . no. . . . He's here in my room . . . yes . . . immediately."

He put the receiver down and took me to the corridor far away from his room. I had to face the wall. He summoned a guard to take care of me. I stood there for half an hour before he called me back and proceeded with the interrogation.

"Don't you ever say a word about what we're discussing now. You understand? Not a word, to anyone, not even the guards—not even the investigators."

"But sir, I wonder, what if tomorrow another interrogator asks me."

"No one will ask you anything," he grunted, "and if anyone does, don't answer; you're playing with your life. Now," he said, "tell me everything you remember about the telephone conversation between Gabor Peter, the AVO chief, and Representative G."

I told him that G was intervening on behalf of two men who had been arrested. One, if I remember correctly, was a well-known lawyer before the war. I didn't remember his name. The other name I couldn't remember either.

"Try to concentrate on it, and tell me what G said and what Peter answered."

I explained to him that as they were talking on the phone I couldn't tell the details.

"All right, all right," the interrogator interrupted me. "Still, the face of G, or his answers, must have given you some indication of what it was all about."

"I got the impression that the men were promised freedom."

"Are you sure?" he asked excitedly.

"Yes, I think so," I added, "for a few days later G made a remark to me. 'You see, if one is smart, one can get things done by the Communists.' "

The detective wrote everything down very carefully. Then he inquired about Kadar. All that I could remember was that Representative G and Kadar seemed to be on good terms, and personally friendly. It was during the interrogation that I heard the rumor that Kadar had become Minister of the Interior. For all I knew, he could still be in that position. Finally I was told to face the wall, and the detective reached for the phone once more.

"Yes . . . it's all done. Sure. . . ." Then silence.

A few seconds later a door opened, and my interrogator got up. I heard some whispering: "No, Comrade Colonel." That was all I could hear.

A strange voice addressed me. "Is that all you know?"

Politely, but rapidly, I wheeled around. The man suddenly disappeared behind the table.

The interrogator shouted, "You look at the wall, or I'll cut you to pieces."

Then the other voice muttered sarcastically, "Don't you be so curious—and be careful. You have to keep quiet about this interrogation in your own interest. It doesn't pay to interfere in our debates. Understand?" he added threateningly. They kept whispering for a while.

Then the door opened, and someone left. "You can turn around now," my interrogator ordered. He took out a match, and lit the papers containing his notes. Carefully, he gathered the ashes and threw them away, then checked for any burnt scraps that remained, and threw them into the stove.

He looked at me. "Now your interrogation begins," he said. "Take a cigarette. What was it about the wife of Bajcsy-Zsilinszky? Wasn't she the one who forwarded your espionage reports to the Americans?"

That was an old charge. But to my great amazement he didn't mind my denying everything.

He put a sheet in the machine and said to me, "So you deny that the woman in question is guilty against the People's Democracy?"

"Yes."

In a few sentences he took down my arguments. Then he wrote down a summary of Bajcsy-Zsilinszky's life. He was a leading member of the Smallholders Party . . . he opposed Fascism . . . he was leader of an anti-Fascist movement . . . he fought against the occupying German army . . . he was arrested with a gun in his hand . . . he was executed on Christmas Eve.

"Why was it," he said, "that the hangman didn't want to do it."

"That's correct, he didn't. The respect for, and reputation of Bajcsy-Zsilinszky were so great that the hangman refused. They got the guard, who for a high price did it," I answered.

He wrote down everything. My impression was that all he wanted was to fill in some data for the time spent. The next day, he summoned me again, and continued questioning me about the anti-Nazi movement. What he wrote down for the record was well known to everyone. Nevertheless, I had to repeat myself.

Finally he asked, "Did you tell the whole truth and nothing but the truth?"

"Yes," I replied.

"Well, you see, here, too, there are people who want to know the truth," he said, but this remark escaped me.

The following day I was taken back to the prison in Vac. The Gipsy greeted me, incredulously, but in a friendly fashion.

"So you weren't hanged."

"Not yet," I answered.

"How was the food?"

"All right, but not enough."

"Orderly," he yelled, "come here immediately. Bring this regular guest of ours a dish of vegetables. Get going," he said.

The following day, with Young Bela, I was taken back to the cell. The four days I spent outside the city were included in my punishment. Well . . . strange happenings. My friends were amazed when a few days later, looking around carefully lest anyone be listening, I told them of my experience. That's it, they exclaimed, there are two lines in the AVO—what are the differences, we wondered? Young Bela argued that one group wanted to be completely controlled by Moscow; the other dreamed of some sort of national Communism, and would like to be more friendly to the West.

"They're all the same. Don't kid yourself," Old Bela grumbled.

10 • THE CRY OF THE BEATEN WOLVES

On a spring day in 1952, some of the inmates were being transferred to another prison under rather mysterious circumstances, and with the use of extreme precaution. Thirty or forty of us, chained together, were herded into a police van. This modern version of slave transportation was highly efficient; it could be carried out easily, with a minimum number of guards.

Several of us knew the area, and, through the small openings in the closed truck, we saw that we were going toward the capital, probably to the large Central Prison, which is used for regrouping prisoners. We had to be careful of our whispers, for being overheard meant the whip—another reminder of Roman times.

Soon we arrived at the enormous Central Prison of Budapest. This "masterpiece" of prison architecture is built like a star, with corridors fanning out from a central glass dome. It looks rather like a modern version of a Greek temple. Every point of this "star" housed a different category of inmates. Those in the right wing were common criminals; those on the left, political prisoners. Under the Communist system the two overlapped, to some extent, for many who had been sentenced for ordinary offenses were actually guilty of sitting on the wrong side of the political fence.

Take, for example, a peasant who was very unpopular with the Communists in his village. The Party Secretary denounced him when he cut down a tree in his own yard. Likewise, city dwellers were charged with dealing in foreign currencies and similar activities, while the true motive for their arrest was undoubtedly political.

The atmosphere of the Central Prison differed from that of our regular "home" in Vac in many respects. Gone was the comparative quiet of the old place. Something was always happening, groups of prisoners kept coming and going. Here, too, the inmates worked in the familiar tailor shops, cobbler shops, bakeries, and in a large button-making plant. The prison was a self-supporting economic unit. The head warden had worked out a system whereby it could be run on the profits from the work of its inmates, and he was anxious to increase the productive capacity of the institution to its utmost.

I was assigned to a lone cell and spent my time trying to find the reasons for my transfer, and my prospects for the future.

Six weeks later I was put to work in the button factory. This was probably one of the most primitive plants in the world. The prisoners were forced to work ten hours a day, and I realized that Marx's theory of the exploitation of workers was indeed carried out—under the Communist system. The machinery consisted of discards from other factories; the production norms were set in such a way that the prisoners could not earn even half their basic pay on those worn-out machines. The building itself was dilapidated, with no heat or ventilation, and some fifteen or twenty accidents occurred every day.

With special deference to my training as a mechanical engineer, I was assigned as helper to an old locksmith. He was a decent old-timer, who had been for many decades a social democrat, and he was rather awed by the fact that his helper was a former mayor of Budapest.

To work again was heaven after the monotony of the cell, and I carried out my tasks with enthusiasm. This new life also gave me the opportunity to reëstablish some human contacts, and to talk to my prison mates.

I had worked two weeks for Uncle Adi and felt that I was becoming a fairly good locksmith, when I was suddenly transferred. It was back to a lone cell for me, with no company but my loneliness and frustration. For long days and nights I kept thinking of my fate, and my thoughts were rather pessimistic. For two and a half years I had received no news of wife and child, and I felt lonely and forlorn. I knew that millions of other people shared my feelings. I tried to figure out how it would be possible to fight with ideas in a world where force seemed dominant, and decided that the solution might be a revolt of all those who were ready to start action on their own, and by themselves, without any previous planning. If they would all revolt at the same moment, I thought, something might be achieved. This was expecting a miracle that had never happened in the bloody history of slavery.

A few days later, my quiet, philosophical life was rudely interrupted. I was taken by the guards to be interrogated. The detectives of the Secret Police were rough and cruel. They wanted an immediate confession. Their charges were centered on my wife and her friends. "There was a conspiracy, wasn't there?" they demanded. They pressed me with hundreds of questions. "No, no, no," was all I could answer. This torture lasted for days until my nerves were on edge. Suddenly, it stopped, as unexpectedly as it had started.

I was already back in the loneliness of my cell when a prison officer visited our wing. "What are you doing here?" he inquired with surprised laughter, as if I had any control over my fate. "Why aren't you working?" "Because you won't let me," I answered. "Who won't let you?" "You," I replied, listlessly, suspecting some new trick. "I'll let you," he answered in a strange voice. "Soon you'll be working as an engineer. You should know that we do not all long to liquidate you. There are good patriots among us too." This made me angry, but he left before I could make any unwise remark. In spite of all the past disappointments I was hoping again. Perhaps I would even be assigned to the Engineering Section, which had a legendary reputation. Some fifteen or twenty skilled engineers worked there on prison construction, and, according to the grapevine, on jobs for outside firms as well. They spent their days behind draft boards; they had access to paper, pencils, and even books. Every prisoner dreamed of being assigned to that office. One reason why I was not too hopeful of getting so splendid a chance was that it was mostly reserved for the National Communists. Perhaps that might be the very reason for my chance, I wondered. Possibly they were interested in establishing some contact with the non-Communists. Perhaps the imprisoned National Communists even had some secret connections with our friends on the outside. Who could tell? Anything was possible. Or perhaps it was just sheer fantasy, the wishful thinking of a frustrated prisoner. We'll see, I decided, there's no other way but to wait patiently, and see what happens.

One day the key turned in the lock.

"Are you 1312?" grunted the guard. We were never addressed by our names, but only by an impersonal number. "Yes," I replied. "What's your name?" he barked. "Jozsef Kovago." He glanced at the paper in his hand and nodded. "Get going." Through long, twisting corridors, we went up to the warden's office. A second lieutenant was waiting for me. His face was that of a stupid, primitive man, and his sense of humor befitted his face. "Listen, goddam you," he started with a jovial smile, "you're going to get a big job, perhaps even freedom to move inside the prison." And he explained that several of the prisoners had reported to the warden's office with ideas for technical innovations and inventions; that the Communist state system was liberal enough to give even prisoners a chance to work out some of their ideas, thereby alleviating their criminal consciences and benefiting the state. He explained that a few years might be deducted from the prisoner's sentence, that he might even be granted visits by members of his family. I immediately realized that not one of the prisoners would be foolish enough to believe in a reduction of his sentence, but that any of them would do almost anything for a chance to see his loved ones.

Then the lieutenant explained what my task would be. I would interview prisoners who claimed to have an invention or a new technical idea, and, once I had the details of the project, I would have to outline and evaluate it from an engineering point of view. I tried to explain that no engineer's training is broad enough to familiarize him with every aspect of his field; I would need books, and a chance to consult prisoners who worked in the Engineering Section. I also explained how risky it would be to give opinions on new inventions, which accounts for the special offices that exist everywhere for this purpose. And as far as my fellow-prisoners were concerned, I suggested that they be granted rights and rewards for their ingenuity, similar to those earned by free men. "You *are* crazy." He stared at me. "What rights and rewards are you talking about?" he inquired laughingly. "Well, they'd get money for their ideas, and the patent rights belong to them," I explained, patiently. Once again he roared with laughter. "You sure have been in prison a long time. Those days are gone for good. Now, new inventions are offered to the state. Of course, some financial reward is given, but that's something we can discuss later, when inventions are reported to us."

There was a new cellmate waiting for me when I returned. I had known him well before our imprisonment.* He explained that he had been assigned to work on the same project, and that he was in charge of the administrative aspect. I used to like him, but now I was afraid of him. He had been convicted of spying for the Americans, and, according to rumors, had managed to escape hanging only by becoming a stool pigeon.

* He was a representative of the Smallholders Party and well known for his strong anti-Communist feelings. He was also very active in city politics.

I felt genuinely sorry for this miserable creature, but decided to be careful.

We visited the various prison shops together. Still wondering whether the Secret Police might have set a trap for me, I warned all my friends in prison against giving me any information, lest I should be forced to confess it. I decided to be careful with all personal contacts for at least a month, and to see what would happen.

A few inventions were reported, most of them ideas which the prisoners had kept in mind for a long time, and were only now trying to utilize.

One of the pleasant surprises of the assignment was meeting an old friend, Jozsef Adorjan. He had been convicted as leader of a military conspiracy in which the Secret Police had tried to involve me. Adorjan was a peasant, with a slight build and a quick mind. After the war, he had been a Smallholders Party representative, and he had a hearty loathing for the Communists. He had almost no formal education, but made up for this with a strong native intelligence. His judgment was virtually infallible.

I met Adorjan when he reported an invention in viniculture; we embraced and were both moved to tears. An instant later, however, he turned to my associate. "I have something to say to you," he said.

"I'm happy to see you again," my cellmate answered, "What is it?" "Aren't you ashamed of yourself?" Adorjan retorted accusingly, in an excited voice, his cheeks flushed. "I heard you've become a stool pigeon, and that's the worst fate I can imagine. How could you stoop so low? Why not at least commit suicide?"

Deathly pale, my associate attempted to answer. "I know about that rumor, Joe, and about that accusation. It's courageous of you to tell me this to my face." "But of course I'd tell you," the little peasant politician continued. "How could I keep silent about such a disgrace? Do you realize what will happen to this country if even anti-Communist politicians prostitute themselves? I would rather face death honestly than resort to treachery."

"It is not as easy as that, Joe," my associate answered. "One day you may discover that perhaps I took a greater risk than any of you. I don't feel I deserve those words, Joe. Another thing. You may not realize it, but this very conversation may endanger my life, while the only risk facing you is ten days in solitary."

For several days after this conversation, my associate kept silent, and I did not bring up the subject again. What was I to tell him? Luckily, the whole invention project came to an abrupt end within a fortnight.

It was mid-July in 1952. The whole prison was plunged into an unusual silence, and we all realized that this was the quiet before the storm.

I listened nervously to any sound from the corridors, but the quiet steps of the guards was all I could hear. It seemed to me that some of the cell doors were being opened very quietly, as if prisoners were walking barefoot in the corridor. Then suddenly the prison walls resounded with a terrible cry of pain; an animal-like wailing that reflected unbearable torture. The cry reminded me of a childhood experience. I remembered a snowy winter when a group of peasants had hunted down a pack of wolves. The wounded animals had been finished off with clubs, and sounds like those they had emitted now echoed within the prison walls. I could hear swearing, blows, submachine guns, and what sounded like mortally wounded animals being tossed back into their cells. Methodically, one after another I heard the cell doors open. They seemed to be approaching our cell.

I glanced at my companion. "This is the end," he whispered, his face deathly pale. "They're shooting men like animals in the center of the compound," I replied in a low voice.

"Yes, and they seem to be coming towards our cell," he said in a voice of despair. "God bless you," I told him, as I offered my hand and said good-bye. "If either of us survives, let's try to inform the other's family."

"Look, Misi," he replied unexpectedly, "I want to tell you something very serious. Now that we are close to death, I want to tell you that I have a clear conscience. It looks as though I am guilty, but I succeeded in fooling these gangsters many times, so help me God."

I looked at him. His eyes brimmed with tears. At this moment we heard the key turn in the lock. "It won't do any of us much good to know this now," I answered, "I doubt if I'll even have a chance to pass it on, and up there they don't need any witnesses. . . ."

The cell door opened, and I heard the voice of the guard who worked on our corridor saying: "These are engineers, don't take them down." At the same instant, two animal-like figures jumped into the cell. They were panting, sweat was running down their faces, and they looked like boxers after the sixth round. They began to slap our faces as hard as they could. "Come on, tell us all you know about the escape," they shouted at us.

They left as quickly as they had come. From the end of the corridor, however, I could still hear the painful howling of prisoners being beaten mercilessly. Then, at last, the prison was quiet again.

We learned the following day that, after an escape from our prison had occurred, guards from another institution were brought in to us with the specific assignment of beating every prisoner. It was our good fortune that by the time they got to our corridor, they were already tired. They also had instructions to go easy on engineers, and to beat them only in their own cells.

That same night my prisonmate was taken away.

The following day, new regulations were enforced in the prison. Motion was even more restricted than previously. Out in the yards we were supposed to keep eight feet away from the walls. Ditches were dug along the walls, and the guards in the watchtowers were ordered to fire without warning at anyone stepping into the forbidden area. All this because of the escape of one single prisoner! His unfortunate compound mates were beaten mercilessly for weeks afterwards, until several of them landed in the prison hospital with serious injuries, and one of them died as a result of his beatings. The warden himself supervised the beatings; he took a personal interest, as he had been demoted in rank because of the escape. About thirty prisoners lost their hearing, and two suffered broken legs. The list of injuries which did not heal for months would be too long to enumerate.

And that is how the famous socialist prison system really worked in the mid-twentieth century, and how the liberal "re-education" principles of the Soviet penal system were actually carried out!

11 • IN THE ENGINEERING SECTION

The great event of my prison life soon followed. I was assigned to the much coveted Engineering Section of the Central Prison, one of the two elite workshops of the institution.

There were several non-Communist members in the workshops. They were permitted to work there, but could not become section leaders or supervisors. Those positions were reserved for the prisoners who were Communist Party members.

Even so, life was so much easier in that section that all prisoners were quite eager to get into it. This at times was quite a formidable task for non-Communists, in spite of their superior technical experience.

It was a mecca for the new aristocrats, the Communist Party members, whose very Party membership carried the occupational hazard of occasional periods in jail. Unpleasant as this may appear to bourgeois observers, it was partly compensated for by the fact that Party members enjoyed special privileges in prison. In the Central Prison, for instance, every shop leader was a Communist.

The other elite workshop was the Translation Bureau. Since the Foreign Ministry and other important government offices often required the translation of confidential materials, why not utilize for this purpose the skills of imprisoned Communists who spoke foreign languages well? After all, what could be safer than a translating office within a prison? Furthermore, it would be inexpensive, as only the prison warden would be paid. As for the prisoners, they would be glad to settle for permission to correspond with their families and some improvement in their meals. This reasoning, based on the full exploitation theory, proved attractive to the prison authorities. As Communists, they were apt to react favorably to such a "capitalistic" opportunity. Once the project had been endorsed, the translators were separated from the other prisoners and remained in contact only with the Engineering Section.

At first imprisoned engineers were used only for prison projects. Soon, however, the skills of its members prompted the warden to seek outside assignments as well. To be in the Engineering Section, therefore, meant not only variation in the drab prison routine, but the much coveted opportunity to acquire outside information. My appointment had been made when two members of the Engineering Section tried to develop a new type of diecaster. They knew that I had some experience in machine tools and requested my assignment as necessary for this important project.

I plunged into my work with great relish, and soon found that I had forgotten a great many things in prison. However, the Engineering Section had some first-class literature on hand, and my colleagues helped to bring me up-to-date. It took all my energies and intellectual powers to reach the proper frame of mind to concentrate on my work.

At the same time, I decided to take up English studies. There were some English books in the Section, and I began reading one of them with great expectations. Unfortunately, I found that some of my studies with Young Bela would not have earned the approval of the Berlitz School. Luckily, there was an outdated English grammar among the books, and I studied faithfully.

Thus I began an intensive work schedule. Every day I concentrated on engineering work for eight hours, followed by two or three hours of English. The food we received was still inadequate, and after eight weeks of this new routine, I felt I was nearing a nervous breakdown. I saw the danger of this, and knew that if I lost hold of myself I might lose everything. I was confined to the prison hospital for a while, and met an imprisoned doctor. Following the usual exchange of political information, which was almost routine in prison, he explained the problem to me:

"To tell you the truth, this is all a matter of nerves. You must pull yourself together, and only you can do it. I'll do my best to give you some medicine, but I must warn you that the only capsules we receive are undated and of dubious potency. I can bear no responsibility as to their effectiveness." He gave me some vitamin B shots, which, along with my own determination, helped pull me through. I was back at work within a few weeks.

By the time I returned to the Section, the project we had been working on was completed, and in order to keep me in the office my colleagues gave me some drafting to do. For those of us who had spent years on fairly high-level engineering work, it took a sense of humor to start out as a draftsman all over again. Some of the best Hungarian engineers, leading construction men, former cabinet members, heads of large engineering consulting firms, were working here as draftsmen. Certainly I could not complain of the company I kept.

The members of the new aristocracy—those who had come from the Communist ranks—sometimes showed a certain amount of tolerance towards the less fortunate of us who had been born on "the wrong side of the tracks." They gave us a hand whenever they could. They knew that I disagreed with them on every political issue, but with a sense of humor and a human approach I succeeded in winning them over, at least on a personal basis. This was probably the reason for my promotion to assistant chief draftsman within a relatively short period of time. This was a great day in my prison life, and I duly celebrated the event with a few friends.

Life in the Engineering Section was a relatively pleasant routine indeed. I became increasingly ambitious in my work. Without hesitation, I would do things over two or three times until they fully satisfied me.

The head of the department was especially pleased with my achievements. He was a member of the new Communist aristocracy, a cheerful fellow with a good bass voice, which he used alternately for swearing and singing.

Another ambition I had at the time was to pry some outside information from the aristocrats. The only way I could do this was on an exchange basis. We members of the "proletariat" also had our sources; there were many among us who worked in the bakery, or as locksmiths, and cleaners. The latter were the most valuable. Whenever they cleaned the quarters of the guards and prison officials, they read all the newspapers they could find. When they returned in the evening, we could determine the degree of their success by the grins on their faces. First and foremost, we wanted to know whether they had actually read the news or had obtained it indirectly. We had to be very careful, for wishful thinking fashioned a wild rumor out of the simplest little piece of news.

Whenever we heard that General McArthur had declared he would level Moscow to the ground unless the Soviets evacuated Hungary, we old foxes just laughed sadly. On the other hand, whenever we got hold of a good news item, we immediately proceeded to "trade it in" for some news the aristocrats were keeping to themselves. To someone who lives in the free world and reads newspapers every day, it must be hard to imagine the joy and satisfaction a prisoner can derive from the tiniest scrap of outside information. Especially when the prisoner knows that the whole Communist system is anxious to keep him isolated from the rest of the world, that he is not supposed to have any news of his family, of his friends, or of the events which are shaping world history. He can only hope that the regime will fall and that he will regain his freedom. He cannot allow himself to believe that a life sentence may really mean spending the rest of his days in jail. Should he believe this, he would concentrate all his efforts on committing suicide. God, however, granted us political prisoners a special blessing. We had been jailed for our convictions, and these convictions sustained us during our prison years. They helped us believe that the regime was bound to fail, and that our freedom would be restored one day.

Once in a while, a prisoner would lose his faith and become, as we called it, "washed up." The first symptoms of this condition were an increasing degree of pessimism, and somber forecasts about our future and the future of the world. The victim sat in his chair, keeping more and more to himself. Many of us suffered such spells but managed to pull out in time. For those who did not, prison was certain to mean death in the long run.

It was pleasant to be allowed to work. It helped us forget. We were permitted to purchase sixty florins' worth of merchandise every month. A list was drawn up by the guard for such personal needs as cigarettes and food items. Cigarettes, of course, were worth their weight in gold. It gave us special pleasure to smuggle a few to our friends who were not fortunate enough to work in the Engineering Section. Sometimes, it took as long as a month to get answers like, "Old Bela received his cigarettes and thanks you," or "Young Bela would like some more cigarettes if possible."

Our regular walks also helped to boost our morale. There were a few trees in the courtyard, and their yellowed leaves told us that fall had come once more. These melancholy signs reminded us that we were wasting away some of our most productive years behind prison walls.

The prison grapevine brought us news of the possible expansion of the Engineering Section. According to rumors, our section was to be enlarged considerably, and might even be moved to more spacious quarters.

Soon we were told that our tasks and projects were to assume increased importance, and that we were about to move into a new compound named "The Little Hotel." We were even promised salaries. Most of us felt rather pessimistic and worried about the forthcoming change. In prison, the human animal has a tendency to get used to the status quo, and any change is feared and suspected. But when we were taken to the small building in the other wing which was to be our new office, I had the greatest surprise in my prison life. There were red carpets on the floors, and it looked like a third-rate hotel in a provincial town, the kind where couples are not asked for their marriage license.

The whole place was freshly painted and cleaned. There was running water in each room, and toilets with doors! This was the height of luxury, by prison standards.

New guards appeared, and when one of them said in a rather friendly, almost courteous, manner, "Please, Mr. Engineer, don't be so loud," we were ready to faint.

"Believe it or not," my friend, the physicist, whispered in my ear, "this man has forgotten how to swear!" Some of us tried to explain all this by claiming that the U.S. Army had occupied Budapest and had forgotten us in prison. But the greatest opportunist in our section, a member of the Communist aristocracy, had a different theory.

"Officer," he said to the guard, "this is really wonderful. This is really a socialist prison. Only a Communist state, where the power belongs to the workers, could create something like this."

"You're a damn fool," the guard said, looking at him in a sarcastic manner.

Soon the translators brought us some interesting outside news. According to rumors, vital struggles were taking place within the Communist Party. Janos Kadar, the Communist Minister of the Interior, had been arrested with several of his associates. Some of us attributed our good luck to those events. Others tied it to the Republican victory in the United States, when General Eisenhower won the presidency. Still others tried to connect our lot with the influence of Churchill and the Conservative Party in England, while another school of thought maintained that all this was connected with the renewed influence of West Germany.

We were granted comparative freedom within our wing, except for one section which was barred to all of us. Rumor had it that the cells in that section were even more luxurious than ours. They were supposed to hold some very important personages.

We soon learned, however, that the section housed the recently arrested Communist leaders, Janos Kadar and his associates. It was rumored that all the cells in that compound were wired, the "bugs" revealing to outsiders every word spoken by the prisoners. We saw the guards carry sumptuous meals to them three times a day.

Meanwhile, we settled down in our "small hotel" to work. I had very pleasant cellmates, who were trying to help me in every possible way. In two of them I finally found people who really spoke English. When they learned about my attempts to study English, they called my attention to the fact that somehow the translators had managed to get hold of a set of the *Encyclopaedia Britannica.* Through these connections we managed to borrow an occasional volume.

Thereafter I could continue my studies from this wonderful work, and at the same time augment my knowledge of history and philosophy. In the beginning it was difficult to follow the text, but slowly my vocabulary increased. From that time on the encyclopaedia was my constant companion in the prison.

Month followed month, and soon the spring of 1953

arrived. The trees in the courtyard began to show their first leaves. It was all very cheerful, except for the sight of the large locked building on the other side of the courtyard. We called it the "house of ghosts," for the corpse of every executed prisoner was taken on a small cart to the basement of that building before it was carried to its unmarked grave in the burial grounds. Whenever we heard the rattling of the cart, we knew that one of our prison mates had left this world. The sound of the cart heard all too frequently meant to us what the obituary column means to those who live in the free world.

One day a sudden change occurred. One of the engineers was walking along the corridor to another cell, to give some instructions to one of his associates. When he passed a guard, who had usually been rather kind, he received a surprisingly strong kick.

"You filthy Fascist dog," snarled the guard, "back to your cell, the good days are over, it's time for you to learn what prison means."

A few days later new guards arrived, all of them rough, and the same evening we heard the woeful cries of beaten prisoners from the other side of the prison. The beatings and tortures had started again. We were sure that something big must have happened outside.

For four days we were not even taken for our routine walks. Then we were told to walk about ten feet apart, hold our hands behind our backs, keep our eyes down, and not say a word. The gruff threats which accompanied these instructions left no illusions as to what would happen if we broke these rules.

On returning from our walk, one of the translators, Pal Ignotus, whispered into my ear at the door: "Stalin is dead."

I can hardly describe the happiness I felt when I heard this news. I was anxious to get back to the cell and tell it to all my friends. So Stalin was dead, the bloody hangman! What would follow, no one could tell.

There would be factional struggles for power, and the Western nations would want to take advantage of this. Nobody knew what approach they would use. They might try a series of political actions, perhaps even combined with military steps. One thing, however, was clear: the Western world would not pass up such an opportunity for action.

We all agreed that with the death of Stalin a new era in world history had begun.

I remember clearly my words that evening: "Please don't be impatient, for it may take quite a while, even years, before Communist tyranny comes to an end. Communism is a bankrupt system, and this is becoming obvious to the whole world. I have no doubt that sooner or later even the Soviet Union is bound to change."

We all believed this, but almost a year passed before we were able to detect any effect of this big change in the Communist world.

12 • A WINDOW OPENS ON THE WORLD

Swallows were flying about the prison courtyard, gracefully returning with the sunshine as they had every year. They, too, were part of our improved status and our new life. The old prison in Vac boasted only sparrows. It was now the spring of 1954.

We were circling the yard one day, round and round, in our daily exercises, watching the mother swallow feed her young, when one of the guards stepped into the center of the court and made the following speech:

"Men," (curiously enough, he omitted the customary "filthy swine") "from now on there will be a new order. We will treat you as political prisoners. You will be permitted to walk together, and to talk to each other if you feel like it. Our purpose here is not to torture you. That's all for today."

The excitement among the prisoners was almost beyond description. What could possibly have happened? Once again rumors were flying. Some claimed that President Eisenhower had delivered a speech in which he had given the Soviet Union two alternatives, peace on honorable terms or the threat of war, and that the Soviets were willing to negotiate. Others explained that the newly organized German army was ready for action. Still others claimed that Beria had been liquidated; that Gabor Peter, head of the Hungarian Secret Police, had been imprisoned; that Rakosi, the faithful satellite of Stalin, was no longer in power; that Imre Nagy, his opponent, had become Prime Minister.

In the days that followed, we succeeded in picking up additional fragments of information about the changes which had occurred. Apparently the Imre Nagy rumor was true. In his inaugural speech as Prime Minister, he had criticized the Secret Police, and announced that concentration camps would be abolished, and that all deportation orders would be revoked.

He had also announced that all political prisoners, non-Communists as well as Communist deviationists, who had been convicted in closed court trials, would be freed, and their cases reopened. Even more sensational was the rumor which credited him with saying that, from time to time, the peasants could leave the collective farms. Allegedly, he had also promised more consumer goods than heavy industrial production, and he had told artisans and small businessmen that they would once more be given the right to operate without state control. All of this sounded fantastic.

Soon, however, a rash of new rumors spread. According to these stories, Rakosi was far from admitting defeat and had claimed that Nagy was taking a dangerous course. Other reports claimed that peasants were rebelling in the provinces, and that Communist Party secretaries had been beaten by the angry populace.

I had a new cellmate at that time—Eugene, a chemical engineer and a real old-timer. He was a Bohemian with a heart of gold, and a highly individualistic person. We understood each other very well indeed. We exchanged language lessons, with Eugene teaching me English, while I taught him French. Our English textbook was still the *Encyclopaedia Britannica*, and with Eugene's help I began to understand the more difficult passages. One evening, after one of my long discussions with a visiting aristocrat, Eugene and I were chatting.

"Are you sure it's right for you to hold all those discussions with former Communists and renegade Social Democrats?" he asked, regarding me intently. "You should be more careful, you might get into trouble."

"Don't worry, Eugene," was my answer. "It's always good to know what they're thinking. Many of them are highly intelligent men, and I think several of them are genuinely disgusted with Communism." He put on his glasses. One of the lenses was broken, and it gave his features a peculiarly forbidding look.

"Do you believe a single word they say? Remember that no one forced them to become Communists. Why did they volunteer to work for those who have now imprisoned them? Naturally, they have softened down a little in prison," he retorted.

"Well . . . don't be mad" I said, seeing he was really angry, "but the contact is useful."

"Well, it's up to you," he said with a smile. I looked at his warm face, and we forgot our flare-up.

The next evening, the "Professor Extraordinary" visited our cell. He was a tall fellow, who had once taught philosophy at the University. He always spoke at the top of his voice, spitting a little with every "r." A nervous man, he was in a state of perpetual excitement, and, according to his cellmates, did not believe in bathing too frequently.

"I tell you," he shouted at me, "that this era of terror is over; and everyone who is responsible will have to face trial." Eugene was in a gloomy mood that evening and forgot about our agreement of the previous evening to be tolerant.

"Can't you be a little quieter?" he interrupted nervously. "I'm certainly not in the mood to be punished if your conscience bothers you."

"Say, Eugene," the Professor answered, "be more considerate. Can't you see that it's only former Communists who can change all this?" This was enough to make Eugene hit the ceiling.

"Of course, what you'll want is a Titoist state, with all of you in good positions, continuing essentially the same treacherous Communist policies you pursued before. Can't you ever understand that no one wants Communism in this country in *any* form? Look at the damages and the losses you've already caused the Hungarian people."

A flood of industrial statistics followed. In this Eugene was unexcelled; his mind was like an encyclopedia. Our guest realized that he was defeated, and after trying in vain to get some backing from me, he left.

Meanwhile, the prison routine remained essentially the same. The aristocrats were certain that they would soon be freed, and were already making tentative arrangements for us to take over their work when they were gone. Of course, no one thought it possible that we non-Communists might also be freed. I was put in charge of designing and directing the chemical factory projects, and thus had less time available for my English studies.

The summer passed by, and the young swallows in the courtyard were learning to fly and preparing for their big journey. Still, no real change had occurred for us; our fancies had moved faster than history.

One evening, the door opened and the prison warden came in with some guests. One of the achievements of the Nagy era was that we no longer had to display our backsides when a visitor entered our cell, but could greet him with a "Good evening." The AVO man who came in, needless to say, did not return our greeting; prison life also has its rules of etiquette.

"We're going to give you some post cards," the visitor announced. "You may write to your closest relatives. Don't write anything about politics, because that means solitary confinement, and don't write anything about packages or visits, because that will come later. Understand?"

"Yes, sir," I replied. "And where shall we address the post card?" Eugene asked.

"To your wife's address, naturally."

"Yes, but how should I know where she is?" Eugene continued his questioning in a cold, almost accusing tone. Our guard became embarrassed, for the warden obviously did not like the whole thing.

"Listen," he said to Eugene, "don't worry, we'll straighten out those minor details. Leave the Comrade Warden alone, he's very busy." Eugene, unfortunately, was in one of his stubborn moods.

"The reason you can't tell me the address," he said to the warden, "is because she was probably deported."

"Well, write to her last address," the warden suggested peacefully.

"That was three and a half years ago," Eugene continued. "I don't know it anymore." Eugene's tone was cold and measured, but his remarks amounted to a provocation.

The warden left, almost running, in a mixture of anger and embarrassment. Soon the guard returned and explained that those details would be straightened out and that Eugene should not worry. They were only following the new instructions. I tried to pacify Eugene, too. After all, here was a wonderful opportunity, the very first, to write to our loved ones.

Who could tell what had happened to our families? I wondered: were my wife and daughter still alive? Were they in good health? What had happened to my aged mother? Thousands of questions came up which I had buried long ago, or which I had not dared ask myself before. I put all my heart and soul into that one post card. From then on, there was nothing to do but wait.

And the answers did come. They were full of love. All the news was really vital—people were well, they had moved, they lived modestly, this and that person had died, the children had grown—and they had a tragic effect on the morale of the prisoners. Now we truly realized that we had all been living in a tomb for many years, and that life—the real life—continued to thrive without us. We also realized that, in many cases, our wives had carried a greater burden than we had. In a way, they too were prisoners. . . . All we had to do in prison was to sit and try to survive. They had to struggle with everyday life, with the Communists, with the whole world, and, last but not least, with themselves.

One evening, Eugene was reading when suddenly he put down his glasses.

"I don't believe," he said in a toneless voice.

"What's wrong, Eugene, what is it?" I wanted to know.

"I don't believe that she is alive, or that she hasn't divorced me." It was my habit to tease Eugene, but I knew that this time I could not do so. I was still waiting for my own answer, and I understood his impatience. The days seemed endless, until the reply came for both of us. In a few lines, my wife condensed the essence of her life: She and my daughter, Catherine, were living in the country, at her mother's home near the water; our daughter had grown up and was going to school.

"I love you and will wait for you," it read. "Don't worry about me, be strong, it will all be over some day."

I made a promise that if I ever got free, I would pamper my wife till the end of my days. Many prisoners did the same. We realized for the first time how heroic those captives of the outside world had been.

Soon the Bulletin Board announced the system of correspondence. Those who were imprisoned for life could receive a visitor every three months, get letters at the same rate, and receive a six-pound package twice a year. Another announcement informed us that from then on, our work would be evaluated in terms of production norms. Those who succeeded in fulfilling 150 percent of the norm could correspond once a month, receive a visitor every two months, and get a package every three months. They would even receive payment for their work, which they could transfer to their family. This was the new prison order, and it was officially ascribed to "socialist legality."

Christmas Eve came, and with it homemade cookies. They tasted wonderful, but they were hard to swallow, for they contained all the love and the frustration which no censorship could remove.

Everyone was looking forward to the great day when the first visitor should appear, but a bitter disappointment was in store for me. It was announced that I had been classified as a "dangerous prisoner" and that until further notice I would not be permitted to receive visitors. I would not be able to see my wife.

13 · THE WIVES

The winter of 1954 was cruelly cold. We shivered on our daily walks, and watched the black crows freezing on the walls of the graveyard across the street.

The cold eventually forced me to become my own tailor for the first time in my life. After long negotiations with the prisoner who was clerk of the stockroom, I succeeded in obtaining some worn-out rugs which had once, in their prime, been socks. Out of these colorful patches I sewed up a sweater for myself. My tailoring efforts greatly amused the prisoners in our section. They kept visiting me to see how my work was progressing. My "heroic" undertaking became a favorite topic.

The greatest excitement occurred on those week-ends when wives, mothers, and other relatives were permitted to visit us. I will never forget the deep emotion we all felt when the first visitors arrived. The meetings took place in a large hall, and a heavy rail separated the prisoners from the visitors. Two guards stood by every prisoner, listening to each word.

To us, these women who came from the outside world seemed the most glamourous beauties we had ever seen. Their visits had varied effects on the prisoners. Some returned in a gay mood, proud of their families. Others came back with a bitter expression on their faces, and we immediately knew who had been told by his wife that she could wait no longer. Some wives complained that they were going hungry; others had been threatened with losing their jobs and livelihoods unless they divorced their husbands, or became the mistresses of their employers; others were just tired and worn-out. We learned during these visiting hours that everyday grind was taking a heavy toll not only of us, prisoners behind bars, but also of them, prisoners in spirit.

In spite of my homemade sweater, I could not battle the cold successfully, and in January I developed a bad case of flu. We needed vitamins and some better food. These were impossible to get. All the dispensary had to offer was aspirin which had been rejected by the hospitals. Our doctors always kept their fingers crossed in the hope that none of the medicine would cause real trouble to their patients. I wore my sweater faithfully, and must admit that I was as proud as a peacock of my creation. This, together with second-rate aspirins and the vitality I seem to have retained even during those years, saved me from complications and allowed me to recover.

My one major grievance was that while nearly everybody else already had visitors, my wife was not yet allowed to see me. I received letters from her, however, and felt that she was the best wife any man could have. We had so many memories in common, and I knew that our marriage was based on firmer foundations than the average marriage. During the difficult Nazi times we had survived together, as well as during our struggle against Communism, and the conflicts had tied us with bonds that no human being could break. I kept sending my earnings to her every month, and I could see from her letters that the money was needed and welcome. One thing struck me as strange in the course of our correspondence—my mother's writing never appeared in any of the letters. It was already spring when the letter came with the tragic news that she had passed on.

Round and round we went on our daily walks, and more often than not my eyes would rest on the walls of the graveyard. I felt that I was growing very old, and I knew that those of us who were spending many of their most productive years behind prison walls, were, in a way, suffering a slow death. I learned of the death of one old friend after another. Old Bela Zsedenyi had gone. He no longer needed the cigarettes I had so faithfully sent him.

Death and hopelessness engulfed us. We began to believe that in spite of the temporary easements, there would probably never be a final deliverance. Why, therefore, should we drag down our loved ones into this suffering? Why should they, too, be punished when their only crime was that they loved us, and would stand by us through everything?

I decided to write to my wife about her future. I told her that she should feel free to remarry. After all, she was young; why should she tie her life to someone who might spend the rest of his days in prison?

I did not feel like seeing or speaking to anyone. Some of my fellow prisoners tried to cheer me up, but to no avail.

I knew it would be from four to six weeks before I would hear from my wife. The agony of waiting became almost unbearable, and when the letter finally came I was afraid to read it. After staring at the missive for a while I opened it. I knew I would have to accept her decision.

My wife said she would not consider divorce, and that she was standing by me not because I wanted her to, but because she wanted to do so. She implored me to remain strong and never to forget that she loved me and that I was not alone.

One day, nearly all the Communist prisoners were released. Apparently this was the result of Imre Nagy's reforms. As more and more of them were freed, a wave of optimism swept the prison. When one or two non-Communists were also released, everyone was overjoyed. Wishful thinking predominated.

Somehow, the rumor got around that anyone who petitioned for the reopening of his case would be given the right to a new trial. After giving the matter careful consideration, I wrote my own petition.

The following week, the prison representative of the AVO who was in charge of political affairs called me to his office. He offered me a chair, and gave me a lengthy lecture on the danger of my request to reopen the case.

"You are a politician—remember that your case is a complicated political affair. You had better wait for your turn," he advised.

"Well, sir," I replied, "if you forbid me to, I will not present my petition." This made him angry.

"I'm not forbidding you to," he said, reddening, "I'm only warning you because I want to help you."

"I will keep your petition with me for a fortnight," he continued. "Should you change your mind in the meantime, let me know." With this he dismissed me.

I did not change my mind, but I never heard any more about my petition. For all I know it still could be in his desk.

God's mills grind slowly but their wheels still turn; so one day the sergeant in charge of the guards came into my cell with a slip of paper in his hand, and informed me that henceforth I would be permitted to receive visitors. He asked me whom I wished to see, and I gave my wife's address. The week that followed was long, and full of excitement and anticipation. I spent most of my free time cleaning my clothes and trying to look presentable to her. My friends unanimously decided that I should not be allowed to wear my sweater creation. Instead, they gave me a clean shirt, and even a beautiful handkerchief.

The day of my wife's visit arrived, and I was taken to the visitor's room. Iron bars divided the room into two parts. I watched the other side of the room anxiously. Suddenly the door opened, and the wives started to come in accompanied by two guards. They filed into the room in a long procession, and finally I glimpsed my wife, her small and slender figure almost hidden by two huge guards.

We looked at each other—for precious minutes we could

not find words, when they finally came, they were more like caresses trying to bridge the gap imposed by the iron bars. We talked about our daughter, ourselves, and our friends, and about the outside world.

Looking back, the conversation was not very dramatic, yet this meeting will always be one of the most momentous events I ever shared with her.

14 • WAITING FOR THE BREAK

One day, the guard informed me that I was to hand my work over to somebody else. This sound like good news, for it was the usual procedure when a prisoner was about to be freed. Once I had complied with this order, I was taken to the infamous political prison of Fo Utca, where I was assigned to a private cell. I was sure that this change meant the reopening of my case according to my request.

This prison experience again differed from the others. The place appeared to be a busy one, and the guards only showed up to hand in my food through the opening in the cell door.

Late one afternoon, I was taken up from my cell for interrogation. The room I entered was full of people, engaged in a lively conversation which stopped abruptly when I came in. In a corner of the room sat a short man in civilian dress, with a sarcastic gleam in his small eyes. Immediately, I recognized that piercing look. It was the Rat.

I was led through the room into a larger study. Behind a huge desk sat the Attorney General, the infamous Alapi, a cruel, intelligent man, fit to serve as model for a statue of Satan. He offered me a seat.

"Why are you here?" was his first question.

"I don't know," I replied.

"Try to think," he ordered.

"Well, sir," I answered hesitantly, "perhaps because I petitioned that my case be reopened; that's probably what you're about to do."

"No one wanted to reopen your case, you were convicted for your crimes against the people," he answered in a sinister voice.

"But how about the appeal?" I asked, "I've been in prison for five years without knowing anything about the outcome of my appeal."

"You'd better leave appeals alone," he answered, "if you know what's good for you. Don't you remember that I also appealed at the trial, and my appeal was that you be hanged? Aren't you satisfied with your life sentence?" he inquired sarcastically. "Well, yes, sir, but I thought," I tried to explain, "that Socialist legality—"

"Keep your mouth shut," he answered, "you don't deserve Socialist legality. We made the law, and only we decide how it should be applied. Besides, we know you have quite a few crimes to your credit which you never confessed."

After these preliminaries he settled down to a serious interrogation. At first, I did not understand why the Attorney General himself was so interested in a few seemingly unrelated incidents from my past. Then slowly the picture began to emerge. They had arrested Andrew Marton and his wife, who were correspondents of the Associated Press. Their activities as correspondents had been thorns in the side of the Communist regime. Now they were trying to link them to me in a false conspiracy and espionage charge, which they would claim was financed by the United States.

I told him that I met the Martons at several public functions. He asked me whether I ever met them privately.

"Yes," I answered. "I played bridge with them once."

"This must have been just a cover—what happened there?" he demanded.

I started to get angry, for after all these years they were still trying to use me to trap other people on completely false grounds.

"All I remember," I answered, "is that I played six spades doubled against him and made it."

This shattered his poise completely.

"You will get four weeks solitary for that," he shouted angrily, and called the guards who took me out of the room. As I walked through the small anteroom, I could almost feel the Rat's bright little eyes boring into my back.

I was taken back to my cell. Days went by and nothing happened. A whole week passed before I was given some exercise again. In comparison with my cell, the small courtyard where I had to walk round and round with my hands behind my back seemed wonderful. More days went by and turned into weeks. The food was inadequate. I was always hungry and had no cigarettes.

During my second week, the prison telegraph spelled out the news that Cardinal Mindszenty had been freed. I was elated because I had always admired him greatly, and, also, because the news indicated a major change.

One day I heard shouts in the corridor. This was unusual, and I listened intently. I could hear fragments of loud phrases.

"I'm Gabor Peter," a voice cried, "You want to murder me, I know it. You want to murder me! Remember who I was, the head of the Secret Police. I order every AVO man to obey me."

Then suddenly a guard must have put a gag in his mouth, for all I could hear was the sound of a struggle followed by silence. I could feel no sorrow in my heart for this gangster who was getting a punishment worthy of his crimes. The AVO men who were torturing him had put to death many an honest Hungarian patriot. The same scene was repeated the following day—shouts, struggles, the loud protests of a man rebelling against a treatment to which he was unaccustomed.

Five weeks passed and then, without further explanations, I was escorted to the prison van. It was a happy moment for me when I was handed over to the guards in the Central Prison.

Back “home,” Eugene and I embraced and were very happy to see each other again. A good chunk of bread and a piece of sausage were brought out for a snack.

“Well, old man, we can start our French lessons all over again,” Eugene said, as he put on his glasses in a manner befitting Mr. Chips.

15 • OUR EYES WERE ON GENEVA

The summer went by quickly. We received a small additional bonus—permission to do calisthenics while we were out in the courtyard. One of the prisoners, a former Olympic champion, took charge of these exercises. We were all enthusiastic, and worked in the summer heat as if we were preparing for the Olympics.

Fall, with its rain and mud, brought this healthy activity to an end.

Our only contact with the outside world was through letters from our families. One day Eugene received a card from his wife, and fell into an unusual silence. Knowing how reserved he was, I felt it would not be wise to approach him with sympathy or questions. It was a whole day before he could speak his mind. During our English lesson, he suddenly blurted it out.

"I can't understand my wife," he began.

"What is it you can't understand, Eugene?" I answered.

"She writes that she wants to buy a new couch. I can't see why, she has a very good bed, and last time she visited me we discussed some other things she wanted to get."

"What reason does she give?" I inquired.

"Nothing, except she said that originally she had planned to buy it in December, but then she decided to postpone it until spring. By then, she feels she will have the money for it. This doesn't make sense to me." I was thinking fast while I watched the worried expression on his face. Then, like lightning, the explanation struck me.

"Eugene," I said, delightedly. "I have the solution, you will be freed in the spring."

"What do you mean by that?" he inquired skeptically.

"Well, don't you remember agreeing with your wife that if there were any prospects of your being freed, she would write about furniture?"

Eugene looked at me, then put on his glasses, and read the post card again: "I cannot buy now, because new difficulties have come up, but by spring I will have saved enough money to get it. You can be sure of this and don't worry." Eugene's features relaxed into a happy smile, and for several weeks afterwards the prisoners greeted him with, "Hello, Eugene, any news about the couch?"

Spring came, however, and still there was no couch for Eugene's wife to buy. Our news from the outside world remained confused and difficult to understand. The Soviet Union was anxious to bring together a top-level international conference; Germany had regained her place in the European community; U.S. atomic weapons were acquiring enormous power; the Atlantic Pact seemed to constitute a formidable alliance of free states. There seemed to be troubles brewing within the USSR, the resignation of Malenkov and the ascension of Khrushchev appeared to indicate internal disorder. Apparently, the vacuum created by Stalin's death had not yet been filled. The best indication of this seemed to be the surrender by the Soviets of industrial interests in Rumania, Hungary, Czechoslovakia, and Bulgaria, to the respective national authorities.

We learned something about the process of de-Stalinization, and our hopes soared. Two pieces of news, however, disturbed us: the resignation of Churchill in England, and that of Imre Nagy in Hungary. The former event, we all felt, meant the loss to the free world of the greatest statesman of our time; the latter seemed to indicate the end of the de-Stalinization process in our country.

When news reached us of the coming Geneva Conference, however, we were enthusiastic and almost certain that this would mean our freedom. The first optimistic news seeped through, indicating that Western diplomacy was proving superior to that of the Soviet. This would give the Soviets a chance for graceful withdrawal. There were some prisoners who claimed that the Soviets would outsmart the West, but theirs was not a highly popular opinion among us at the time.

The biggest bombshell of all, we felt, was the visit paid by Khrushchev and Bulganin to Tito. One of the prisoners compared it to the pope visiting Martin Luther. This event again appeared to us as a sign of weakness within the Soviet body politic. What could result from all this, we argued, but a gradual withdrawal of Soviet imperialism to Russia itself?

16 • THE FIRST RUMBLINGS

My friends and I were convinced that there was more to the Geneva Conference than the facts disclosed by the official communiques. We placed all our hopes on secret clauses, and looked forward to the coming conference of foreign ministers which would settle the details. We were certain that freedom was very near, and we felt that this would not result from the actions of the Communists but from Western pressure.

Such was our mood as we awaited the great Hungarian national holiday on August twentieth. That day is dedicated to St. Stephen, who, as first king of Hungary, introduced Christianity to the pagan Magyars a thousand years ago.

It had been a colorful occasion in the past. From all parts of the country people came to Budapest to take part in the celebration. The Prince Primate of Hungary led the grand procession with the Head of State, the Cabinet members, and other prominent figures. As Mayor of Budapest, I had participated in two of the processions. The Holy Dexter, a relic of St. Stephen's hand, was carried around the beautiful Hungarian capital, and the day was brought to a close with a splendid display of fireworks and general merrymaking.

Inside the prison, St. Stephen's Day in 1955 dawned far from merry. The weather was hot and humid, and the colorful memories running through our minds made our loneliness and isolation even more acute than usual. All of a sudden, somewhere in the prison, a warm baritone intoned the ancient religious hymn.

"Where art thou, King Stephen, the Hungarian people long for you," came the hallowed words.

One after another, as if by previous arrangement, other voices took up the tune, basses, tenors, and even sopranos from the women's wing. It was the most beautiful choir I have ever heard. Twice we sang the ancient hymn, ignoring the panicked reaction of the AVO men and other Communists who were held accountable for our actions. They did not know what to do. Obviously this was not a prearranged revolt, but a spontaneous demonstration springing from the very depths of our hearts. All the values and traditions of a thousand years, all the loyalty of the Hungarian people to the West, were expressed in the outburst of this cherished melody.

We could hardly believe our ears when some of the guards joined in the singing. All this took but a few minutes, and a dead silence followed. Afterwards loud swearing and cursing was heard, but we did not care. We felt strong and very happy.

Several months went by, with our hopes slowly waning. The Foreign Ministers had met, only to decide that they had nothing to decide. Nevertheless, prisoners continued to be freed. We also heard rumors that some of our previous Communist prison mates had been appointed to high governmental and Party positions. They had wasted no time in starting energetic attacks against those Communists who had caused their imprisonment, and against the regime of terror which had tortured so many of them.

The long cold winter passed, and the spring of 1956 found us full of optimism once more. Rumors were flying. It was said that Rakosi was being attacked within the Party, and that there was mounting pressure to force his resignation. This stubborn, shrewd gangster held on desperately to power.

Our visitors from the outside world brought us further heartening news. The Communist Party secretaries in plants and offices were acting in a more restrained manner. People were no longer forced to attend the Communist Party seminars against their will. The over-all picture seemed to indicate that some form of National Communism might take over in Hungary, as well as in Poland and other Eastern European states, that it might develop sooner or later into parliamentary democracy.

I could distinguish three distinct threads among the skein of rumors and fragmentary news. They were the stresses and struggles within the Soviet body politic; the mounting pressure from the Western world; and the reawakening of nationalism within the satellite countries.

Soon more exciting news filtered into the prison from outside. We learned of the Poznan riots, which proved that violent outbreaks could occur at any time.

The summer of 1956 arrived. Most of the Social Democrats had already been freed, along with some other non-Communist prisoners, but the turn of the former Smallholders Party members had not yet arrived.

An important piece of news followed a few days later. Anna Kethly, the foremost Social Democratic leader, who had left our prison in November, 1954, had already been asked to join the Government. According to rumors, however, she had declined this offer, demanding first the release of all political prisoners, and also other changes guaranteeing political freedom, even the multiparty system.

Within a few weeks, other important news followed. Several years ago, influential writers and Communist intellectuals had formed an organization called the Petofi Circle. Under the leadership of Tibor Dery they now became very outspoken and were attacking Rakosi in open debates. Then came the bombshell. Rakosi himself, the Hungarian Stalin, had been forced to resign. This was almost too good to believe, but it was true. He was succeeded by a close associate, Gero, whose prestige was not as great, but whose policies were not essentially different. Yet we felt increasingly convinced that events were being influenced by forces deeper and more powerful than the will of any of these men.

D-Day finally came for Eugene. He was called to the warden's office with all his belongings. Apparently, his wife had finally managed to buy the couch. Our farewell was emotional. We embraced and in that moment realized how close we had been.

The next day, Bandi was freed. He had been in charge of the Engineering Section, and we all loved him for his good nature. For years he had talked of the day when he would go home to his wife and two children, even though his life sentence had not made the prospects too hopeful.

In the days that followed, more and more friends were freed, but still no word came for me.

Summer passed, and there was nothing for me to do but wait on a day-to-day basis, with every nerve strained for the slightest indication that the time for my release had finally come. Yet it was but a continuance of the seemingly endless, drab, suffocating prison routine. Having glimpsed the first ray of hope, prison life became more intolerable than ever.

Exciting rumors came with the fall. After the Poznan Revolt we feared that the repercussions of that outbreak might prolong our imprisonment. These apprehensions proved mistaken. More and more names were called, and more and more of our friends left prison.

Then came the Suez crisis and the nationalization of the Canal. Our political debates became more vehement than ever. The Soviet Union was forcefully approaching the important Middle East area. We were all convinced that England would not tolerate such effrontery.

Another Sunday arrived, and once more I would see my wife. She seemed to be in high spirits and obviously she wanted to tell me something of importance. She kept glancing nervously at the guards, hesitating to speak. Finally, she told me that a new Attorney General had been appointed, who respected me for my anti-Nazi activities. She had visited him the previous day, and had come away convinced that I would be freed without any further delay. I had heard this many times, but I managed to look happy and to smile, because I did not want to hurt her. If all went well, she said, I would be freed the following day. Then she gave me some news about our daughter, and the visit was over. Back in my cell, I was depressed and felt sad for her.

The following day was Monday, September 18. That evening I heard my name called. I could hardly believe my ears. My name was repeated, and I rushed out to the guards.

17 • "LAZARUS, COME FORTH . . ."

I marched down the corridor with the other men whose names had been called. We were taken before a fat major.

"All right, hurry up with the processing, or else you won't get home in time today," he said.

"Are we being freed?" we asked in unison.

"Of course," the major said. "We just received instructions from the Attorney General that you were to be freed immediately." In the excitement my heart thundered against my ribs. Two more prisoners were called to join our group. To my great delight, one of them turned out to be Bela Padanyi-Gulyas. His hair had turned gray, and he had several days' growth of beard. I was delighted to see him and could not resist embracing him. Some of the guards muttered that we should behave and try to maintain discipline.

We learned then that it is as complicated to leave a prison as it is easy to enter it. We were given civilian clothes which had to be gathered from the stockroom. They were dirty and needed pressing, but the tailors did not work evenings, and they were not permitted to leave their cells even on the Attorney General's orders. We hurriedly slipped on the dirty old rags only to be informed that it was too late in the day for us to be freed anyway, and we would have to wait until morning.

We were taken to a special part of the prison reserved for prisoners who were about to be freed. I shared a cell with Young Bela, and we spent most of our last night in prison wondering what kind of life awaited us. We hardly slept at all that night, but talked on and on about politics, old friends, those who had been freed before us and those who had passed on, until our great morning dawned. We had to fill out endless forms, and signed, almost automatically, whatever was thrust into our hands. We were taken to the comptroller's office, where we collected the balance of our earnings. One of the secretaries turned to me.

"Are you Jozsef Kovago?" she asked. "There is a message from your wife asking you to meet her at her friend's house downtown." My wife had a close friend in Budapest, with whom she always stayed when she came to the capital.

Finally we stood in front of the fat major, washed and shaved, wearing well-pressed suits, and feeling very handsome indeed. The major went through our personal data. As we were all married, he inquired whether our wives had waited for us. We replied that they had. We could see that he had something to say, and finally he blurted it out:

"My best advice to you is to forget about the time you spent here," he told us. "Maybe you were here without a reason; if so, it's not our fault. We only do our duty. When they told us to treat you badly, we treated you badly. When they told us to treat you well. . . ."

"This never happened," one of the prisoners interrupted, "you had no such problem to cope with."

"My, my," the major tried to laugh that off in an embarrassed way. "In any case, a new life is beginning for you, and I want to ask that if we ever meet outside, say, on the streetcar or in a bus, let's not look upon each other as enemies. We're all human and we all make mistakes. True, I wear this uniform, but still I don't regard myself as an evil man. Whatever I do, I do in good faith."

Bela could not control himself.

"That may be true," he remarked, "but it's hard to believe." The major's face grew sad, and he gave up.

"Well, in any case, let's go," he said, and took us to the prison gate. There, another high-ranking AVO officer checked our names and personal data as if the prison authorities knew nothing about us. Then each of us was handed his discharge papers.

The AVO officer called the guard, who took us out to the gates. Once again our names were checked.

"You are free to go now," the guard informed us. "Don't go out in a group," he added. "Leave one at a time."

It seemed to me that he, too, was moved. Apparently, he had never thought that he would see us walk freely out of that gate.

I tried to be calm, but the inner excitement overwhelmed me.

A few seconds later, I stood in the street. It seemed incredible that I was free again and that the prison was now a thing of the past.

Bela soon joined me. He talked with great animation, but I was so excited myself that I couldn't say a word, and I hardly knew what he was talking about.

We decided to take a cab. We had no cigarettes, and we asked the driver to stop somewhere so we could get some. He turned toward us.

"How many years did you spend in prison?" he wanted to know.

"Six and a half," I answered.

"Well, 2,608 days," Bela told him, "that means seven years and fifty-three days . . . exactly."

"That's a long time," the driver remarked in a friendly tone. Then he reached into his pocket.

"Won't you please have some of my cigarettes?" That was our first sign of friendliness in the free world.

The cab drive was like a dream. We were seeing things that had been long forgotten during the prison ordeal. People walked freely, unaware of the great blessing they enjoyed. There were parks we used to frequent.

The city of Budapest was even more beautiful than we had visualized it in our fondest memories.

And there were colors. In prison everything seemed to be gray, brown, or black, but now we were seeing women in gaily-colored dresses, the color of their flesh giving us quite a shock.

Entering a park, we saw some flowers, and they immediately suggested a plan. Let's take some home, we thought, so that we can arrive like gentlemen, returning with a present after a long, long journey.

We turned to the cab driver and commanded: "Take us to the best florist shop. Does Malvin Gelb still exist?"

"The shop is still there," the driver explained, "but under another name. It was taken over by the State several years ago."

"Well, let's go there anyway," Bela said.

We bought some flowers, and a few minutes later I stood in front of the house where my wife awaited me. I ran up the steps and rang the bell. The door flew open and two arms reached out for me; the flowers fell to the floor.

"Lazarus, come forth," said the Lord, and Lazarus rose from the dead.

PART II • THE VOLCANO ERUPTS

"Budapest is no longer merely the name of a city; henceforth it is a new and shining symbol of man's yearning to be free."

—President Eisenhower

1 • THE GRAY EMINENCE

Loss of one's freedom is a hardship, but regaining it is not an easy undertaking either. For the first few days I was dazed by all the new impressions. Life seemed to be so vibrant, colorful, full of tension; and it often seemed confusing. I knew I was supposed to forget prison and look forward rather than backward. It was natural, though, that I should want to know what had happened to my loved ones since I last saw them. My wife, Lonci, was reluctant to talk about those difficult years. To make a living took quite a bit of effort. For years after I was arrested and sentenced, she could not get a job in spite of her Ph.D. in chemistry. The minute she gave her name to a prospective employer, she was sent away. She was told many times that if she would divorce me she would get a job, but she was unwilling to pay that price.

After two years, she had decided to leave Budapest and join her mother in the country. She tried to make a little money by knitting sweaters. In addition to paying poorly, the work was hard on her eyes, she admitted, and it gave her too much time to think.

"What did you know about me?" I wanted to know.

"Nothing at all," she said, trying to maintain her self-control.

Years later, she had gotten a job as a bookkeeper with a small agricultural firm. She had been working there ever since. Most of my friends and relatives were frightened at my fate. A few of them, however, loyal friends like Robert, Peter, Alicia, and some others, always stood by her. When I started sending her money home in the later years of my prison life, her financial situation improved somewhat.

At first we were interrupted by constant ringing of the phone. Friends and relatives had heard about my new freedom and kept calling. Lonci was decidedly cool to some of them, and it wasn't difficult for me guess why. My two good friends, Peter and Robert, soon dropped in. They explained that something was in the air, everybody knew that something was about to happen. People felt free to criticize the regime. The loosening of the grip of the Communist terror machinery encouraged people to think and talk more freely. This period of the thaw was sensed by everyone. Peter and Robert kept arguing about the possible explanation behind the Communist concessions. Lonci was more skeptical and regarded the whole thing as a Communist trick. Robert reacted emotionally.

"How could you regard this as a trick?" he asked Lonci. "Remember what happened in the Petofi Circle? Or remember the last few issues of the *Literary Gazette*. Lonci," he added, whipping out the latest copy of the newspaper, "these writers are almost openly criticizing the regime."

Both Robert and Peter agreed that a change was about to occur, and that, sooner or later, a freer and more democratic Hungary would emerge. They attributed this to the well-planned diplomatic pressure of the Western world on the Soviet Union.

Meanwhile, we had quite a few things to do in connection with my new life. I had to report at the police station and get my all-important identification card. As we wanted to travel to the country, we needed a special permit for that, too. Lonci and I went from office to office for our permits. I enjoyed seeing the beloved streets and buildings of Budapest. Still, all the traffic and movement made me slightly dizzy. In the offices the clerks were courteous, sometimes openly friendly to me.

Lonci told me more about our little daughter. I wanted to buy her a present. I knew she didn't care for dolls, but I knew she collected miniature toy animals. When we passed a shop window downtown, I decided to go in and buy a little lion I saw in the window. I saw that Lonci was happy, for this was the first step in which I had taken the initiative since I had become a free man.

The second evening some old friends of mine gathered for dinner. It was a lovely meal, and we all made an effort to be gay, talking of bygone times. I made a special effort to smile and be cheerful to Micko, the widow of Endre Bajcsy Zsilinszky. From a beautiful, gay woman she had become a haggard, trembling old lady. It shocked me to see such a change in her. I was careful not to give her any hints about how much the Rat had tortured me on her account.

At the end of dinner the phone rang. My wife answered it, and, after taking the receiver, she turned to me.

"L. F. wants to visit you."

"Who is L. F.?" I inquired.

"Don't you remember? He is the Gray Eminence." Now I remembered the man. I was surprised.

"But why should I see the Gray Eminence?" I said. "When does he want to see me?"

"Today, if possible," Lonci answered, "by tomorrow at the latest, before we leave for the country."

The name of the Gray Eminence had upset my friends. Contempt and sarcastic laughter was their reaction to the mention of his name.

I glanced at Micko and saw the anger in her face.

"Don't meet that gangster," she whispered.

Peter, too, was red with anger. Robert, however, held a different view.

"Remember Misi, you are a politician. You shouldn't avoid a meeting like this. Besides, we have no proof that the man is dishonest. Sure, he changes colors like a chameleon, but he has his own schemes," he said.

"Nonsense, he writes editorials for those in power," Peter countered with contempt in his voice.

"On the other hand," Robert said, "he does have the ability to bring about compromises. After all, politics consists of facing reality."

"Yes, but one should draw the line at treason," Micko remarked angrily.

I didn't enter the discussion, but I whispered to Lonci to invite him for coffee the next day. Needless to say, I had my own opinion about the Gray Eminence. In fact, I had given him that name. He was typical of the "powers behind the throne" who exist in every country. He operated in the historic tradition of Machiavelli. The Gray Eminence was the silent man of influence and power who always stayed in the background, letting others strut on the stage, shaking hands and acting important, while he manipulated affairs from behind the scenes.

I remembered the first visit he had paid me ten years ago. I still remembered his tall figure, always stooped a little, as if he were apologizing to all the shorter men because he had succeeded in growing so tall. His face made him look older than he was, his hair was carefully combed over his forehead, to camouflage its height. His glasses partly hid the searching glances of his big blue eyes. His hands felt strangely damp and his handshake alternated between limp and surprisingly firm. I have learned that this depended on my situation in politics at any given time. Like a barometer, his handshake indicated the security of my political position.

His speech, like his movements, was slow and deliberate. He spoke in even tones, emphasizing the end of words. His appearance, as well as his name, was insignificant. He rarely stepped into the limelight, for he preferred to stay in the background. Those high in politics, cabinet members, associate State Secretaries, knew him well. He wrote articles and speeches for many of them. He lent his pen and talent, but only to those who were in power or who were about to get power. He had amazing political instincts; he could learn new names surprisingly fast and forget others just as rapidly. When any of his "candidates" were defeated, he never forgave them. He always felt that the reason for their fall was failure to accept his advice. By that time his handshake was rather limp. A few days before I was arrested, I met him on the street. He buried his head in a newspaper and pretended not to see me.

Robert's sharp voice interrupted my thoughts at this point.

"Don't be childish. You can be sure that the Gray Eminence doesn't come of his own accord. Some people are sending him to see Misi. The Gray Eminence may bring him the very message which might influence his future."

"Why complicate the situation?" Peter argued. "Maybe he just senses that things are changing, and he feels that this is a good opportunity for him to renew his acquaintance with Misi."

"Whatever the truth is," Robert concluded, "there's no point in refusing to see him."

"Robert, you were always one for compromises," a lady remarked. "I hope that Misi will refuse to participate in any public role with Communists who dare to call themselves Hungarians. Just a few years ago they wrote odes of praise to Stalin."

"What Misi will do," Lonci interrupted, "will be to leave Budapest with me. He doesn't have to decide right now. Let's give him a chance to rest and see the situation more clearly."

The next day I received permission to leave Budapest for the country. We could stay a month. That evening the Gray Eminence arrived exactly on time.

He was dressed in dark clothes and acted ceremoniously. He stopped at the door as if he couldn't find words, trying to control his emotions. Without saying anything he embraced me. Then he took off his glasses and started to wipe his eyes.

"Welcome, Misi," he said, visibly moved.

I stared at him in amazement. There were tears in his eyes, real tears. I could not help but admire his magnificent acting ability. Apparently he really "lived" his role.

He sat down in an armchair and spoke to my wife and to me in quiet tones. He oozed humility and spoke in a conciliatory tone. He knew that both of us suspected him, and that circumstances seemed to show him in an unfavorable light.

He proceeded to give a brief summary of the past few years, how Moscow tried to exert pressure on the regime, and how a few of them fought an almost hopeless battle trying to retain a measure of independence for the country. He explained that he had worked to get me freed. I would never know how hard he had worked, he said. He didn't want me to thank him for this; that wasn't the reason he mentioned it.

I kept quiet, darting an occasional glance at my wife. I remembered her telling me that two years earlier she had telephoned the Gray Eminence trying to get his help. He hadn't even come to the phone.

He talked for hours. By now, however, I knew his tactics. All of this was to wear me out. He would come to the point later on.

"Many people are waiting for you," he droned in a monotonous voice, "they expect you. You have a fine character, a clean reputation. Everyone knows how much you suffered for your democratic beliefs. Now, it's time for you to enter the political arena again. You must have noticed that things have been happening. A new era is about to start. Of course, a Western type of democracy is merely wishful thinking," he emphasized.

"The West will not liberate us," he added, with sarcasm, emphasizing every word. "Only the old guard reactionaries dream about such fantasies. Today reality means coexistence. This means a certain amount of freedom and a certain amount of independence from Moscow. One thing, however, we must never forget. We must go on building a Socialist State."

"And what does that mean?" I inquired naïvely.

He was ready with the answer. "You might call it Titoism, or Gomulkaism."

Now I knew why he had come. His purpose was to sell me, if possible, on the so-called National Communism. I fully realized that my future was at stake and the extent of the risks involved. They could still take me back to prison. I remained quiet, however, and let him go on talking. He was somewhat discomfited by my silence. He looked at me and continued:

"Of course you would have to receive ample financial compensation for your sufferings. You would receive a fine home in Budapest since you would have to reside in the capital."

This sounded like a clear-cut proposition. I was curious what the alternative would be, but I knew that he would let me know it in due time. Instead I asked him:

"And tell me, are you sure that's what the Hungarian people want?"

Obviously he didn't like the question, for he smiled engagingly, and became even more benign in his attitude.

"Well, the people . . . you know the people. They want what they are told to want. If people like you, and some other non-Communists whom they trust would explain things to them, they will understand, and that's exactly what should be done."

I glanced at my wife. Her face was anxious. She understood the full implication of the visit, and was worried lest I give an angry answer. However, I kept silent, staring at him with a fixed, indifferent smile on my face. I made him continue with his talk. Now he was name-dropping.

"Zoltan Tildy, Dobi, Bognar, all agreed on these things. The Communists are willing to let them participate again in public affairs. They all knew that you planned to leave Budapest.

They all felt that this was a good idea for the time being, that you should have a rest, and then, perhaps, they could come down and visit you," he told me.

"But, by the way," he added, "they are also in touch with Bela Kovacs. They visited him in the country, too."

I was immediately conscious that his answer did not mean that Bela Kovacs was in agreement with them.

Now at last I knew who were the persons who had sent the Gray Eminence. The only question unanswered as yet was what would happen if I refused his offer. In no time he volunteered information on that point too.

"Of course, don't hurry with the decision. For the time being all you need is a good rest. You must get back into shape. If, for the time being, you would prefer to work as an engineer instead of entering public life, we understand. Even then we could keep in contact and chat from time to time. Of course, you must be very careful of one thing." Now again he emphasized his words as if underlining their significance. "There are some crazy people with crazy ideas. They are the ones who always want more. To them the natural way of progress is not fast enough. That's bad," he said, "it's very bad. One should not play with fire. That might only help the Russians."

This was a clear warning. I should not demand more concessions than the regime was willing to make. He had warned me without mincing his words. Then he changed the subject, and I knew that his mission was over. He gave me some advice on my health, what I should eat, how much I should sleep. He told me that I should not worry or get excited. And above all, I was always to remember that I could count on him. He was my loyal friend who was always willing to help me. Once in a while, however, I was a bad boy, for I had always been a little stubborn. But now, we would work together. After all, none of us had become any younger in the last few years. He, too, had gone through much. In fact, his heart was giving him trouble.

Now I knew that the visit was almost over, for that was always the case when he mentioned his heart.

"There, think it all over," he told me in a mild voice. "After your little rest in the country, we can chat again." He rose and embraced me again.

After he left I kept on thinking about his words. I realized that according to rational logic he was right. Whether I liked it or not, all trends seemed to indicate that our future lot would be some sort of National Communism. Maybe that could be a comfortable and safe way towards more independence from Moscow.

Lonci was sitting quietly, for she knew what I was thinking. Finally she spoke.

"I don't want to influence you," she said gently. "I am sorry that this gangster put such a burden on your mind so soon. Please don't try to make a decision right now. Let's go to the country. I think you will soon discover how people really feel. They loathe Communism in any form or shape. They want to be free, really free."

"Well, feelings and political realities are two different things," I answered resignedly.

"Please forget about politics for the time being. Just be a husband and father. I will always love you even as an unknown engineer, but I will always look down with contempt on political opportunists," she replied.

She was putting the cups away as she spoke these words. I looked at her slender figure and suddenly understood how much she must have gone through in the last few years to make her speak like this. I felt that I understood, and I loved her very, very much.

2 • IN THE COUNTRY

The following day, September 22, 1956, we left Budapest for the country. I was anxious about meeting Catherine, our daughter. She had grown from a small child into a schoolgirl, and after all these years, I wondered how she would face a reunion with her father. After all, she must have heard about prison being the place where evil criminals are locked up. Would she be able to understand that in the present period of our country's history, patriots went to prison?

It was a delightful discovery that, thanks to her mother's intelligent approach to the problem, she welcomed me with all the love of a daughter, and soon we became better friends than I would have dared to hope.

One circumstance helped to give me a flying start. When I entered the garden, our dog, Betyar, recognized me immediately. Lying at my feet as he always had, he spoke to me with that wonderful combination of whining and tail-wagging which only happy dogs can display. Catherine volunteered to translate them for me:

"He is very happy that you are back. He doesn't know what to do, he's so glad. He's never been so happy in all his life."

When I handed her the toy lion she was delighted. We became fast friends from there on, and wonderful days followed. I breathed in the fresh air, enjoyed my books and nature, the sunset, and all the beauties of country life. In the evenings I walked up to the hill above the village, and looked down on the beautiful lake. A happy routine developed in the days that followed. Mornings, I accompanied my wife to her work and picked her up for lunch. We were the honeymoon couple of the village and enjoyed it thoroughly. In the daytime, while Catherine was at school, we used to talk and have a good time with my mother-in-law, who had a wonderful sense of humor. Once in a while my heart ached when I spoke with her, remembering my own mother who had passed on while I was in prison.

The following week Peter, my friend, came down from Budapest. He took his vacation then so that he could spend some time with us, talking about old times. I told him some of the problems I faced. Sometimes prison still haunted me. Some insomnia and restlessness were unpleasant leftovers that I couldn't quite shake off. We discussed this problem, and the way of adjustment to normal life.

A few days later, my other good friend, Robert, came from the city. He brought interesting news. Things were happening, something was in the air. In our previous discussions, Peter and I had wondered whether we would live long enough to see our country free. Robert told us that the Communists, for reasons of their own, decided that they wanted to share the burden of government with non-Communists. This gave us a chance for possible Party activities, at least on a limited scale. Some sort of a Patriotic Front was to be organized in Hungary, something like that in Poland. Several people, Robert said, were inquiring about me, especially one of my former political associates, Zoltan Tildy. As the leader of the Smallholders Party he had been first Prime Minister, then President of Hungary, between 1945 and 1948. His reputation with the people was rather low. Most persons regarded him as a weakling and a politician always ready for concessions. In fact they assigned him a large share of the blame for making it easy for the Communists to take over in Hungary. One of the tragic incidents which contributed to his poor reputation was that he let his son-in-law be tried by the Communists. A diplomat, who had formerly served in Washington, D.C. and in Cairo, Tildy's son-in-law had been lured back to Budapest and arrested for espionage. Even Tildy was unable to prevent his execution. The general consensus blamed him for this execution. Tildy himself was under house arrest in 1949 until the very end of 1955. Nevertheless, people could not forgive him.

Another person, Robert told us, whom the Communists were trying to approach was Bela Kovacs. This man was, in 1946, Secretary-General of the Smallholders Party. Of all the leaders of the Party he was the man who could never be intimidated, and who had been willing to start an open fight with the Communists for the Party ideals. He did everything to prevent the spreading of Communist influence, and insisted that the peasants and the middle class should have equal rights and opportunities with industrial workers. He also insisted that the different political parties should share power in the government in proportion to their success in the elections. This, of course, seemed intolerable to the well-disciplined and well-organized minority group of Communists, who were ready to do anything in order to gain power. As a result of his brave stand, Kovacs was openly arrested by the Soviet Army in February, 1947. With his arrest, the independence of Hungary as well as its stake in a free future, suffered considerably. Subsequently, Soviet courts sentenced Kovacs to fifteen years for espionage, and for a long time after no one heard of him. Around 1955, some news was circulated that the Soviets had handed him back to Hungary, and early in 1956 he was set free.

The reputation of Kovacs was legendary. With Cardinal Mindszenty, he became the symbol of Hungarian freedom. According to my friend Robert, he now lived in his village with about thirty AVO men keeping an eye on him. Nevertheless, some of his friends and former political associates had visited him in the past. Recently, leading Communists had gone to see him too, probably trying to win him over to the new combination of forces in this present period of political thaw. For the time being, Kovacs refused all such commitments, claiming that his health was not good enough for active political participation.

I asked Robert if he thought Kovacs was really ill. He told me that this, unfortunately, was a fact. As a result of torture and lengthy imprisonment, the strong, charming man we had known in the past had become a moody invalid, with high blood pressure and heart trouble. This was sad news and I decided to try to visit him. Robert cautioned me to think twice before doing this. If I went to his village, I would draw the attention of the AVO. Why not wait, Robert advised, for a little while? Bela Kovacs planned to go to Budapest soon to be examined by the doctor, and then I could go to Budapest, too, and there we could meet without being too conspicuous.

I also discussed with Robert and Peter the problem of my own future. As for politics, there was no chance to follow my honest convictions, therefore we felt that the best thing for me to do was to lead a quiet life as a father and a mechanical engineer.

This problem was greatly influenced by a letter that came some days later. Some of my old engineering associates wrote, inviting me back to Budapest and offering me a leading position as an engineer. The job seemed very interesting and full of promise.

The next few days were spent in planning. Lonci was somewhat reluctant to give up the security of her job and would have preferred that I stay for a month or two in the village. She felt that the country air was better for Catherine, too. But my one month's permit to stay in the country had expired and could be extended only in the capital.

On Sunday, October 21st, Lonci and I started for Budapest. On the train both of us felt nervous with unexplained forebodings of what the future might bring.

3 • A SHOT IN THE WINDOW

When we arrived in Budapest, there were many invitations awaiting us. All of my wife's relatives and our circle of friends were trying to get in touch with us to arrange a reunion. They all wanted to see me after the years I had spent in prison.

On October 22nd the Gray Eminence telephoned me. We were out when he called, and he left a message, saying that he was anxious to speak with me. If there was any way that he could be of assistance with the authorities, he would be happy to help. In any case, he earnestly suggested that I speak to him before taking any decisive steps. I found the message puzzling. There was no hurry, I decided, and planned to wait for a few days until I saw how I stood.

The next day, we went to visit some relatives outside Budapest. I was anxious to see their daughter, Judy, whom I had only known as a child. Now she was nineteen years old and a medical student in Budapest. When we arrived at our relatives' house, we received an enthusiastic reception. The table was set beautifully, as it had been years ago in normal times. I asked for Judy, as she wasn't there.

"Haven't you heard?" they queried in surprise. "Today the university students are demonstrating."

"Oh, yes, I have heard about it," I said.

"Well, then, you know of all the excitement, don't you? The university students have presented demands to the government which the regime refuses to fulfill."

"How interesting," I said in an offhand manner. "Frankly,

I don't believe that they can achieve much. I know that an AVO man walks next to every student." Changing the subject, I asked, "Why don't you tell me what you've been doing?"

Conversation followed and time passed quickly. We all grew hungry, but the hostess obviously delayed the dinner for her daughter's arrival. Finally, we started without the girl. It was a good dinner, and we were already having our coffee when Judy rushed in with all the excitement of youth. She wore red, white, and green rosettes on her blouse and shouted at the top of her voice.

"Uncle Misi, it was just wonderful," she said, in a high pitch of excitement. "It was tremendous. We stood in front of the Parliament and lit some newspapers, carrying them as torches, and sang together, 'We are not comrades. We are not comrades.' We also sang the national anthem and the national prayer. It was just wonderful, I'll never forget it. It is a wonderful feeling to be a Hungarian."

I was moved by her emotional outburst and kissed her cheek.

"Of course, Judy, it is a wonderful thing to be a Hungarian, but I am afraid it will be a long time before we can become Hungarian. The Russians are still very much with us."

"But I just remembered," she interrupted laughing, "we also kept chanting, 'Ruskis, go home.' "

Her mother came in with some food, but the girl said she was too excited to eat. All she wanted was a little rest, and then she would go back to the demonstration. All the other students, she explained, had stayed in the demonstration line and they planned to march all over the city.

Suddenly the noise of the radio added to the confusion. I laughed. This was a favorite joke of our host. Whenever the guests became noisy, he put on the radio as an additional fillip.

"Quiet, quiet," he shouted. His wife laughed.

"Forget about it," she said, "we would rather talk; we don't want that radio."

"But it's Prime Minister Gero," Judy exclaimed. "He just returned from Yugoslavia. We must listen to this. Now he'll have to make some concessions."

"Concessions," I muttered, "do you really believe that? For God's sake shut off that set. Don't ruin our lovely evening by forcing us to listen to that gangster Gero. He's one of the worst."

Our host turned the set low so that we could go on with our conversation. He continued to listen to the speech. Suddenly, he turned the volume up high. Gero was angrily belittling the university students, calling them to task for their demonstrations. I clenched my fists. My face must have turned pale, for our hostess suddenly rose and, without comment, turned the radio off.

"Here are your concessions, Judy," I murmured in anger. "These are the gangsters who are leading you. You see now why we cannot live like Hungarians."

The room became hushed and the atmosphere tense. We all felt depressed. The endeavors of the hostess to cheer us were fruitless. We went to the living room and had some liqueurs, trying to talk about bygone days.

It must have been about midnight when we started home, taking the streetcar. When we neared the city, people seemed to have been walking for a long time. A contagious excitement was in the air, and we could hear shots. We saw people running along the street. At one stop passengers boarding the streetcar told us about some street fights. The driver was muttering, debating whether or not he should continue. Finally he decided to go ahead, and we reached the ruins of the Elizabeth Bridge, one of the few remaining scars of World War II. By now the sound of shots seemed to be very close. We saw people running from all directions, some of them shouting.

We alighted from the streetcar and started walking with the crowd towards the heart of the city. More and more people came running from the side streets. The shots were very close now. I glanced at my wife; her usual composure seemed to have fled. Apparently the many years of nervous strain had taken their toll on her, too. Without saying a word we started toward the apartment, walking at a fast pace.

Our friend and hostess, Alicia, was waiting up for us. She was greatly excited.

"Big things are in the offing," she told us.

We started questioning her, but before she could give us a coherent picture of what was happening, the doorbell rang and friends arrived. The news they brought was really sensational—if it was true. According to them, the university students were besieging the headquarters of the State radio. We turned on our set and tried to get some details of these events. Meanwhile, more friends arrived with later news. They told us about the open battle raging between the youths and the AVO, the dreaded secret police. We still didn't realize that we were about to participate in one of the greatest historical events of the twentieth century.

It was well past 1:00 A.M. when Robert arrived. His boyish face was usually smiling. Now he was deadly serious. His eyes were blazing, and his whole personality seemed to have undergone a change. Most of the group realized that something momentous must have happened to turn this witty, charming man into a deadly serious, tense person.

"What happened? What's the news?" they kept asking him.

"That's a good question," he said slowly. "You are sitting cooped up here, when a revolution has just broken out."

There was a silence in the room. Finally Alicia broke it.

"Sit down, Robert," she said, in an effort to calm him. "You seem nervous today."

"Nervous," the newcomer replied with a trace of his old sarcasm returning. "That's a good way to put it. For God's sake, don't you realize what's happening? The volcano has erupted.

The whole city has risen against the Russians and the Communists."

"That's wishful thinking," I heard my wife remark.

"I wouldn't say so," Robert answered, obviously trying to control himself. "Don't you understand that there is a revolution?"

"You mean Poznan?" my wife asked incredulously.

"I can't believe it, Robert," I spoke up. "I always try to separate my dreams from reality."

"Okay," he replied, "you're just about the only one in this room who has a right to have doubts."

"Robert," I continued, "let me explain to you why I can't believe it. I know something has happened, I have seen a little of it myself today. But, believe me, I know these gangsters better than you do. You can't shake off the yoke of Communism from inside. They will arrest the student leaders and that will be all." I heard my wife seconding me. The others in the group nodded in agreement.

"Well," Robert answered, in a quiet, even tone, "that's one way of looking at it. Of course you can't deny everything the way the Communist radio does. But that still doesn't change the facts. In any case, there's no point in wasting time and words. If anyone really wants to know the truth, he should go down to the street and see for himself. Come, if you want to see a few sights worth remembering for a lifetime.

"Soon the radio station will be taken from the Communists. The crowds are already trying to topple the gigantic statue of Stalin. Maybe by now they have brought it down. Quite a few strategic locations in the city have been occupied by the Revolutionaries, and every minute dozens more are joining them. When the sun rises, in a few hours, the whole Hungarian nation will have risen against the Communists," he continued.

"Let's go, let's go," some members of our group urged.

"I don't want to go anywhere," my wife said nervously.

"We have to go," Robert replied in a quiet tone.

"It's not just a matter of going," I replied, "it's a matter of believing."

"Those who don't believe don't have a country," Robert remarked to me significantly. The words had a familiar ring. This had been one of my favorite sayings years ago.

"Well, all right," I said with a smile, "let's go."

"You can't go," my wife shouted excitedly, "there's no point to it. You just got out of prison. I won't let you go!"

"I know, dear, that I shouldn't; you're right," I answered. "But I have to go. You know I'm not a child any more, I'm not looking for adventure, but I want to see what's happening."

The others, who wanted to go promised that we wouldn't go near any danger, and that we would be back in half an hour or so.

The streets were thronged. Like ants, people swarmed all over, and from a distance we could hear volleys of shots and the rumbling of tanks. From the direction of the State radio station, people came bringing the news that the Revolutionaries had captured the station. The Communists seemed to have been prepared for such an emergency and were able to continue their broadcasts from another, unknown station.

According to some rumors, the gigantic statue of Stalin, the symbol of tyranny, was lying on the ground surrounded by rejoicing people. According to our promise, we returned home within half an hour.

"Well, what's new?" the women inquired.

"Perhaps Robert is right," I said. "Though I still don't believe it." In my heart I knew that it was true, but it sounded too beautiful to put into words.

We went to bed, tired and excited. My wife nestled close to me.

"I'm worried about you," she whispered.

"Don't be silly," I said. "Sleep well, we will see clearer in the morning."

In a few minutes' time I was fast asleep.

A sharp noise woke me. It sounded as though somebody had dropped a glass and stepped on it. It seemed to have happened on the floor near my bed. In a daze I sat up.

"What happened?" I heard Lonci ask in a frightened voice.

I put on the light and looked around in the room. Then I stepped to the window and pulled the drapes aside. There was a small, round hole in the middle of the glass panel. From a distance I heard the noise of a plane.

"Do you see anything?" my wife inquired nervously.

"Nothing at all. It probably was the building superintendent or someone on the street who knocked over a garbage can in his enthusiasm."

"That's a relief," she sighed, reassured.

Before turning out the light, I carefully picked up a bullet from the floor and put it in the ashtray next to my bed. Before falling asleep it crossed my mind that this shot was almost like a message, warning me that great things were in the offing, and that I could not hesitate to take my part and do my duty.

Next morning the super's wife came up and told our hostess that, for several months, an AVO officer lived in the apartment across, one floor up. He had left during the night, taking all his things.

By then, the AVO's lot was far from being a happy one.

4 • THE STRUGGLE FOR FREEDOM

I will never forget that morning. It was probably the most hectic one of my life. It began when our hostess rushed in.

"Misi, Lonci," she exclaimed. "Get up, the Russians are on the run! Imre Nagy is Prime Minister."

"That sounds good," I answered. "But what about the Russians?"

"A lot of things happened while you were asleep," she explained. "There is no question that a Revolution has broken out."

In a few minutes some other friends showed up, as well as an elderly lady who had gotten stuck on the west side of the city, unable to cross the Danube to Buda. I begged them to explain what they knew.

All throughout the night, they said, people were fighting the AVO in many places throughout the city. At dawn, Russian tank units arrived, and now the Freedom Fighters were fighting those. As a result of the pressure from the young people, Imre Nagy became Prime Minister.

Somewhat later Robert arrived.

"You're a prophet, Robert, you're right, there is a revolution," we shouted to him. Somebody turned on the radio.

"The sneak attack of the Fascist Counter-revolutionaries caught the government unaware," the announcer's voice said in a matter-of-fact way; "therefore, under the Warsaw Pact it requested the help of Soviet troops to restore order."

"Imre Nagy is a gangster too," Lonci cried. "I told you not to trust him."

"He should be hung next to Gero," someone else added.

"Don't be so upset," Robert said. "Imre Nagy's personal character doesn't matter now, let's not waste time thinking of that."

Everybody in the room disagreed with him, and the argument continued. Meanwhile, the shooting and the gunfire seemed to have drawn quite close and the windows shook. Robert suggested that the men should try to talk by themselves, for it was impossible to reason with the nervous women. Why didn't they go to see how our food supply stood, we suggested, since the trouble might last for quite a while. This indication of male egotism drew angry protests from the women on their way to the kitchen.

Robert started by giving his analysis of the situation. He felt that the government had committed a serious error by asking the Russians to help quell the insurrection. The people might have been contented with some sort of a minor revolt. Now, the whole nation would join the freedom fight against the Russians.

Peter had spent the night on the Buda side. He told us in detail about battles raging in several places, and about Soviet tanks guarding the bridges across the Danube. He had considerable difficulty getting over to the Pest side. Between his account and Robert's I started to see the total picture more clearly. By now I had no doubts that this was a full-fledged fight and would have far-reaching effects.

"Where do they get their weapons?" was one of my first questions.

"First you must understand that there is no single person in charge of the Revolution. In fact, that is part of its strength," I was told. "As far as the guns are concerned," one of them said, "they have just a few rifles, pistols, and hand grenades which they got from the army and from worker units. That's how it started. By now, the soldiers are joining us. They say that the barracks are also supplying munitions."

The phone rang. George took the receiver.

"No, he's not here," I heard him explain. "I don't think he's in Budapest. No. Good-bye."

He put down the receiver and turned to me. "A man whom I know to be a fanatic Communist wanted to speak to you."

Again the phone rang. Again somebody wanted to talk to me. I was trying to figure out how they had learned of my whereabouts. Most of the people who had called were types whom I did not want to know where I was. Finally we realized that waiting like this was impossible.

"Let's get out of here," Peter said. "We can't talk anyhow. Why don't we go and see?" Before we reached the door the women saw us going.

"Where are you going?" Alicia asked.

"Down to the street," Peter explained.

"You can't go!" Lonci cried.

"I have to go!" I answered in a determined tone.

"You can't go. Don't you understand?" she said. "Don't you see that this whole thing is a Communist trick? They are trying to use this to suppress Poland and Hungary even more. They called the whole thing de-Stalinization, or something like that. It's one of their devilish tricks."

"What trick, Lonci?" Robert interrupted in a sharply sarcastic tone.

"This whole crowd," she retorted, "the Communist rioters are only confusing people, making them excited, so they will be victims of the Soviet tanks. That's just the excuse they want to find for their long-range policy. If men like you show where you stand and what you are doing, you will give them an excellent excuse to liquidate you once and for all. That goes for Misi and all of his friends above anyone else. Are you crazy, that you can't see all this?"

"Lonci," Robert replied, "you are talking nonsense. This is a spontaneous outbreak of a whole nation. You can't prearrange a thing like this."

I listened and felt that her words made sense. Her feverish eyes and excited words were very convincing.

"Oh you men, you can be so stupid," I heard Lonci say again. "Don't you remember the words of the Gray Eminence? All this revolution is no good to anyone except the Russians. Anyhow—you have to choose between me and the street."

"Look here, Lonci, don't worry," I tried to reassure her. "I have to go and see for myself. This is not a matter of choosing between you and the street. I just have to see for myself what goes on."

"They might shoot you. Please don't go," she begged.

"If they want to shoot me they can do it any time. Last night they almost succeeded." This gave the whole conversation a new twist. I went to the bedroom, brought out the bullet and showed it to everyone. Lonci, too, became quieter.

"All right, then, let's go, just to look around a little bit," I said.

"You are hopeless," Lonci said. "Not even prison has changed you."

"Well, look," said Peter in a pacifying tone, "would you love him if he changed?"

"I hate you all," Lonci said. "If anything happens to Misi, I will . . ." she burst into tears and ran from the room.

At last we were down in the street. I wasn't in a good mood. I reviewed our conversation to myself. Maybe she is right—the Russians have set a trap for us all, I thought. George explained that if we could put up one more day's resistance, then we could be sure of Western aid. He had already listened to Western broadcasts in English as well as in German. Everybody talked about the Hungarian battles over the radio.

"We will be a front-page sensation all over the world," he said with laughter. "What do you think of that?"

"Well, the revolt at Poznan must have made the front pages, too, although at that time I was still at the spa and they forgot to mail us the Western papers there," I said sarcastically.

"The Kovagos are a hopelessly pessimistic lot today," Peter retorted.

"Apparently the prison has worn Misi out," they teased, laughing like schoolboys.

All over the city, as we walked, we saw signs of the battle, broken cables, bullet holes in walls of houses all over the place. Crowds of people swarmed the streets. On the corner of Museum Avenue we saw a deserted Soviet tank. Everybody seemed to be wearing the Hungarian colors and rosettes, and there was universal gaiety. Near the Hotel Astoria we saw three children with guns going toward the university. Then, suddenly, we heard the rumble of tanks in the same direction. One of the huge monsters appeared, followed by another. People pulled into the doorways.

"Ruskis, go home," someone shouted, and others repeated, chanting, "Ruskis, go home." This gave the street almost a carnival atmosphere. One of the tanks stopped at the intersection. As a former soldier I knew that it was getting ready to fire. A group of men was heading toward the tank on the wide avenue. We saw with horror that the huge turret gun of the tank turned toward them.

A little old lady walked up to the tank and explained that all her group wanted was to have the Russians go home.

"We don't want to occupy their country, so why did they want to take ours?" she asked. One of the Russians listened intently, and then he declared that he would not fight crowds or shoot children and old women. Here was the tank at their disposal. He offered it to them and volunteered to take them anywhere they wanted to go.

"Good Ruski," the people shouted. "Let's go to the Parliament."

They climbed on the tank, as many of them as could find room.

"Step on it, Ruski," they yelled. "Show us how good a cabbie you are."

From the direction of Museum Avenue another tank showed up. People were hailing it as if it were a taxicab. This one, however, ignored the crowd.

"Apparently there's a cease fire," somebody said. "Imre Nagy did it."

"Don't mention that traitor, fellow citizen," someone else argued. "He's no good. He's the one who called in the Ruskis."

Peter was roaring with laughter.

"Did you hear that?" he asked. "Fellow citizen, instead of 'Comrade.' That's something new, isn't it?" Walking up to the other man, he said: "Tell me 'fellow citizen,' do you, by any chance, know what's going to happen in front of the Parliament?"

"A demonstration, of course. That's why everyone is hurrying there. Everyone's demanding that the Ruskis go home."

"All right, then, 'fellow citizens,' let's all go."

With this we started. The streets were alive with the news. Everything seemed wonderful. The youth of Budapest had scored a victory over the Ruskis. Soldiers of the regular Army had joined the insurgents. There were rumors that in the Kilian Barracks some soldiers were handing over weapons to the Freedom Fighters. The same happened in Buda in the Radetzky Barracks, too. Even among the Russians, there were many who didn't want to fight.

The government issued a ban on public gathering, but in spite of that the streets were crowded. We sent George back to report to the women that we were still alive, and then we continued. Near Elizabeth Square there was a group of armed men in front of a new building which I had never seen before.

"These are those damned AVO men," Peter muttered. "They are the ones who should all be shot."

Near police headquarters a truck was circling round and round. There was an atmosphere of excitement in the city. Once in a while a voice in the crowd would yell "Ruskis, go home" and the crowd would take over, chanting the demand. From a distance, one could hear gunfire.

Around noon we reached Freedom Square. A large crowd was demonstrating in front of the American Legation. "This was a peaceful demonstration right here in front of you," I heard the speaker say. "You have seen how they massacred men like cattle. It was cold-blooded murder."

Peter took hold of my arm and led me across the square.

"Sit down here, Misi," he said. "We don't want you to participate in a demonstration in front of the American Legation. I am sure there are AVO men in the crowd. Robert and I will come back and tell you all about it afterwards."

I sat quietly on the bench when suddenly someone embraced me. It was a man sitting on the other side of the bench who used to be a prison mate of mine.

"Isn't it wonderful, what the young people did?" he said proudly. "It's hard to find words to express it. I would love to do something, anything, if someone would just tell me what. But during the eight years in prison I have lost contact with the outside world and with the people. I don't even know the names of these youth leaders."

I understood well how he felt.

At that point my two friends returned. They gave me a brief account of the demonstration in front of the U. S. Legation, how people had spoken out. Then they suggested that it was time for us to leave; something was wrong. People swarming toward us from the direction of the Parliament said that Parliament Square was barricaded. A short time ago, the AVO and the Russians had massacred a crowd of peaceful demonstrators, several hundred people had been killed in a few minutes' time. This was an outrage by any civilized standards. Something had to be done.

"Let's take Misi home immediately," Robert suggested.

"Leave me alone," I said. "I'm not a child anymore." With that I started towards Parliament Square. On the corner two armed soldiers stopped us. In spite of the protest by my two friends, I tried to go on. "No one can cross here," the soldiers shouted, pointing their guns at us. They were backed by Russian tanks standing by, ready for action. My friends berated me.

"Lonci was right, you are a damned fool to get mixed up with them again."

"Keep quiet," I said. "These kids taking on the Russians virtually barehanded are running a greater risk. What matters now is that everyone who has courage be on the street; and that everyone who can get hold of a gun should fight. I'm convinced that after this blood bath, events can no longer be stopped."

Walking toward home we saw yet another change in the streets. The national colors of Hungary were everywhere, and houses were suddenly bedecked with red, white, and green flags. On the walls we saw hastily printed demands of the Revolutionaries. Children were running up and down, some of them armed. Tension mounted.

"The AVO murders—" we could hear people murmuring. The news of the massacre on Parliament Square went round like wildfire. New crowds came to the streets to demonstrate, demanding that the Ruskis go home. People defied the government orders. They felt that the best help they could give the fighting youth was to go out into the streets. It seemed that an avalanche had started. People were no longer afraid. This was something new, this was something no government orders had power to stop.

When we reached home the women told us that Tildy, former President of Hungary, had spoken on the radio. Apparently, they tried to use *him* now. The phone kept ringing. The Russians were on the retreat all over the place.

"It's still a dirty trick," Lonci insisted. "This will be a devilish trap which will end in the massacre of the people. Don't you remember the Russo-Finnish War?" she asked impatiently.

Someone came in with the news that Yugoslavia's attitude would force the withdrawal of the Russians. A visitor gave us details about the regular Army units continuing to join the Freedom Fighters. I tried to get a clear picture of events, separating fact from assumption. This was far from easy. We tried to get Radio Free Europe, Voice of America and B.B.C. broadcasts, while some of our group went down to the streets to gather information. I realized that the most important thing to do now was to get a comprehensive view of the situation. To anyone who asked my advice about what to do I said:

"This is a revolution for freedom. No one should expect orders. Everyone should try to fight for himself. Those who don't have the weapons can still help the cause by disobeying the orders of the government and going to the streets to demonstrate."

Late at night a young man visited us. He had been behind a tank on Parliament Square during the horrible massacre that day, and he told us all the details. It was from the gigantic building of the Ministry of Agriculture across the square that the AVO opened fire. The Russians had begun firing only after that. Some of them actually shot at the AVO men.

"Are you sure of that?" I asked incredulously.

"Absolutely. In fact, a tank behind the one where I was fired at the AVO, too."

That report explained quite a bit. The Russian tanks, some of which we met during the morning, had been heading towards Parliament Square and had gotten mixed up in the massacre quite innocently. The AVO started the massacring and some other Russian tanks helped them.

Some telephone calls later on gave me additional information about these dramatic events. Like a jig-saw puzzle, I put together all the available bits of information, filling in events which related to the over-all picture. To me the most significant thing seemed to be that these Russians who joined the Freedom Fighters did so genuinely, and not with any Machiavellian motive. I felt this to be of paramount importance because if I had found the Russians joining the insurgents as part of a fraudulent scheme, that would have been an obvious indication that there was a gigantic trap set for the Hungarian nation, that the Imre Nagy affair was also a trick, and that Imre Nagy himself was a traitor.

All throughout the night the battle continued. The Freedom Fighters, increasing in number hourly, used hand grenades. They put to good use the military skill which they had learned in the Communist schools. They had also been taught how to make primitive weapons and fight guerilla warfare. This was practically the order of the day.

Around midnight we went down the street again. I was convinced that when the outside world learned about the massacre of Parliament Square, United Nations' observers would be dispatched without delay.

The street was full of news. The National Museum was on fire, but the radio apparently was in the hands of the Revolutionaries. The workers started a strike, insisting that the Russians leave. Public tension was ready to force the hand of Imre Nagy. The mood of the street was enthusiastic and defiant. It was around dawn when we returned. Peter wanted me to go to bed. He said he had to return to the streets for a little while. I knew he was determined to get some weapons and fight.

"Let's go," I said. "Both of us."

"You won't go anywhere," he said. "You did your share. You

spent enough time in prison. We don't want you to get caught in battles and killed by a stray bullet. Your seven years in prison will have been in vain. We need your head for better tasks."

"What we need now," I interrupted "is men who fight, not heads. Let's go!"

"Nothing of the kind," he insisted. "You'll stay here even if I have to fight you to hold you back. The time will come when this country will need honest leaders like you. I won't let you go."

"Then you won't go either," I said angrily.

"All right," he said with resignation. "But what a shame. I certainly feel like taking a shot at those gangsters."

5 • "EVERY HUNGARIAN IS WITH US"

Early in the morning of October 26th the battle raged again fiercely close to our apartment. The walls shook with the vibration from the gunfire. Our fellow tenants were afraid and wanted to use the air-raid shelter.

Peter and I walked down the street. Just as we reached the next block, the house across the street was shattered by the blast of a direct hit. Then we saw a gigantic tank racing at full speed toward the bridge, as if it was fleeing. Young Freedom Fighters ran from the house, throwing what was probably a homemade grenade at the tank. It exploded.

As we reached the Astoria Hotel, that old landmark received another hit. The crumbling walls fell on a deserted tank. Some of the wounded were taken out of the hotel. Near the museum, the sight was horrible. The streets looked like a nightmarish battlefield. Houses and tanks were reduced to rubble with the dead lying all over.

"Let's go home," Peter suggested. "Let's hear what the radio says." We found the ladies ready to tell us the latest news.

"The whole country has revolted against the Russians and the Communists," Alicia said. "The AVO men are on the run everywhere. The Army is joining the Freedom Fighters. All the police are aiding them, too. People are no longer afraid, and everyone disregards the Government's instructions. Public opinon will sweep out Imre Nagy unless he accepts the demands of the people."

The women decided to go out to buy some food. We went

to the store with them. There was a big crowd in front of the State store. We saw our friend George giving orders.

"Fellow citizens," he cried, "let's open the door and sell the merchandise!"

"The boss isn't here," somebody shouted. "We'll have to wait. Say, who are you, fellow citizen?"

"I come from the Revolutionary Committee for Public Supplies," George answered, confidently.

"Just open the store. We don't need the boss." Robert walked up to George and patted his shoulders.

"Well done, George," he said. "But what if they had demanded documents?" George laughed.

"Then I would have shown this one," he said, whipping out a document with a red, white, and green flag across it. George explained that the night before two university students had visited him, giving him the document and asking that he have some food stores opened for the Freedom Fighters. They pointed out that the population needed food supplies.

The women stood in the long line and we left them there, since it looked safe. We walked toward the area where a battle had been raging a few hours ago. We saw a dead boy of about twelve years, lying on the street. He was covered with national flags and flowers. There was a box next to his body to collect donations for his family. It was full, not only with coins but with notes as well. The money was unguarded.

In the next block I saw a jewelry store with the glass broken. Expensive jewelry was without any protection. No one had touched it.

"Take a good look at this," I told my friends. "This jewelry store will go down in history as a symbol of the idealistic purity of the Hungarian Revolution. There are no thieves or burglars in this city now. At this moment everyone has but one cause, and that is freedom."

We felt a wonderful pride. We recognized then the high principles and the nobility of our people.

We arrived at Deak Square. On the top of the police headquarters building there was a gigantic Soviet star. People eyed the hated symbol helplessly.

"Let's take down the Red Star. Let's take down the Red Star," I heard Peter shout.

People took up the slogan, chanting. The crowd grew, insisting that the Soviet symbol be removed. Some police officers appeared at the window, talking to the people.

"Don't talk so much," someone said. "Let's pull down that star right now."

Suddenly on the top of the building a lone figure appeared. He was climbing toward the star. The crowd greeted him with loud roars of enthusiasm. He was tugging at the star while the crowd encouraged him. Then, spontaneously, many hundreds of people took off their hats and sang the National Anthem. Slowly the star began to move. The man worked feverishly. The star was well attached and difficult to move. A foreign movie-camera man started to make a newsreel of the crowd. Peter stepped in front of me, murmuring, "There's no need for you to appear in that film. Who knows what will happen to it?"

Finally, the star started to topple, and it fell the six floors to the pavement. Everyone cheered. Peter and I continued our survey of the streets. Stars were falling all over the city, Soviet stars, that is. The national flags hanging from the buildings all had a round hole in the middle. The hated hammer and sickle was cut out, like a cancerous spot. This was another symbol of the Revolution which we will never forget.

The mood of the people was exciting. The determination of the people was a powerful force ready to sweep away any government which did not act fast enough. The wrath of the people had turned against every reminder of the hated Soviet oppression. A bonfire of Communist books had been lighted.

The afternoon broadcasts gave a number of confusing and conflicting government orders. The government ordered the Freedom Fighters to lay down their arms, but it was obvious that nobody believed that this order would be obeyed. The regime itself realized that what was being challenged was the whole Communist state system and philosophy.

The hospitals were crowded. The wounded and dead were in every house. The barracks became temporary graveyards. The flower of the nation's youth shed its blood for Hungary. Black drapes appeared next to the national flags.

Late in the evening there was shouting and noise from the streets. We opened the windows and looked out. An enormous crowd was approaching, led by young men pushing bicycles, carrying an enormous national flag. In the center of the flag was a blood stain. Hundreds of bicycles followed, all flying the national colors. Behind them, marching in ranks, were men, women, and children. Well-dressed and ragged people marched together; national flags were in every hand. The angry murmur of the crowd could be heard clearly.

"AVO murderers," rumbled from a hundred throats. "AVO murderers. Every Hungarian is with us. AVO murderers. Every Hungarian is with us!" The rumble swelled to a roar.

"Let's go," we all said, and without losing any time we rushed down to the street. Lonci joined us too, full of excitement, her eyes sparkling. "Let's go too. We are Hungarians."

Down in the street we became part of the crowd and took up the chant. We had a wonderful feeling of identification and of challenge to us all. All of us were shouting. The demonstration headed towards the U. S. Legation. We were carrying the feelings, dreams, anger, and determination of a little nation to the representatives of the greatest power on earth.

Near Elizabeth Square the demonstrating crowd almost walked into a raging battle, and, learning that strong AVO detachments were about to arrive, we dispersed. Soon we converged again and with more people joining us every minute, we continued to march toward the U. S. Legation. It was an exciting and inspiring crowd. As we marched toward the American diplomatic building, my eyes suddenly came upon a familiar gaunt figure. Electrified I was shaken out of my enthusiasm right into memories of my imprisonment. It was Daddy Longlegs, demonstrating as one of the most enthusiastic men in the crowd.

"Anyone who is Hungarian marches with us," I heard him chant. With grim satisfaction I listened to his rather convincing shouting, "The AVO are murderers, the AVO are all murderers." He certainly ought to know, I thought.

We reached the building where the American Legation was housed and made sure that the voice of the people of Budapest was heard by representatives of the United States.

On my way home I still thought of Daddy Longlegs. There was an AVO man demonstrating against the AVO, shouting at the top of his voice. Remembering Daddy Longlegs and my experience with him in prison, I could believe that his sentiments were sincere. This apparent contradiction was one of many which threw light on the complexities of these events. After all, who were the ones who turned first against the Russians and the Communists? They were the youngsters, most of whom had been forced to join either the Communist Party or one of the Communist-sponsored youth organizations. Their minds had been crammed with Communist ideology day and night. The healthy resistance of these young minds and hearts shook off the veneer of indoctrination almost overnight. They were the backbone of the Revolution. They had had enough of the Communist lies. They were hungry for the truth which their leaders had failed to give to them. With the strength of youth, therefore, they reached out, searching for truth, unaided. No force could halt these young men.

The ordinary citizens of Budapest, suppressed longer by the Communist regime, were infected by the enthusiasm of the youths and filled the streets, demonstrating, fighting in this way their own battle against Communism and the Russians. It was the youth who manned the guns. The older citizens' fight consisted of less dramatic weapons, but their behavior contributed considerably towards the annihilation of the regime. They disobeyed the government's orders and filled the whole capital with their demands, demonstrations, and shouts. The role they played was similar to the chorus in Greek drama. The aid from the citizens boosted the morale of the Freedom Fighters, and helped immeasurably in the battle. The mood of the people was a clear indication to the Freedom Fighter that they were behind him and that he was a cherished champion fighting for liberty. The same attitude on the part of ordinary people—men, women, and children—frightened the AVO. Where could they run? Who would take them in?

Soon it became clear to me that yet another powerful force lined up for the battle: the industrial workers. Every plant, large or small, organized its Revolutionary Council. After many years of make-believe trade unionism the workers really had a say in their own destinies. At last they recognized the strength they possessed. No Russian tanks or AVO submachine guns could stop them. The workers made it clear that they identified themselves with the Revolution, ready to threaten any government which hesitated to accede to the demands of the risen population. The workers were powerful in more than one way. Organized, they had control not only over raw materials, but also over the means of transportation. Their behavior must have been one of the greatest shocks to Communist theoreticians. This was an example from modern history where the workers openly revolted against the "dictatorship of the proletariat."

Late that night the city knew that the people had won. The AVO machinery, organized and armed for years at huge expense and with much effort, disintegrated in a few hours. Fear and guilt feelings had weakened their ranks as effectively as the armies of the Freedom Fighters. Some AVO men even turned against their own officers.

That night I felt it was time for me to sum up the essence of the Hungarian Revolution. The picture began to take shape.

The first wave of attack against Communism was waged by the writers and intellectuals. They were the much-pampered elite of the regime, and the Communists for years had tried to woo them into service.

This wave of attack was followed by youth. They were the ones who actually took up arms against the regime. For years the Communists had given free scholarships, education, and the possibilities of great careers to the young people, hoping to win them over.

The workers, who were supposed to be the new leading class under Communism, had turned against the regime, organized and in an overwhelming majority.

The Army, that much-pampered Communist Army of the Hungarian People's Democracy, also proved unreliable for the regime. First individuals—then organized army units—joined the people, identifying themselves with their demands. Most of the officers who turned against Communism were working-class men especially trained by the Communists for key Army positions.

In other words, it was not the embittered and suppressed middle class, nor the frustrated peasantry, regarded as the arch-enemy of Communism, who had started the Revolution. They joined the Revolution wholeheartedly, but the pampered children of the Communist regime were the ones who turned first and most effectively against the Party of the Soviets.

On October 27th the might of the demonstrations increased further. All the street signs and walls were plastered with posters demanding freedom and concessions from the government. The government-controlled radio station continued to blare against the demonstrating people as "bandits and counter-revolutionary

Fascists." None of this kept the people from demanding more freedom from the Communists. There was an amazing unanimity in the voicing of these demands. The wording was simple and clear to anyone: "Ruskis, go home; Hungary should leave the Warsaw Pact; October 23rd should be declared a national holiday; all fighting should be stopped; the Hungarian national emblem should be used, instead of the Soviet star; the Army should be under Hungarian control; the workers should be given their just rights, and Russian should no longer be a compulsory language in the schools." The demand for free elections was heard more and more frequently.

With all my friends we covered every part of the city, trying to get a clear picture of the demands of the people. None of us ever saw or heard a single demand which indicated that the Hungarian people wanted to go back on any of the social reforms affected since World War II. There were no posters demanding restoration of the monarchy, nor of feudalism. No counter-revolutionary "Fascist" forces appeared. No one demanded mass liquidation of Communist Party members or any sort of white terror. In fact, it was touching to see how much respect people were ready to give to religious beliefs of others. There was no trace of anti-Semitism.

While the Revolution was an elementary force shaking the very foundations of Communism and Soviet power in Hungary, there was a certain dignity as well as moderation in the demands voiced by the people.

The lack of food forced long lines to stand in front of the food stores. There was unparalleled patience and good will among the people waiting for hours in these queues. I often saw someone with two loaves of bread handing one over to an old woman, a complete stranger, just to save her the trouble of standing in line. People were helpful and cooperative with each other. The word "comrade" seemed to have disappeared from the Hungarian language; "fellow citizen" or "mister" replaced it.

As the hours wore on, the demands of the masses became more and more insistent. It became obvious that very soon all of Imre Nagy's prestige would vanish unless he acted fast, to satisfy the demands of the people. Announcements which the government repeated to the effect that "the leadership of the Communist Party has been reorganized under Janos Kadar," made no impression on the people. They were no longer interested in reshaping events within the framework of the Communist political system. People were much more concerned about the possible arrival of U. N. observers and some indication of Western help for the Hungarian Revolution.

Finally, at noon, the radio announced that Imre Nagy had organized a new government. After his silence—which gave birth to many rumors about his possible arrest by the AVO, as well as his alleged role in calling for Soviet help—this news was rather reassuring. We were not surprised to see the name of former President Zoltan Tildy in the new government. The name of Bela Kovacs, however, electrified us. To us, this was a clear indication that the Communists realized that they could not control the situation with a Communist or pseudo-Communist government. They badly needed men in their ranks whom the Hungarian people trusted. One disappointing fact was that the announcement of the new government was not followed by any declaration of policy. Rumors circulated to the effect that Bela Kovacs didn't even know about his appointment to the government; that he still resided in a small village in southern Hungary. Another disturbing note was that the Minister of War had ordered the Army to liquidate armed insurgent groups. It seemed that he was the only one who was not aware yet that the Army had joined the Revolutionaries and that the Revolution had been won. One piece of good news announced was that the government had accepted the legality of the Workers' Councils.

The basic question, however, still remained open. Would

the Revolution have effective political leadership to take control of the situation and enforce the demands of the Freedom Fighters? Our fear was that if no such step was taken, passions might tend toward the extremes, and the demands of the people would move away from clear reason and reality.

6 • A CALL FROM PARLIAMENT

Robert suggested that we go down the street and take another look at the city. He thought that we should try to reach the Kilian Barracks. That was where the strongest battles were being waged, and it seemed that a military leader of the Revolution was emerging there. His name was Pal Maleter, and his name was on everyone's lips. Another potential leader was Jozsef Dudas. Peter and Robert argued about the relative merits of these two. I couldn't resist putting in my two cents' worth. It will be Imre Nagy, Tildy, or no one else, I felt. In any case, we all agreed that the mood of the street was one of excited anticipation. Everyone was curious about the ability of the new government to fulfill its promises. The greatest hopes were pinned on Bela Kovacs. The only problem was that no one knew whether he had actually accepted participation in the government or if his name had been included without his permission.

It was difficult to make our way through the crowded streets. The city looked like a gigantic ant hill turned upside down. We met many friends. Everyone was full of enthusiasm. They proclaimed that the Russians had already been beaten, and that those who were left would be taken care of by Maleter, with the help of the Army, the youth, and workers. Everyone was delighted by the display of Hungarian unity.

Some others told me of the Revolutionary Councils now being formed everywhere. I was invited to several of them; apparently the Smallholders Party planned to reorganize within a few days. Friends insisted that I be there among the new leaders.

In the center of the city the fighting had died down. The streets looked like a battlefield, and we could smell the acrid smoke of countless gun battles among the ruined houses. There were long lines in front of the shops. From far away we heard the battle raging. We started toward the noise, and as we reached Museum Avenue we ran into a small group of armed seventeen- and eighteen-year-old boys. They were heading toward the Kilian Barracks to join the Freedom Fighters there.

"Whose orders are you following?" we inquired.

"Orders?" one of the youngsters replied. "No one waits for orders here, Mister."

"Well, who gave you the weapons?" we continued our queries.

"No one in particular," the boys replied. "Find some for yourself, that's your job."

"Okay," we said, "there is somebody you have to report to when you want to fight, isn't there?"

"You can, if you want," the youngster answered with a wide grin on his face, "to the good Lord, Himself."

I couldn't help liking these boys. Up to now they had been fighting in Buda, but now the job there was over, so they were heading towards the Kilian Barracks, for they figured that they might be of help there.

While I was thinking, the boys decided that it was their turn to tease us.

"Well, Uncle, you are no good for fighting any more, you're too old for that. All you can do is to yell. That's good, too, we need that help. Let's not give these AVO gangsters a peaceful minute."

We were already on our way and the youngsters continued to fill us with information. In Buda, where the Revolutionaries had secured an overwhelming victory, the AVO men had tough going. Some of them were captured, but most of them had fled. At the Grand Boulevard we turned from the group. We decided to take a look at the building of the *Szabad Nep* which housed the most powerful Communist newspaper. In the last days, t building was occupied by the Freedom Fighters and became place of legendary fighting. The building still showed sc yesterday's fighting.

We got home late, tired, and happy. It definitely looked lik a day of victory. The news pouring in from the provinces alsc showed that the country had risen, united against the Communists and the Russians. Apparently the critical historical moments were those of the Communist-initiated massacres. In addition to the Parliament Square blood bath there had been others, the most revolting of which was the one at Magyarovar. After those horrible outrages the people rose like one and joined the youth.

By now even the most pessimistic realized that victory was in sight. My friends and I tried to be realistic in our conclusions. We listened patiently to the free radio stations in Hungary, as well as to the Western broadcasts. We spent considerable time on the streets, talking with people, and trying to gather all possible information. It was still impossible to form a clear picture on the fighting itself, for it seemed to change with the hour. New elements and new groups showed up unexpectedly. The situation was in a state of flux. The individual's initiative, courage, and heart were apparently the paramount factors. Nevertheless, we could sense a yearning on the part of the people for a national leader. Everyone realized that after the completely scattered and decentralized freedom fight there was a need for a national leader. People were not sure about Imre Nagy, but they still hoped that the government under him would do something.

Although Revolutionary Councils formed all over the country and were organized locally, the ideas behind the revolution and the political program was everywhere identical. This was one of the most exciting aspects of these unsettled days. The demands of the people were still just and reasonable. It could be hoped that Imre Nagy and the government would realize that ublic opinion could not be resisted. The skeptics who claimed hat Nagy and former President Tildy were weaklings, still ered about the role of Bela Kovacs. No one knew how he d come into the picture, but everyone wanted to find out. obert suggested that we try to reach him in the south, visit him, or invite him up to Budapest. If anyone could do it, he could salvage the government.

By evening I slowly but inevitably came to the conclusion that I, too, should have something to do with this. What would my contribution be? Where could I do the most good? The phone rang and shook me out of my reverie.

I heard Alicia, our hostess, talking.

"Who is it?" I heard her say. "Dobi? Istvan Dobi wants to speak to Kovago."

"Istvan Dobi?" I repeated. "I don't remember his name."

I heard Robert whisper, "Don't be a fool. You know exactly who Dobi is."

Needless to say, I knew. Dobi used to be a member of the Smallholders Party and was notorious in giving in to the Communists and finally the regime made him Head of the State. He was still, nominally at least, in that top position. I still insisted that Alicia ask him and I heard her cool voice politely replying.

"Mr. Kovago doesn't know a Mr. Dobi . . . oh, I see. Good evening. I am sure he will remember you."

She turned towards me.

"It is Zoltan Tildy. He says you surely remember him."

I could feel the tenseness of the hushed silence in the room. I took the phone and heard the friendly voice of former President Tildy. He expressed his delight in hearing my voice and in speaking to me after so many years in prison. I was determined not to fall for any persuasive friendliness and answered in a cold voice.

"I am glad to talk to you."

"In these historic hours," Tildy said, "I wanted to call you among the first ones. You know, of course, that I assumed a highly responsible position in this difficult situation."

"So I understand."

"I want to ask you to help us in this task and join us—" I couldn't help interrupting him.

"I am glad to be able to tell you right now that you haven't the faintest idea what's happening. None of you has any notion what the people want, and your information is far behind events. The will of the people has already overtaken you. The storm of the Revolution will blow you away. I have quite a few conditions to be filled, without them I can't help you."

"Don't set demands now," he replied. "We realize and—"

"Is Bela Kovacs really in the government?"

"How can you ask such a question! Of course he is, and we hope he will soon arrive."

"In other words, he isn't here yet. Well then, if you don't mind, I will continue to explain my view." He tried to interrupt but I continued in a firm voice. "I think that after so many years of prison I have a right to voice my opinion."

"But, Misi, there are thousands of things to do now. Why don't you tell me this tomorrow morning, for I wanted to ask you to—"

"I'm sorry. I have to tell you this right now, during our first conversation. You all will be swept away by the storm of the Revolution unless you have courage and take over leadership of the Revolution itself. I mean genuine leadership. In order to do this, however, you have to declare immediately that those who are fighting are the heroic sons of the nation. You have to declare that those who fell are Hungarian martyrs. You will have to withdraw immediately from the Warsaw Pact."

"Please stop," he interrupted nervously.

"Wait, I'm not through yet. The most important point is yet to come. You should declare immediately the right to organize free political parties, for only reorganized political parties can fill the vacuum left by the collapse of the Communist state structure. Otherwise there will be chaos and irresponsible factions will destroy all the achievements of the revolution. Declare a free election and ask the U. N. to step in immediately." I took a breath and felt happy that I could compress so many essential points into such a short conversation.

"Well," he replied, "will you please come to see me in Parliament early tomorrow morning? Then we will talk all this over. We, too, . . . I, too, have quite a few ideas. I agree with you that the motivating force of these events is the very essence of the Hungarian nation. Still, the foreign political situation—"

I couldn't help remembering earlier conferences with Tildy. I knew immediately that whenever he started to make references to foreign political aspects he was ready to accept some compromise. Therefore I interrupted.

"There is only one question now. Will the wrath of the people sweep you away, or will you be able to become a genuine Revolutionary government? There is no time for hesitation. What we need is not forecasts but help to tackle the situation."

He answered in a quiet voice.

"Look, Misi," I heard him say in a warm voice, "I know that you are motivated by honest patriotism but let's not continue this conversation now. Come in tomorrow morning. I will send a car for you."

"Don't send one, thanks. I like to walk. At least I learn what people feel. Believe me, the only place where one can get the true picture is on the streets. It might be a good idea for you, too, to mix with the people."

"All right, then, may I see you at eight in the morning? Then we will have a chance to speak about everything."

"Yes, I'll be there. Thanks for the call. The only thing I want to be sure of is that I will be able to tell you my opinion very frankly. I don't feel I want to hide any of my convictions."

"All right, then I will see you in the morning."

When I put down the receiver, Alicia and the others rushed up to me, embracing me and offering congratulations.

"You really spoke as a good patriot. It was time for them to hear these things."

"Don't worry. They had already been told about this. The delegations of students and workers made their feelings clear in no uncertain terms."

Still, it felt very good to tell them how I felt. That's all I could do in this situation and that's what I did. We would see what would happen.

Lonci did not like these latest developments at all. In a reserved manner she refrained from making comments of her own.

"Lonci, if I were you I would be rather proud," Alicia said, unable to resist the remark.

"I don't want to be proud, I'd rather be happy," Lonci retorted. "I would rather see Misi concerned about his child, not about Tildy."

We ate in silence. The gunfire could be heard punctuating all of our conversation. And, of course, the phone hardly stopped ringing. People whom I hadn't heard from in many years telephoned. Several of them mentioned in these conversations that the Smallholders Party should soon reorganize.

While I was in prison, we had a fairly good channel of information with regard to happenings in the world. We knew precious little, however, about how individuals had behaved and resisted Communist pressure.

Late in the evening, a friend of mine who lived close to the Kilian Barracks called on us. After complaining how hard it was to reach our number he furnished me with some details about the fighting there. The most interesting part of his information was about Pal Maleter, the heroic military leader of the Freedom Fighters. This man's prestige seemed to be increasing day by day. We discussed events that evening in some detail.

In a cool and almost detached manner, Lonci explained why

she was convinced that what was happening was nothing else but a repetition of the Russo-Finnish War. According to her the Soviet tactics seemed to be obvious. The Russians gave some leeway to the insurgents and allowed a feeling of victory to the patriots involved in the Revolution. At a given time, they would suddenly swoop down and take away all the concessions made prior to the Revolution and in the period of the thaw, too.

Robert's viewpoint was that this was all nonsense.

"There is no similarity whatsoever between the Russo-Finnish War and these events," Robert stated. "If the Soviets decide to intervene in this fight with major military forces, this would immediately bring the West in."

"That is a fairy tale," Lonci retorted. "The West will not go to war because of Hungary. All these children will die, and there will be lots of talk and no action."

"Are you trying to say that the whole Revolution is pointless?" Robert asked, irritated.

Peter intervened. "Remember that revolutions are the results of emotional factors and not pure reason," he suggested.

"This will be the greatest event of the twentieth century," said Robert, his voice rising in a tone of deep conviction. "This will be the very glory of the Hungarians."

"Those are all beautiful words," Lonci answered. "In 1848, when the Hungarians shook off the Austrian yoke, Petofi and his friends did the same. And what happened? For twenty years afterwards the nation was suppressed. I don't want to go deeper into this discussion," she added. "All I am trying to do is to keep Misi out of this. He did his duty ten years ago. He went to prison for it, too. Whatever has happened since is not his doing, so why should he join the fight now? How about all those Communists who wrote beautiful poetry glorifying Stalin? Let them go to the barricades and die. You can be sure that most of the people who were just freed from prison will not participate in the Revolution."

"Well, that's probable," Peter said. "People react differently.

Misi would deny his whole past if he withdrew now in a cowardly manner."

Lonci interrupted: "And this way he will deny his family."

"Don't get so upset," I told Lonci. "All I'm doing is to attend that meeting tomorrow in Parliament. That doesn't make me a hero, and it's nothing to my family."

"Sure, provided you return from the meeting. Remember that the Parliament is full of Russians, Communists, and probably AVO men, too. And besides, you know well that such conferences are only the beginning of a chain of events," she countered.

The roar of guns from nearby silenced our debate. Soon we heard the voice of one of the free Hungarian broadcasting stations. A hoarse voice exclaimed: "Let's stop the massacre of Hungarian youth in Hungary. Let's hang the AVO men. The government should take notice that it is all the Hungarian people who are fighting for freedom, and they will not give up." With this the station stopped abruptly.

Meanwhile, another friend of ours, a university professor, had arrived and sat down, listening to the broadcast. After it was over he spoke up.

"There's more trouble too."

"What?" Robert wanted to know.

"The Revolution broke out as a direct result of the writings of the Communist authors and under the leadership of Communists. Now, however, we are fighting for freedom. How can you imagine that a Communist, Imre Nagy, could become a leader for a fight for freedom when he was not even able to become leader of the Revolution?"

"That shouldn't be too complicated," Robert answered. "All he has to do is identify himself and his government with the demands of the Freedom Fighters."

"Yes, but remember that among these demands you'll find not only points such as leaving the Warsaw Pact and withdrawal of Russian troops, but also free elections. And remember that one of the cardinal rules of the Communist form of government is that there must be a one-party system."

"Well, still," Robert replied, "I can see the possibility of a special Hungarian solution permitting several parties but exercising moderation on questions to which Communists react sensitively."

"That's a contradiction in itself," the professor replied. "You either have a free political system where every party can promote its own program, or a one-party system that is Communism. And you must agree with me that the Freedom Fighters would never accept this. The Soviets will never permit the democratic way of life in Hungary. And remember, if the other parties existed but acted as you said, with a measure of moderation, how could they deviate from the Communist programs to any considerable extent? For such a peaceful modification of the Communist system there would have been no point in starting a revolution."

"You're right," Lonci interrupted. "You have the right idea. You put into words what I was trying to say all evening."

"If this government goes beyond a certain limit which the Soviets will still tolerate, then Russian power would suppress everything . . . and if the government does not pass that certain critical point," our professor concluded, "then the wrath of the people will sweep it away. This is the unavoidable dilemma of the Hungarian Revolution and the fight for freedom. Unfortunately, I cannot see any way out."

"I am ashamed of you," I interrupted. "The streets are full of dead children, and you are having academic arguments here. Action is what we need. First the government has to identify itself with the Freedom Fighters. Then negotiations must follow to see if a measure of coexistence can be reached between the Communists and the non-Communist parties."

"Of course there will be need for moderation, and remember that many of the changes which occurred under long suppression may be retained," Robert put in.

"The Soviets won't accept such promises of moderation. And

besides, remember that's not what the Revolution was started for," the professor coolly replied.

"The Revolution was started in the hearts of the people," I answered in anger. "No one person started it. No one organized it. It came like a storm and now it's a fact."

The debate would have probably become even more heated but the doorbell rang. The arriving guest was an old prison mate of mine, Steve, the flyer. He was all excited, and he started talking immediately.

"I was looking for you everywhere. You simply must do something. Are you politicians? Can't you stop this blood bath? What are you waiting for? Are you waiting for the youth to pull the chestnuts out of the fire for you, while you will simply take your seats in the Cabinet?"

I embraced Steve and laughed at our professor friend.

"You see? Here's the classical argument against you."

He rose and remarked, "It's the classical, dramatic approach. It has precious little connection with reason." With this he left.

"Who is that idiot?" Steve inquired.

"A friend of ours, an intellectual from the streets," I replied.

"Nonsense," he answered. "He's an intellectual from a dusty old library."

"Well, for those who want to know more about politics," Lonci spoke up, "it may not be such a bad idea to spend some time in libraries instead of shouting on the streets." With this she left the room.

"Your wife doesn't seem to be in a good humor," Steve remarked. "I am sorry that I made her angry."

We put his mind at ease and explained that he was not the guilty one. I was the culprit, for I had gone down into the streets and taken a big breath of the same air of freedom that the ten million Hungarians were now breathing.

7 • REJECTED ADVICE

Early the following morning I started toward the Parliament building. The streets were comparatively quiet at that hour, but I could hear noise of the battle in the distance. Parliament was surrounded by tanks. For a moment I was frightened. Once again I felt that chill of fear that I had known in prison. I felt a strong urge to turn back. Was it worthwhile to take risks again? Lonci may have been right. Why should I do all this? Self-preservation should be everyone's first instinct. See if the Revolution gains international recognition, I thought. Then there would still be time enough to step forward and offer my services to my country.

As I was standing around, somewhat hesitant, I noticed a group of four youngsters marching with guns on their shoulders. Probably these four had been among those who had demonstrated a few days ago at the statue of the Polish hero of freedom. I remembered the statue very clearly. The Polish hero pointed toward the Danube and the statue bore the inscription, "Forward, Hungarians, if there is no bridge, there is no country." Apparently these boys had learned their lesson well. Whatever happened to them, they were determined to do nothing less than march forward. I realized that this was the answer to my problem, too, and I started out again toward the Parliament.

When I reached the tanks at the entrance, I saw that the soldiers in them were Hungarians. Across the square, however, I thought I saw the Russian units. I could not be sure; they all looked alike. When I reached the main entrance the place was familiar. I used to be a member there myself and I had entered that gate many times from 1945 to 1947. I gave my name to the guard and informed him that I wished to speak to Zoltan Tildy. A high-ranking officer, wearing the long-banned uniform of the Hungarian Army, stepped forward and told me that he had been sent by Tildy to wait for me. We started up the stairs. All over the staircase and corridors soldiers were swarming, staring at me. I had an uneasy feeling. I wouldn't have been surprised if one of them had stepped to my side, pressed a gun barrel against my ribs, and whispered: "Forward, you dirty Fascist traitor."

My guide, a general, told me that President Dobi had asked him to invite me to stop by in his room before I saw Tildy. We arrived at the Speaker's Room. I knew that room well, for back in 1946 and 1947 we held long and friendly visits with Bela Varga who had been Speaker at the time. He was a leader of my party, and he could avoid arrest only by fleeing abroad. I left my coat in the anteroom, and in a minute Dobi came out to greet me. He shook my hand in a friendly manner, and said that he was glad to see me again. I wasn't sure that he meant it, but it sounded sincere. He invited me to have some coffee and brandy with him.

"Thanks, I will have some coffee but I'll have to decline the brandy," I said with a smile. "You know, the sanitarium where I spent the last seven years was controlled by prohibitionists. So I'm no longer used to drink."

"Yes, naturally, of course," he answered, much embarrassed. "You know I really suffered when I thought of you, and that I couldn't do a thing for you."

"That's understandable," I replied. "After all, how could the Chief of State be expected to intervene for prisoners who were unjustly imprisoned? It's good of you even to have thought of me."

"The coffee will be here in a minute," he said, trying to change the subject. "I am sure you see the Revolution more clearly than we do, and perhaps it makes more sense to you, than it does to us; for I must admit I didn't realize that the people hate Communism as much as they seem to. I figured that about thirty to forty per cent of the peasants, who received rough treatment, loathed them."

He gulped down his brandy, wishing me good health. I sipped my coffee and relished the idea that I was sitting across the table from the Chief of State who drank the greatest amount of liquor but possessed the least influence. Except for the beautiful carvings and the antique furnishings of the room, I might have believed that I was talking in prison with a newly arrived, frightened prisoner who didn't know yet how his prison mates would react to him.

"Look here," I heard Dobi say, "I fought against feudalism. I knew, of course, that it wouldn't be easy to build up a new world. The Russians made it impossible for us to build a Socialist regime in the Western sense of the word. They wanted Communism. I didn't know they were such evil people. They insisted that we become Communists too. They wanted the peasants to join collective farms. But those people just won't accept collective farms here. I thought that they would get used to it or that the Communists would tire of all the pressuring and that a healthy state of affairs would develop. I tried to help people myself. I told Rakosi not to allow this terror, but you can't talk to him. I tried to talk to the people, too, but they wouldn't believe what I said to them. They don't seem to be too fond of me."

I listened and then answered in a quiet voice: "Well, at least you can see now that the peasantry does not want the collective farms and that the Hungarian people don't want Communism."

"No, I guess you are right," he said, gulping down another drink, and continuing in a quiet tone. "They just don't want Communism. They don't seem to be able to adjust themselves."

Suddenly we heard the roaring of the guns from the other side of the river.

"All this bloodshed, all this trouble," he said, "we must put an end to it. Perhaps Imre Nagy and his new government can tackle the situation. Some people suggested that I resign. But after all, there must be a Chief of State. Who would swear in a new government if there were no such person? Then the government wouldn't be legal."

"The Revolution has its own legality," I answered with a smile, "but let's go to Tildy now, for I have to speak to him."

"I know, I know," he replied in a strained voice. "If you are in such a hurry, then, let's go."

"Good-bye," I said, offering my hand. He suggested, however, that he accompany me. We walked quietly through the long corridors. I was thinking of this pathetic figure beside me. He was the living image of consistent concessions, a man without a backbone. Undoubtedly he was a good man at heart; it was just that he didn't believe in putting up any resistance. Probably he was not the first head of State in history who had similar attitudes.

As we were walking along the corridor he turned to me and asked: "Tell me frankly, you think that I am absolutely rotten and no good. Right?"

I started laughing.

"Well, Istvan, the question includes the answer."

"You know I am not really evil or bad," he said sadly. "Maybe I was mistaken in my interpretation of events. But, to me Socialist Law makes more sense than the Revolution."

I didn't answer his remark. Meanwhile we had reached Tildy's office. There was great activity here, many people coming and going, all very busy. Several secretaries came in and out telling people to be patient. The air was charged with electricity. It was obvious that the person behind these double doors had power and influence.

I was immediately shown in to the inner office. Three cabinet members were in conference with Tildy. I recognized two of them, Erdei and Bognar. They were virtually permanent fixtures of any Communist regime, as they were well-known pseudo-Communists. When I entered, Tildy rose. He was a small man with graying hair and enormous eyes. He came forward to greet me. I felt moved. He had tears in his eyes and he embraced me.

"Welcome, Misi," he said, moved.

After a few minutes of casual chat Tildy requested the others to leave us alone, for he had important things to discuss with me. Dobi, who stood silent next to me, seemed hesitant.

"Istvan, we would like to be alone," Tildy suggested.

I thought that we were alone until, from a corner of the room where I hadn't even noticed him, a tall, gaunt figure rose. He walked towards us.

"Welcome, welcome," he said. "I am so glad that the two of you are reunited." It was the Gray Eminence.

"I have to go see Imre Nagy," he said, by way of apology for leaving.

"Yes, yes," Tildy answered, "and remind him to issue orders to the peasants."

With this the Gray Eminence said good-bye.

"We will see each other quite a lot from now on," he said to me and left the room.

"I feel it important," Tildy explained, "that our first orders pacify the people in the provinces."

"That's a good idea," I countered, "but there are a few other important things I mentioned to you over the telephone."

"Sure," he said, "but before we get down to politics let's talk about ourselves first."

He told me in some detail how the AVO had kept him under house arrest and of the difficulties and unpleasantness he had encountered. Still, he explained, he had no hatred in his heart. These were things he must forget, otherwise much valuable time would be wasted.

I told him briefly what had happened to me, and he inquired about my wife and daughter. The door opened and his wife entered. An old, haggard woman, she was thin, with trembling hands. I hardly recognized the Mrs. Tildy who used to have beauty and poise. She, too, was very kind. They had moved into Parliament, for they lived far away in Buda, and transportation was difficult in the city.

"After all," she said, "I had better stay with my husband, because he needs care nowadays. He is no longer what he used to be. He was tired and sick, and still he came, for he has the interests of Hungary at heart and he was ready for self-sacrifice."

Her husband joined the discussion. He told me that he had been asked to come. He felt that every honest Hungarian should assume his share of the work, for the situation was very serious. The Revolution was, he believed, the finest period of Hungarian history.

While they talked I looked at this old couple. They treated me like an old friend. It would have been nice if I had been able to respond with the same warmth, which actually I felt in my heart toward them, but I was afraid to show it. I was determined not to fall under the influence of Tildy but to follow my own instincts. Back in the years from 1945-1948 he had been ready to make far-reaching compromises which I didn't believe in.

While we talked I wondered whether the two of them realized how unpopular they were with the people. Did they know that people were almost unanimous in disliking them, and that many regarded Tildy as one of the traitors of the nation? I wondered if there was any way of telling him of this and warning him that this time he should seize the helm of history with a firm hand, otherwise the nation would never forgive him. It seemed to me that his very friendliness almost obliged me to be frank with him. After all, he had many people surrounding him who gave him nothing but compliments and praise.

We started talking politics. Tildy hinted that he would like to have me as a close associate. Would I consider joining the government or taking another similar high post? As for membership in the cabinet, I declined it immediately and without hesitation. I told him that probably I could do more good by helping to reorganize the Smallholders Party.

"Would you be interested rather in becoming Mayor of Budapest again?" he asked with a smile.

"Well, I could hardly think of a greater honor than to head this great city once again," I replied, also with a smile. "But now we have a Revolution, and it is much more important that we have political parties in good hands." Patiently I repeated once again what I told him the previous day over the telephone. I tried to sound convincing in describing the dangers I saw awaiting the government and the whole country unless the regime identified itself with the demands of the Revolution. Then I brought up the name of Bela Kovacs. I felt that his presence in the government was most important.

"Bela is an important man," Tildy replied, "but people overestimate his importance. He should realize that there are hours in history when one should help with the great tasks without hesitation. I should be sorry if he declined to come to Budapest, but we can't wait for him until doomsday."

"I am convinced that you can't gain the confidence of the masses without him," I replied.

I could easily see that my answer did not please him. Obviously, he would have preferred to hear that his name would pacify the people.

He was in agreement with me on some other points. He believed that the Freedom Fighters should be regarded as good patriots and the heroes of the nation. That it was ridiculous to call them gangsters and Fascist counter-revolutionaries.

"This is the finest national revolution of Hungary," he said with confidence in his voice.

As far as the withdrawal from the Warsaw Pact and free

organizing of political parties was concerned, he was much more hesitant. It was obvious to me that he would prefer to leave these sensitive questions alone for the time being. I insisted, however, that he listen and consider my arguments, for I was convinced that this was what the people wanted. Unless the government gave freedom to other political parties and proclaimed a free election, the Revolution would take its own course, and the government might forfeit all chances of winning the confidence of the people.

The secretaries waiting outside must have been bored by this long conference. The Gray Eminence entered the room and left with Mrs. Tildy. A few of the cabinet members also returned, and I gave them the same advice that I had given Tildy.

Tildy requested that I keep in close contact with him. He wanted me to be available to him at any hour. He thought that we should work out some way of meeting every day. He asked me to become an advisor to the government.

"Believe me," he said, "it's good to hear an honest opinion like yours. You can be sure that whenever it's possible your suggestions and advice will be taken."

Then he inquired whether I wanted to meet Imre Nagy and the other members of the cabinet. I suggested that we leave this for another occasion. I didn't want to hurt him by saying that I had little to discuss with them, or they with me.

On my way out I repeated once again, "So I am to understand that tomorrow a plane leaves for Bela Kovacs?"

"That's correct," came the answer. "Believe me, we wish that he was here now."

8 • REBIRTH OF POLITICAL PARTIES

The next day came and still Bela Kovacs had not arrived. Rumors were flying that he was reluctant to become a member of the government. Meanwhile, the battle raged at the Kilian Barracks. The name of General Maleter had become a household word throughout the country. His fight had become identified with the fate of the Revolution.

The government made the first concession. Around noon on October 28th it ordered a cease-fire, and people said that Imre Nagy would speak on the radio.

Meanwhile, our food supply was growing short. The food lines were long, but as we went to market with the women, it was obvious that everybody in the street felt happy and victorious. When we returned, I was told that somebody from City Hall had phoned. The name wasn't clear to Alicia, who had answered the phone, but the man on the line was obviously someone in authority. He wanted to report to me that the public utilities were functioning properly. He expressed the hope that I would take my place soon and would fire the Communist city administration. All this sounded like good news; even Lonci seemed optimistic. I promised her that we would call her mother and our daughter and tell them the good news.

Some former prison mates, whom I met on the street, were less optimistic.

"Be careful," they warned me. "The show is not over yet. The worst is yet to come. Do you really think that the Russians will give up so easily? Remember that it hasn't been long since you were in prison."

Early that afternoon we listened to Imre Nagy. He was enthusiastic, and though he was cautious on certain crucial issues, it was obvious that he identified himself with the Revolution.

The people of Budapest were divided in their opinion of him. Some, like myself, rooted for him, because they felt that he could find a way out of our difficulties. Others were bitterly opposed to him. After all, they claimed, wasn't he the one who had called in the Russians? He should resign as soon as possible, and someone with a clean record should take his place. Nevertheless, even these people acknowledged that he had recognized the Workers' Councils, as well as replacing the hammer and sickle with the ancient Kossuth symbol. The withdrawal of the Russian troops had also made quite an impression on the skeptics.

Tildy's speech tended to increase the number of Imre Nagy's supporters rather than create a following for Tildy. People were cautious with their forgiveness. The National Guard was organized under General Bela Kiraly, a former prison mate of mine. The armed youth, instead of surrendering its weapons, decided to join the Guard. Everyone was proud of them. Most of us were virtually glued to our radios.

We learned with great excitement of the United Nations Security Council's meeting discussing the Hungarian problem.

The following day, the 29th, Tildy was anxious that I come to see him without further delay. I arrived there quickly. Tildy was extremely busy. Secretaries were coming and going, cabinet members received their instructions, and he seemed full of energy and activity.

"I am glad to see how busy you are," I told him, "but I would be even happier if I heard over the radio that we have withdrawn from the Warsaw Pact, and that the Government has proclaimed the right to organize political parties and to hold free elections."

"Be a little more patient," Tildy advised. "We can't move too fast."

"Time is running short," I warned.

He wanted to know my opinion of the situation. I immediately spoke against the Hungarian United Nations delegate, Peter Koos. I felt that he had betrayed the Hungarian cause in his speech to the Security Council.

"Why don't you get decent representation at the U. N.?" I inquired.

He promised that the man would be recalled, but said that we would have to be a little more patient. The situation was still chaotic, and there were still many unreliable elements in the government.

Then he said good-bye, as he was already late for an appointment.

In no time the Gray Eminence came in. He begged me not to be harsh with Tildy. After all, he explained, the man was doing his best. Rome wasn't built in a day. The Communists, themselves, needed some time to swallow these changes.

"To me it's obvious that the government is lagging behind the people and that it is unable to take the initiative and leadership. Instead of acting with courage and imagination, they hesitate. Take, for example, the organization of parties. Don't you see that it's imperative? If the government is reluctant to permit this, we'll take the initiative ourselves. Right now I'm restraining myself, for I feel that it's my duty to summon the members of the Smallholders Party in Budapest," I answered.

The Gray Eminence was not pleased.

"How about Bela Kovacs?" I continued.

"I know," he acknowledged. "We need Bela. In fact, we telephoned him. He doesn't feel well. His health isn't any too good."

"Can't you understand," I pleaded, "that the very existence of the government, and perhaps the nation, may depend on the presence or absence of Bela Kovacs?"

"He's not well, and his health is troubling him," he replied.

"Even if he's sick you must produce him," I countered. "Otherwise you'll lose whatever prestige you have."

"Don't you feel that the speed you are dictating is dangerously fast?"

"It's not I who dictate this speed, but the Revolution. Delay may lead to catastrophe. In fact, to give you just one example, here is the problem of the Security Council Meeting—"

It was quite late when I said good-bye.

In the morning I walked again to the Parliament. I still preferred my constitutional walk. I was glad I had gone, for I met General Maleter, an extremely handsome and impressive person. He was speaking to a group on the military aspects of the situation. He did not believe the Russian promises, and therefore had decided that his tank units should guard all the main arteries leading into Budapest. I suggested that after the Russians actually withdrew, he should stop sending his tanks to the streets, too. Some people may mistake them for Russian units, I suggested, and in any case, the city had its ears full of tank rumblings for the last few days. The city was quiet, and, in case of emergency we had the newly organized National Guard. Maleter didn't understand my presence at the meeting. After all, I was not a member of the cabinet; in fact, I had no official status. Tildy realized the awkwardness of the situation and explained who I was. Then he called me aside and asked me whether I was planning to go to the Smallholders meeting that day.

"Of course I am," I answered. "I have been asked by several people to attend it."

"I'm so glad," he replied, "because I want to be sure that nothing rash is decided."

"Nothing foolish will happen," I assured him, "but the party will organize itself."

Again I warned him that the government should not delay in declaring the right to free political organization. He was evasive in his answer, but he ordered the officer in charge of the Guard to supply me with a car and chauffeur for the day. As the meeting of the party was to take place in Buda, and there were no streetcars or buses, I was glad to accept his offer of transportation this time. Before leaving, I joined Maleter and his group for a few minutes longer. I was anxious to get their evaluation of the military situation. The picture they drew for me in a few words was dark. The Russians were moving in new units. I was on my way out when President Dobi stopped me.

He was worried about several things. Primarily he was concerned about his own personal relation with the newly organized Smallholders Party. He was afraid that the party might expel him and fire him from his position. He had every reason to be worried. His performance during the past years had not won him any sympathy from honest Hungarians.

The second problem, however, concerned me also. It was a basic question whether the number of political parties should be limited to the ones taking part in the coalition of 1945-47. These parties were the Smallholders, the Social Democrats, and the Peasant Party.

There was no easy answer to this. In principle we were for complete political freedom. But at this point we felt that a large number of parties advocating principles distasteful to the Russians would jeopardize all the accomplishments of the Revolution. I felt that we should not challenge the right of the constructive opposition parties which used to serve an important function during the time of the coalition. These represented the

Hungarian line of thought against the policy of compromises which unfortunately were unavoidable during the coalition period, in the shadow of the Russians. On the other hand, this was no time for a political free-for-all.

The apparent first step was to get the reorganization of the traditional democratic parties on its way as soon as possible.

In the car I realized additional difficulties I was facing. With my presence at this meeting I would be responsible for the reorganization of the party. If things went well, the Government would graciously approve everything. On the other hand, should things go wrong, I would be blamed.

On the way I picked up Peter, for I felt it was better for him to be there, too. He was glad to come.

We drove along in a good mood. It was the first time in eight years that I had sat in a car with a chauffeur to drive me wherever I wanted.

Our meeting took place in a private house, and some five or six rooms were crowded with from one hundred to a hundred and fifty people. They were all enthusiastic; many of them had come on foot from a considerable distance. To participate in that meeting took some courage for everyone, for the Revolution's political victory was far from being definite, and no one knew what the Soviets or the defeated AVO forces might decide to do. Many of the men I saw had suffered considerably in the last few years. But there were some faces I was not sure I should trust. When I entered the room, the meeting was already in session but the group gave me a standing ovation. I was embarrassed but moved at this warm welcome.

The speakers were moderate. All of them seemed to agree on two points. One was that the party must be organized and must help the Revolutionary forces in solving the political problem. The second point of general agreement was that there was prevailing bitterness against Tildy and hatred against President Dobi. Many people felt extremely bitter against them and against some of the minor figures who had collaborated with the Communists. To the majority, these men, especially Dobi, were traitors.

The chairman immediately wanted me to take over. I requested, however, that a few more persons speak first, for I wanted to get an idea of the situation.

Finally I rose to speak. It was the first time in eight years that I had addressed a group. I started out by exclaiming that, as far as I was concerned, the leader of the Smallholders Party was Bela Kovacs.

The spontaneous applause revealed that the gathering was in complete approval. This way, the party had a leader acceptable to everyone, and the difficult problem of analyzing Tildy's role or the question of a purge was avoided.

The party would be finally organized when he joined us. Until then, we would have to do our best by pressing the government to take over leadership of the country with endorsement of the demands of the Revolution. "Let's begin by organizing the party and establishing contact with the young people and the Revolutionary organizations, as well as the other parties," I advised.

Some speakers demanded that the newly organized party expel some of the former leaders who had collaborated with the Communists until the end. My answer was that in the present fluid situation such steps would do more harm than good. Take the example of President Dobi. He was in Parliament as head of the State, serving the Revolution just as faithfully as the regime of terror. Proceedings to remove him would start a chain of complications, from a constitutional point of view. In fact, we might create a situation in which the Soviet Union could attack the Revolution on a point of public law. In any case, I told them that this was not a time to pass judgment on human behavior.

I knew that should such a procedure be started, the people

would demand the head of former President Tildy. This would automatically deprive the Imre Nagy government of its most active and probably its ablest member. Therefore, I suggested that our policy should accentuate the positive, rather than the negative of deciding which heads must roll. I called for a motion to elect a new Executive Committee of the party. This proposal was accepted and a committee was formed to nominate candidates.

The slate was as follows: "Jozsef Adorjan, businessman and former member of Parliament; Dr. Janos Csorba, former Presiding Judge at the High Court of Administration; Sandor Kiss, former Director of the Peasant Union and former member of Parliament. (Kiss was prevented from attending the meeting by reasons beyond his control, and I suggested that this worthy man should be elected.); Jozsef Kovago, former Mayor of Budapest, former member of Parliament; Dr. Imre Nemeth, lawyer, former member of Parliament; Tivadar Partay, journalist, former member of Parliament, and former Deputy Secretary-General of the Party; Istvan B. Ratz, former Youth Leader of the Smallholders Party and former member of Parliament; Istvan B. Szabo, former Cabinet Member; Istvan Szemes, furniture maker, former head of the Artisan Section of the Party, and former member of Parliament."

The election took place in an orderly manner. Toward the end, six men, suspicious-looking and unknown to anyone, appeared. We thought that they were AVO men who had come to cause trouble. In any case, they were too late. The meeting was over, the newly elected Executive Committee decided to meet the following day to get the party fully organized and ready for operation. Two men received the assignment to reoccupy the former party headquarters building in downtown Budapest. I was named by the group to make known to the government demands of the Smallholders Party for the freedom of party activities as well as the other demands of the Revolution.

It was a real pleasure meeting several old friends. I stayed with them for a while.

I arrived home late and tired. An excellent dinner and even better news awaited me. Imre Nagy and Zoltan Tildy had given beautiful speeches. That day was the crucial day in the history of the Revolution. The leaders of the government identified themselves with that cause. This step prompted even Communists to step forward. Kadar made a speech in which he said, referring to the Communist Party, "The party rank and file will become loose."

Late that night I met one former leading personality of the Communist Party. He had tears in his eyes when he told me, "I hope that now even you believe that we, too, are Hungarians."

I was touched, and I tried to believe it.

9 • DAYS OF GLORY

From that day on events moved rapidly and the picture was one of excitement and confusion. Everything seemed to happen at once. Everyone was working, running around doing something. There was meeting after meeting. By the time we had a chance to check the enforcement of a new order it was superseded by a newer decision.

The Imre Nagy government opened its doors not only to Smallholders Party representatives, but also to the Social Democrats and to the Peasant Party, which was in the process of reorganizing as the Petofi Party.

The Social Democrats elected highly respected persons into new leadership, headed by the great names of Anna Kethly and Gyula Kelemen. The free Trade Unions also started to operate again. The newly organized Petofi Party expelled its former collaborationist leaders, and, in their stead, elected Ferenc Parkas and some others among the best Hungarian writers. The Christian parties and Christian youth organizations were in the process of reorganization. Thus, by now, the Revolution of the youth was supported by the workers and by the traditional political parties. In addition, local organizations and new administrative units had begun operations.

The radio adopted a new tone, promising its listeners to broadcast the truth. Indeed, the tone of the broadcasts, as well as the contents, had changed considerably.

The whole country felt elated by the news that Cardinal Mindszenty, the most respected spiritual leader of the nation, enjoyed full freedom. He had returned to Budapest and planned, shortly, to resume his duties as Prince Primate of Hungary. The other churches, too, sprang into action after many years of terror and intimidation.

Imre Nagy's government took a firm stand on the question of withdrawal of Soviet troops. The whole nation insisted that the Russian soldiers leave Hungarian soil. A general strike had been called. The workers refused to work until the Russians withdrew. Rumors were flying that the Russians had seemed willing to negotiate the withdrawal. This was a happy hour in Hungarian history. The Revolution and the fight for freedom had been won. The streets were crowded with happy people.

The only reason that people went to their offices was to pick up pay checks and to help repair damage caused by the fighting. The hitherto highly secret Communist files on personnel—the so called cadre cards—supplied fascinating reading. Party secretaries felt it safer and more comfortable to stay away from their offices. Workers organized armed guards to protect the plants. Public safety was protected by armed military units and university students wearing civilian garb.

The Communist press had disappeared. Some of the old-time fourth-estaters, veterans of many years of honest newspaper writing, were able to return to their profession once again. Youth aired its views in its own publications.

The Army was reorganized. General Pal Maleter became First Deputy of the Ministry of War. I was happy to see the name of General Bela Kiraly among the new Army leaders. He took command of the National Guard.

In the morning I went to Parliament. Tildy had crowds of people congratulating him; it was obvious that he hadn't had much sleep the night before. I joined the well-wishers, mentioning, however, that the Government still lagged behind in announcing Hungary's withdrawal from the Warsaw Pact. At that point the telephone rang. Tildy was angry at the interruption, for he was busy. The door opened and the Gray Eminence entered.

"It's Mikoyan's secretary," he told Tildy and took the receiver. A hushed silence followed. Everyone realized that a top Soviet leader does not phone without a serious reason. They all listened to the Gray Eminence talking.

"Yes, indeed. I will discuss it with the Minister immediately . . . to the Soviet Embassy . . . yes. . . . We will call you back."

"Mikoyan is in Budapest," we heard the Gray Eminence inform Tildy.

The silence became even more hushed.

"He would like to speak to you," the Gray Eminence said to Tildy. "He wants you to visit him at the Soviet Embassy as soon as possible. Right away."

"The Soviet Embassy?" Tildy asked. "Right now? Is there an interpreter available? And a car?"

"I don't think that a car or a suitable interpreter are available right now," the Gray Eminence answered. "After all, we need the best interpreter in the Foreign Office," he continued in a quiet voice. "In fact, I wonder if such a conference is a task for the Prime Minister himself."

Tildy looked at him, then glanced at me. After some thinking he made the decision and spoke.

"Get a car with a reliable chauffeur. Call the Foreign Office and tell them to send over a first-class interpreter. As soon as they are ready return Mikoyan's call."

Then he turned to us.

"I am sorry friends, I need a few minutes to think the matter over. This conference may be the most crucial of all. We'll see. I always got along with Mikoyan in the past," he told us.

The telephone rang. It was the Foreign Office calling, informing us that the interpreter would be over in a few minutes. Then Mikoyan was called, and Tildy himself took the receiver.

We heard him say that he was very glad to meet Mikoyan again but that it would be hard for him to get away from the Parliament right now for he was very busy. He would be very grateful if Mikoyan would be kind enough to visit him here, and they could have their discussion in the Parliament building. Mikoyan, however, insisted that Tildy should go to the embassy. Tildy was obviously trying to avoid the trip to the Soviet Embassy and asked if a halfway point such as the Foreign Ministry building could be their meeting place. Apparently, a place was agreed on. Tildy did not repeat the location aloud. All he mentioned was the time of the meeting. When he hung up there was dead silence in the room. We all started to leave, but he asked me to stay behind. He also motioned to the Gray Eminence to remain. He was thinking aloud.

"I will suggest that, once order has been restored, we will go to Moscow as a friendly delegation. Instead of our membership in the Warsaw Pact we will be ready to complete a new agreement on the basis of equality and mutual respect of sovereign rights. I hope he understands the situation." Then he turned to us.

"What do you think of it?" he asked us.

"To withdraw from the Warsaw Pact," the Gray Eminence replied in a slow tone, "is a long and complicated procedure. All the signatory powers have to meet and agree to it."

I could not resist interrupting.

"The procedure may be a long one but giving notice for our withdrawal should be done right now, without any delay. The survival of the government depends on that. Mikoyan, too, has to understand—"

"—that the government does not want to lose the friendship or to incur the hostility of the Soviet Union," Tildy interrupted, completing my sentence.

I swallowed, for I would have finished the sentence differently.

"The government will have to conclude a separate, friendly

treaty with the U.S.S.R." Tildy said. "It might be a good idea to inform the Soviet government of our intentions right now."

"That's all right to present as the intention of the government," I countered, "but right now the most important thing we have to accomplish is to persuade the Russians to withdraw their troops and accept the fact that the Hungarian nation has fought for its freedom. Tell him that the monopolistic tyranny of the Communist Party is over, and that from now on we will have a democratic multiparty system, and that we are preparing for a free election."

"The election is still far away," the Gray Eminence answered, "and let's make sure that we permit the activities of only those parties which accept basic social reforms," the Gray Eminence said.

I felt my face grow red. Tildy remained quiet, looking at both of us.

"The date of the election should be as soon as possible," I told them. "As far as the political parties are concerned, they should proclaim and promote their own independent programs."

At that point the interpreter arrived. Former President Tildy left to change before his visit. I couldn't resist speaking to him before he left with Mrs. Tildy.

"Be sure you get an answer as to whether they agree to full political freedom for the parties and free elections."

"I will discuss it," Tildy answered, already on his way out. "Please be sure to regard our conference as being confidential."

I had to admit that it was significant that Mikoyan wanted to meet with Tildy. At the same time, I wondered how I could possibly report on all this to the leaders of the Smallholders Party without giving them the details. I realized how difficult it would be to convince them that they should give Tildy their full support. After all, Tildy's intention was not to betray the Revolution to the Russians, but to save the newly gained Hungarian freedom from Soviet suppression.

On my way out I met two leaders of the Social Democratic Party who had come to negotiate with Tildy. They were former prison mates. We embraced each other warmly. Naturally, the only subject to discuss was the present situation. I asked them if they were planning to participate in the government. They were not yet sure, they told me. We agreed somewhat jokingly at this point, that any party joining the government would actually lose some of its popularity with the masses.

The Gray Eminence came in.

"What's wrong?" I inquired.

"We have another complication," he said, "the only condition on which the Social Democrats would be permitted to enter the government is if the Socialist International agrees."

"Why don't you find out?" I suggested.

"Well," he answered, "as a matter of fact, Anna Kethly would need a passport to go to Vienna to attend the congress there, and I wonder whether, in such critical days, it is wise for one of the top leaders of the Social Democratic Party to leave the country."

"Why shouldn't she go?" I queried. "After all, the Soviet Union seems to be in a conciliatory mood. The Western world will get some much-needed firsthand information from her. Today the whole world follows the Hungarian problem with attention and concern."

He looked at me and then answered in a quiet tone.

"The big ones often don't like it if the small ones ask unpleasant questions."

I left him and on my way out, I saw Tildy returning.

"Well, what happened?" I inquired.

His eyes were sparkling. "Mikoyan accepted everything," he said.

With this good news I left for the Smallholders Party meeting. By now volunteers of the party had repossessed the party headquarters which, for the past seven years, had housed the

Soviet Hungarian Society. The news about the Smallholders Party reorganization had spread like wildfire. There were so many people in and around the building that I could hardly get in. The nine-member Executive Committee was besieged, there were so many things to do; volunteers were everywhere.

Journalists representing foreign papers came to us for information, as well as hundreds of people with problems, all urgent and important. There were many newcomers, who were not acquainted with the old-timers, and there was the usual amount of friction, unavoidable in any undertaking.

I decided to find out the answer to the question most important to all of us and put in a long distance call to Bela Kovacs. Nobody thought it would work, but I had luck and finally succeeded in reaching one of his friends.

"How is Bela's health?" I inquired anxiously.

"He's all right."

"Tell him to come up to the capital for God's sake; his presence is of utmost importance."

The man explained on the phone that Bela Kovacs was reluctant to come to Budapest, but that he was anxious to establish contact with me. I earnestly requested that he inform Bela to leave immediately for the capital. The man promised to do his best to persuade Kovacs to start the following day.

The next day, November 1st, was pregnant with fateful events.

Early in the morning, a phone call informed me that Bela Kovacs and his friends had left by car, and that they should arrive in Budapest in the late afternoon.

Tildy informed me confidentially about very bad news. General Maleter reported to the government that, according to aerial reconnaissance, major Soviet tank units were on their way toward Hungary.

The direction of their move was to Tatarhago via Szolnok, while other tank divisions were preparing in Rumania, too. Hungarian airports were taken by Soviet units by surprise.

"Well, so there is no way to send somebody to the U. N.—" I said with a sinking heart.

"That's right," Tildy said and continued with his information. When the government tried to reach the Soviet Ambassador to get an explanation concerning the new troop movements, the Ambassador could not be found. After a long search he was discovered in the basement. The messenger who was dispatched by Imre Nagy explained to the Ambassador that unless the Soviets supplied a satisfactory answer about the troop movements, the government would announce it to the public.

We got a vague explanation which characterized the troop movements as preparatory to withdrawal. This was probably contrary to the truth. Tildy had to leave for a cabinet meeting called in the face of danger. He wanted to know my reactions.

I told him that in my judgment only firmness could save the situation. This blackmailing should be counterattacked by decisive political steps. It was high time to state what the Revolution demanded: Hungary's withdrawal from the Warsaw Pact. We also should appeal to the U. N.

He agreed but he did not know what particular steps Imre Nagy had decided to take.

I called his attention to another danger. The Soviets would search for pretexts to intervene. The most conspicuous one would be if they could claim that there was chaos in Budapest, and the government was not in control of the situation. The important thing to do right now was to concentrate all our energy toward restoring complete order. My suggestion was to ask Cardinal Mindszenty and other respected church leaders to come immediately to the government's assistance by speaking to the public over the radio. Bela Kovacs, Anna Kethly, and a few of us who enjoyed some reputation, must do the same. He agreed and asked me to prepare my statement as soon as possible.

I had to rush to the party headquarters. Naturally, the party was not yet functioning satisfactorily. There was no lack of zeal but rather a lack of order and discipline. It was not easy to create order. Sometimes I had to be harsh. Too many people wanted to see me. Everybody thought that his problem was the most important to talk about.

It was relaxing to meet my old friend, Bela Padanyi-Gulyas. He warmly congratulated me on the fact that I had not yet gone mad in this chaos. He wanted to concentrate on foreign affairs again and try to reorganize the Foreign Office. I gave him my wholehearted approval, appreciating the fact that at last somebody with knowledge would proceed to this important spot.

I was called by phone to go to Parliament. It's very urgent—the message said.

Before rushing there, I asked all members of the Executive Committee to gather for a very important meeting when I returned.

In the Parliament everybody was in a fighting mood. Tildy was stern but depressed.

"The die is cast," he told me.

"What happened?" I asked him.

"The Soviet threat is very serious. Imre Nagy is angry and has decided to take a bold and serious political step."

"The bolder the better," I murmured.

"You'll be satisfied now," he told me, but without a smile. "It is still confidential. The government has decided to declare Hungary's withdrawal from the Warsaw Pact and the neutrality of Hungary. It will also request the U. N. to defend Hungary's neutrality."

"This is the solution!" I exclaimed, my voice full of joy. At last, a bold and wise step. This would halt the Soviets. It was just the right step.

Tildy was serious and he looked tired. He asked me to make order in the Party. "We must end all personal disagreements. We are all Hungarians," he said.

On my way back I was exuberant. I knew we had reached the climax. I firmly believed that we had found the best solution.

We provided an excuse to the West to interfere, and we gave the Soviets an opportunity to save face while giving up Hungary. I was sure that the free world's diplomacy would act quickly. The precedent of Austria's neutrality was before my eyes.

I had yet to learn how difficult it is to arouse the Western giant.

I asked the Executive Committee to come out with a public statement in which the Smallholders Party would give firm backing to Zoltan Tildy. In a stormy meeting, I had to exert all my influence and eloquence to win the battle. I did.

Then I asked them to gather again at 7:00 P.M. Bela Kovacs would be there. After giving instructions to the secretariat and the guards that after 6:00 P.M. nobody but the members of the Executive Committee and a few members of the secretariat must stay in the building, I went home tired, but full of optimism.

By the time I returned home everybody had heard the news.

Imre Nagy declared personally: "I called Mr. Andropow, the Soviet Ambassador—"

He declared Hungary's withdrawal from the Warsaw Pact, Hungary's neutrality, and he had sent a cable to the U. N. asking that body to protect this neutrality.

Budapest was gay. The Prime Minister's statement had echoed sentiments close to the heart of the Hungarian people.

At home everybody was elated. Alicia embraced and kissed me happily.

Lonci was the only one who still remained somewhat of a pessimist.

"Don't worry," I said, "we are free and neutral . . . we have a government and by tonight Bela Kovacs, too, will arrive."

"He's just one more naïve idealist," she countered. "He would have done better to stay in the country, and we would have, too."

"That certainly is a heroic philosophy," I answered, annoyed.

"I never claimed to be heroic. All I said was that naïveté will not solve the Soviet threat," she continued. She saw my face.

"Please don't be angry," she said, embracing me. "I am just anxious to save you. It would be so nice to live in freedom once again."

10 • A GREAT PATRIOT

Late the same day I had to rush back to Parliament for a meeting with the leaders of other parties. We were discussing how to set up a really representative coalition government.

When I returned home, Alicia congratulated me.

"Misi," she said, "I heard that you will be Mayor of Budapest again."

I felt a pang of guilt for neglecting the city, but my mind was occupied with other vital problems.

In a few minutes the message came that Kovacs had arrived, so I left in a hurry.

A few minutes later I embraced him. He was a changed person. He had lost his robust health, and his eyes had grown cold, his features hard. He rarely smiled. Many years of prison had changed him into a reserved, somber person. When we started talking about the past few years, he began to thaw out. Then I decided to bring up the subject most important to me, that of governing the country and his possible participation.

"You came at the right time, perhaps at the last possible minute," I told him. "The government is slowly gathering strength, and it needs help badly."

"I don't want to participate in the government," he answered deliberately.

"What do you mean?" I said. "That's impossible!"

"I can't work as much as a cabinet member should. I'm no longer healthy," he replied. "Besides, I don't see the entire situation clearly."

He began walking up and down the room.

"Bela, you must recognize the situation," I told him in a low but firm voice. "You have no time to hesitate anymore . . . you almost came too late."

"Why do you push me to decide?" he said angrily. "Why does everyone urge me to become a member of this government?"

"You must feel that it is the urgent appeal of the nation," I countered.

There was a silence. I could not help but admit that his position was far from simple.

There was a government with about twenty Communist members who had not resigned yet and whose records showed bloody crimes committed against the Hungarian nation. There was only one man in the government who never was a Communist, Zoltan Tildy. His name, however, created doubts and uneasiness in Bela Kovacs' mind. In the eyes of the people of the country the government was still bearing the stigma that some kind of responsibility rested upon it for calling the Soviet troops.

Bela Kovacs broke the silence abruptly. His voice was almost harsh, and he looked at me with tormented eyes.

"I feel alone. I have to decide alone. Nobody can help me, and I can not trust anybody. I am suspicious of everyone and everything."

"Then Bela," I told him slowly in a low voice, "my mission is finished. I am not offended. I understand you. I am terribly sorry that suspicion entered your soul. This is the result of nine years of constant torture. I feel it myself sometimes. I know what it means. You can not trust anybody."

"I trust you," he broke in. "I know you are an honest Hungarian," he continued and embraced me. "You know that your call was responsible for my being here, and now here I am. Remain and listen carefully. Help me to find the right way. You must recognize how difficult my position is."

We began a long and friendly talk. Slowly his warm human personality broke through the discipline he had imposed upon himself during the long years of suffering. He knew, as I did, that the whole Hungarian nation wanted to be rid of Communism forever. There was no doubt whatsoever that this included national Communism also. But his main argument was that he knew the Russians better than I or anybody else. All this could be a Russian trick. The Soviets would never permit a small nation under their domination to regain her freedom. Why then should he lend his name to this government which could not identify itself with the demands of the whole nation during the precious days of the Revolution? As a consequence of this it has a very doubtful future.

His other worry was that even by joining the government there would be no opportunity to represent the real feelings and will of the nation, for the present status of external affairs was very dangerous, and after long years of oppression the internal problems were too complex to solve satisfactorily. Take, for instance, the large number of former Communist Party members. No matter how enthusiastic they were right now, they would never accept a clearly Western type of democracy. His view was that the revolution must forge its own order of state with bloody sacrifices. In his eyes it seemed that this new order would not resemble a clean Western type of democracy. It would be something new in which, despite our opposition, institutions and customs established by the Communists would still remain in the social and economic life of the country. He was convinced that even the new order of state which was created in relative freedom in the years of 1945-46-47, belonged to the past. Terrible years went by during which people had to face new realities daily. The Revolution forged the whole nation into a sacred unity against Soviet domination. It would not be so easy to find the same unity when searching for a synthesis of the free enterprise system and socialism. Such a synthesis would be suspected from outside by both the West and the East. It would also be suspected from inside because it would satisfy neither the non-Communists nor the former Communists.

We faced a grave contradiction and had to accept a realistic solution, namely, that the people did not want to tolerate any kind of Communism. They wanted to be free. But they had lost their belief—whether they realized it or not—that we could turn back to live in a Western type of democracy in the shadow of Russia. The economic and social innovations of the years of Communist domination were too deeply woven into the life of the country. Furthermore, it was generally recognized that the Soviet Union was always ready to fight the reestablishment of a Western-style democratic country on her border, while it was very doubtful whether the Western powers were ready to risk a new world war.

Bela Kovacs was very pessimistic about this last aspect. He had grave doubts of any quick action by the Western powers.

I countered with my firm belief that we would get political and diplomatic help from the West. I explained to him that the declaration of our neutrality gave a unique opportunity to the West for intervention, while it gave the Soviets a good chance to save face and withdraw.

He was pleased by my argument but he was far from being convinced.

I had to admit that his analysis of the internal problems went far deeper than mine. Here he interrupted me, and expressed his doubts that even I could understand that if the freedom fight were successful, then I would have to sacrifice my typical Western ideas for political reality.

I went on and told him that I did not believe that all these complex problems were to be solved right now. My approach was simple. We have to solve them step by step. In my judgment two things were the most important: To have a government which would represent the demands of the Revolution and which would lead the nation toward consolidation. The second problem was to make preparations for free elections, which would mean the reorganization of non-Communist parties. In both respects his role was of paramount importance. This he could not deny.

During the long talk he became a little gayer. Soon he even teased me, saying that while I did not want to be a member of the government, I pushed him.

"Sure," he said, "you again want to be Mayor of Budapest. That is your love," he continued jokingly, "and no one can separate you."

"That's correct," I answered. "But you have to admit that I made great sacrifices by initiating the reorganization of our party, instead of rushing my re-election as mayor."

In this way we came back to our main problem. I explained to him that although it was a personal sacrifice to take part in party politics, I firmly believed this to be our duty. To have a democracy, you must have parties.

"Let's go, Bela, to meet the leaders of the Smallholders Party," I suggested. "They are waiting for you."

"I am not even a member," he replied. "They expelled me."

"Don't be silly, Bela. You know very well that it was a different Smallholders Party. They were under tremendous pressure."

"Eleven years ago my friends expelled me, so I am no longer a member," he said firmly.

I must have seemed depressed at his answer.

He changed the subject. He sensed the great respect and warm feelings I had for him. He told me how he was treated in different prisons. He asked me to talk a little about my own life. We felt mutual sympathy for our bad years and felt close to each other. We realized that the separation of long years had brought us even closer in friendship than before.

"Tell me how Tildy behaves," he wanted to know.

I knew we had come to a very delicate subject.

"Frankly, Bela," I said, "I can tell you that he is behaving as a good Hungarian patriot should. He has courage, resolution, and brains. Without him the government wouldn't be half as good as it is."

"I am very glad to hear this from you," he said.

"No one wants to believe anything good about Tildy," I replied. "The feeling against him seems to be running rather high, especially in the Party. It is important that you give him your backing."

"That is quite a request," he said.

I knew he was convinced that Tildy had played a part in his arrest eleven years ago. That would be hard to forget.

But every honest Hungarian, even Tildy, had a lot to forgive and forget. This idea gave me an argument which seemed to break his hesitation. I told him there had to be a general and noble forgiveness for everybody. Hatred and the spirit of revenge were not strong bricks with which to rebuild a country. He fully agreed. He considered it most important not to have any purges of Communists and not to frighten the former Communist Party members.

"No more political trials," he said. "Continue along the noble way of the Revolution."

Our long talk came to an end. He could not give me a definite "yes" to my political requests but at least he promised to reconsider the situation and to discuss it further with Imre Nagy, Tildy, and other members of the government. He reluctantly agreed to start for the meeting with the Executive Committee of the Smallholders Party.

We walked along together for a few blocks. No matter how he tried to conceal his feelings, he was deeply touched when we approached the building which used to be his headquarters.

He was received with warm respect. He came back as a king to his kingdom. He was touched, but he imposed again upon himself his mask of discipline. The members of the Executive Committee one after the other made short speeches. They all asked him to take the chairmanship of the party. He thanked them for these kind words but coolly refused to accept the unanimous offer.

The conference was interrupted by Tildy's telephone call. He wanted to talk to Bela Kovacs.

"Tell him I'm busy," he replied coldly. "We are in conference."

"He wants you to go to Parliament immediately."

"I'll take my time," Kovacs replied, "and go when I'm through here."

A few minutes later Tildy called again, urging Kovacs to come. But Kovacs wanted to know about the Smallholders Party program. I explained to him that we had not issued a program at that time. We had identified ourselves with the demands of the Revolution, and we would give a detailed political program in the election campaign.

"All right," he said, "but I have my own ideas about a party program. I'm not sure you'll agree with me," he continued. "I have discovered that you can never turn back; even our 1945 program is dated now."

"All right," I said. "We'll have time to discuss that later on."

He then explained that, for the time being, he would not accept the leadership of the party under any circumstances. He needed a few days to think and to see the situation clearly.

"Now we can go to Parliament," he said to me.

"Don't you want to go alone?" I asked him.

"No, you have to come with me." On the way I spoke to him.

"Bela, if you don't want to join the party or the government, I'll leave the party, myself, and organize another party with some friends. Without you I can't carry the burden of the party's past record."

"You certainly know how to press people, Misi."

Then I explained to him again that his presence would secure the government's position.

When we arrived at Parliament they waited for us with great respect. Bela didn't like it a bit, his manner was cold and formal. Tildy received us graciously while Bela was cold as ice.

"It's fine to see you here," Tildy said. "We are doubly glad, for this way you'll be able to participate in the cabinet meeting tomorrow morning."

"I'm not a member of the government yet," Kovacs replied. "Besides, I don't even know what you have been doing up to now."

Tildy started to give him detailed information. Kovacs thanked him and suggested that he would prefer speaking to Imre Nagy. The Gray Eminence entered the room and inquired whether he could inform the press that Bela Kovacs had joined the government.

"You'd better wait," Kovacs said, "until I have spoken with Imre Nagy."

"Yes, but it's near the press deadline," came the reply.

"Then they'll have to wait. Tomorrow is another day," Kovacs said adamantly.

"Public opinion would be very much pacified if people could read in the morning papers of your intention to join the regime," the Gray Eminence pleaded.

"There will be no declaration of my intentions in the morning papers," Kovacs answered in a determined voice.

Then he rose to go over to Imre Nagy's office. Tildy offered to accompany him.

"No, thanks," Kovacs replied. "I want to speak to Imre Nagy alone."

After he left Tildy did not hide his hurt feelings.

"Bela still carries the marks of prison," he said. "He's so suspicious."

Then we started discussing the problem of the Soviets. I suggested once again that the United Nations should have a special Hungarian representative. He said that he was thinking of me as the U. N. representative, but Imre Nagy wanted to represent Hungary himself. Once again he urged me to join the government. I explained that I didn't want to become a member of the cabinet, for I felt that my task lay in putting the party in shape, and then I'd go to the City Hall.

The Gray Eminence asked me to join him for a talk.

"Zoltan feels very badly about the fact that the Smallholders Party does not back him. In fact, the Communists have asked him whom he represents and on whose behalf he speaks. You can't leave him in the lurch in a situation as difficult as this."

I let him go on with his talking and didn't tell him that I had in my pocket the Party resolution backing Tildy. I was determined to make the document public only after Bela Kovacs agreed to join the government.

The Gray Eminence changed the subject. He explained that they would like to know what post I was willing to accept. Would it be in the cabinet, or the United Nations, or would I like to be the Mayor of Budapest once again? I gave him a specific answer. I would not accept a cabinet post in any circumstances. I would be willing to become Mayor of Budapest but only by election, not by appointment of the government. This had always been my ambition, although if I could benefit my country at the United Nations I would go.

In about an hour and a half Kovacs returned.

"Did you get all the information you needed from Nagy?" I inquired.

"Yes," he replied in a firm voice. Then he turned to the Gray Eminence. "Prepare a release saying that I agree to become an Observer-Member of the government."

The Gray Eminence tried to explain very politely that he could be either a Minister or an Observer, but not both.

"Well," Kovacs replied, "prepare the release in any case. Then we'll see."

Dobi appeared, ready to administer the oath of office to Kovacs. I was happy that I could play my modest role by assisting this fine patriot to serve his country in an hour of need.

We parted late at night. I couldn't resist remarking, when we said good-night: "Very few Hungarians made such a sacrifice for their country as you did by becoming a member of the government. God bless you for it."

"All right, all right," he muttered. "But now you have to do your share. You won't have time to be mayor now, you must help me in the party and in the cabinet, because my health is not strong."

"All right," I agreed. "I'll do it, at least for the first few days, until things are back to normal."

11 • BEFORE THE STORM

When I arrived home an old friend was there. He had been waiting for hours and apparently was determined to sit there until he could speak with me. I hadn't seen him for ten years. I was so tired that I would have preferred a bed, but common courtesy forced me to sit down and learn why he had come.

"Misi, you know I have never requested anything from you," he began.

"That's very true," I replied. "In fact, you have often helped people when I couldn't."

"Thanks for remembering that," he replied. "As you know, I have never mentioned this."

"True," I conceded.

"I'll tell you something else that no one knows. You wouldn't have known it, except that we are in a tragic situation and I want you to listen to me. I know you are stubborn," he added, with a smile. "Therefore I want to put down all my aces."

"You don't need to but go ahead."

"It's about those small sums your wife received from an anonymous donor while you were in prison." He seemed hesitant, then he continued. "I was the one who sent those sums."

"Thank you very much," I replied, greatly embarrassed. He sounded embarrassed, too.

"I hate bringing all this up but I have to, because I want you to listen to me."

"Go ahead, what do you want?"

"I want all of us to get into a car tomorrow morning, with

both our families, and leave immediately for Austria. We can't stay here for another minute. The Russians are coming."

The request sounded preposterous to me. I was convinced that we could handle all these difficulties and I was trying to find the right words with which to refuse him without hurting him. He read my thoughts.

"Don't hesitate," he said. "I mean well to you and your family. Leave everything here and come."

"No, I can't," I said with determination. "I will stay here and do my duty."

"This is a crime against your family and yourself," he replied in an excited voice.

"I still prefer it to a crime against my country and my people."

"The country," he replied quietly, "is something intangible. Your family is a reality. They are a part of the country. Your primary obligation is toward your family. Everything else comes after."

"I can't argue with your convictions," I said. "Besides, I'm much too tired to argue. There are thousands of things I have to do, and I need all my energy."

"I'm sorry," he answered. "I see that you're a hopeless idealist. This is commendable but it's not practical. Above all, it's unfair to your family. Let me take your wife and daughter at least. Then you can do anything you want to."

I suggested that he discuss this with Lonci and said goodnight to him.

I had to work on my radio speech, but things were so hectic that I had to retire with my typewriter to the only place where I still could find privacy, the bathroom.

Early in the morning two university students came to call. They were determined and wanted to know the Smallholders Party views on two questions. Would the formation of political parties threaten the political unity of the Revolution? They wanted to know. Was the government determined to fight the Soviets again, in case they attacked the country? The restlessness of youth prompted this visit, because the U.S.S.R. had occupied all the airports in the country, yet the government had not issued any orders for defense. My answer to their first question was that a multiparty system was necessary for a free election, which was, after all, one of the most important political demands of the Revolution. As for the second point, I explained that I was convinced that Imre Nagy genuinely represented Hungarian interests, and that those Smallholders Party members who were in the government guaranteed, by their very presence, that they would do everything possible to protect the country.

The boys accepted my first answer. They were, however, not reassured by the second. They told me of large-scale Soviet troop movements. The way they saw the situation, the primary problem was military and not political. I had to explain to them that I did not know how much military power General Maleter and his associates could muster. Should a large-scale Soviet military attack occur it would mean a massacre, and we would have no chance unless we received outside help. I promised them to alert the government to the military danger.

The boys had hardly left when the phone began to ring. Several people called from the party and from Parliament, requesting that I come, that it was vitally important. I hurried to party headquarters. When I arrived, everybody rushed up, offering congratulations. I was surprised, and I didn't understand it. They showed me a morning paper with headlines announcing that Jozsef Kovago had become Mayor of Budapest once again. This was exciting news, and a great moral victory for me. The Revolution had sent me back to the same office from which the Communist terror had expelled me nine years before.

Finally, the repeated pleas from Bela Kovacs made it necessary for me to leave for Parliament. My friend Peter accompanied me, telling me that the city was full of rumors to the effect that

I was receiving a cabinet position. He also told me that Lonci was anything but happy about this possibility.

"Don't worry," I said. "I won't accept such a position. Didn't you read in the papers that the National Committee of Budapest had elected me chairman? That means that I am mayor again. That is what I want to be. As soon as the government is reorganized and the party is in good shape, I will occupy my chair in City Hall."

"When will that be?" Peter inquired.

"Monday, I hope," I replied, "by Monday at the latest."

"All right," he replied, "just be careful that the Ruskis don't arrive before you."

He told me that the general mood of the city was to fight the Russians if necessary. The workers were organizing, there were armed detachments, and they seemed determined to resist any attack. It was almost a miracle how everybody, without any central command organization, had thrown out the Reds, both physically and emotionally. Patriotism had replaced any other feeling. Communist Party secretaries were vanishing or, in some cases, trying to apologize for their past actions.

"There has been no violence anywhere?" I inquired anxiously.

"Oh, no, they simply threw them out. They are not needed any more. The workers are electing their own men. Many old-time Social Democrats are now in labor positions and quite a few deserving engineers, too." He listed a few names I knew and I relaxed.

We stopped on our way to Parliament to meet a friend of ours who had come in from the country. He had arrived in the capital bringing two truckloads of food as a present to the people of Budapest. This sort of thing had been going on for days now. The peasants had sent food to Budapest, not expecting any payment. My friend was one of these kind volunteers. In addition, he told me some good news about my daughter and my mother-in-law. They were both well. He also told me of the attitude of the peasants toward the Revolution. They simply left the collective farms and took back their own land. That was their way of supporting the Revolution.

We continued toward Parliament. In the car Peter told me that my friend of the previous evening had spoken to Lonci about leaving for abroad. He had received a prompt refusal. She would not leave without me.

When we reached Parliament we found a tense situation. We were concerned with the reorganization of the government and the distribution of cabinet seats among the parties. I felt that the Smallholders Party which, in the free elections of 1945 received fifty-seven per cent of the votes, should have its proportionate representation. Tildy resented my insistence that the Smallholders Party have what I regarded as a fair share in governing the country. I explained that giving the Communists a significant role in the government would not serve the interests of the country either at home or abroad.

Tildy's view was that the Soviet Union would be more likely to accept the government in Hungary if Socialist Parties were in a majority. He felt that the Soviets' attitude toward us was crucial. In contrast my view was that if the Soviets interfered and crushed Hungarian freedom they would not care in the slightest about the composition of the government. To prevent any Soviet danger the government had to take immediate diplomatic steps. A good United Nations representative might be of greater help now than the whole government. Kovacs persuaded me to yield and accept Tildy's view. We ended our debate in a sombre mood.

Tildy seemed to be much more concerned than the rest of us. We did not know it then, but he had probably heard that Janos Kadar had disappeared mysteriously the night before. A Soviet limousine had picked him up.

Things were really chaotic. All over the country Revolutionary groups were organizing, issuing reports and new orders, and starting newspapers. The youth organizations and workers' councils all had their problems and demanded quick solutions. Former prison mates wanted legislation that would rehabilitate and compensate them.

I was on the verge of complete exhaustion, and some of my friends advised me to take over City Hall and abandon all of these feverish activities.

A friend of mine, also a member of the Executive Committee and an expert on city problems, however, convinced me that I should stick to my present job. Bechtler, the vice-mayor, was able to cope with the problems of the city and could go on for a few more days while I established order and a functioning administration in the Smallholders Party. It was extremely important to keep the party united and to keep individual members from letting their own enthusiasm run away with them.

There was also the question of liaison with other parties and leading personalities.

Several people stressed the importance of paying a visit to Cardinal Mindszenty. Some people thought that all parties based on a Christian ideology should join forces. When this idea was brought up to Mindszenty, the Prince Primate explained that he stood above parties, and that he could not change this policy. I sent a message of greeting to the Cardinal, telling him that I planned to pay my respects the following week.

Bela Padanyi-Gulyas wanted to speak with me. We met, and he presented his views on the international situation. He felt that a Soviet attack was near. He was truly convinced that without the immediate help of the West we were lost. He wanted a car to leave for Vienna. He offered to take Lonci and my daughter, too. "After all," he argued, "you have to have a reliable representative outside."

"Look, Bela," I replied, "if I did what you suggested I would betray those who have died for their country. I would show that I don't believe in our country's future, I would just give validity to the charge against politicians that they are seen and heard only when glory awaits them."

"You too," I added, "are needed here at home. If you leave, you should be going as a United Nations representative. My understanding, however, is that Imre Nagy, as Foreign Minister, wants to be our spokesman at the U. N."

"Do you know that a number of people of all age groups are already fleeing towards Austria?" he asked. "They are convinced that a Russian attack is inevitable."

"You're mistaken," I pleaded. "The Soviets must know that Hungary is a sovereign state like Austria and any military attack might involve the Western world," I said. "The United Nations Security Council is about to meet any hour now—"

"—And will not accomplish anything," he broke in. "You are now caught in the fire of enthusiasm, and so are all patriots. You assume that the Western world burns with the same fire."

"The West must be convinced that what is happening in Hungary is a decisive blow to the Soviet Union and to Communism. If we can consolidate our position, introduce a multiparty system once again and have free elections, then we will have shaken the very foundation of Communism," I replied.

"You're right," Bela said. "Of course you're right. Your analysis is so correct that the Soviet Union sees it as clearly as you do. That is precisely why they will crush Free Hungary. It will take quite a while for the West to discover that they have missed a unique chance," he added. "However," he conceded, "I will stay here if you feel that strongly."

That same evening I held a conference with two leading economists. They were pessimistic. People were not working, production was almost nil, and the government was not taking any constructive steps. This might cause a tragic inflation.

"What do you want?" I asked.

"That we submit a series of instructions which the government should issue," they answered quickly.

"Why don't you go to the government?" I asked.

"They are much too busy organizing themselves. The Economic Ministries don't function; there should be a top Economic Council coordinating the work of different financial and industrial organizations of the country. Strong political leadership is needed. Experts are fine," they added, "but theorists should be on tap, not on top."

"Why did you come to me? I'm not even a member of the cabinet."

"Still you are a person of influence. Your decisions will be accepted by the government," they replied.

"I have no right to such a post," I protested.

"It's not a matter of right, it's a matter of need. We have to create order out of this chaos."

"All right, I'll speak to the government," I told them. "Call me tomorrow." They thanked me and left.

A number of other delegations were waiting outside. I was hungry and tired. Robert rescued me, for Bela Kovacs wanted to speak to me immediately. I could speak to Lonci for only a few minutes. She had talked to her mother on the phone. She and our daughter were well, but there were many Russian tanks traveling from that part of the country toward Budapest.

Later that night Bela Kovacs called me up. He was wrestling with his conscience and had come to the reluctant conclusion that he should contribute to the establishment of complete order. Therefore, he was willing to accept our suggestion and assume the leadership of the Smallholders Party. He felt that his personal prestige would help the government to cope with the situation. He felt that the Smallholders Party was amiss for not supporting strongly enough the social and economic reforms. In his view, this was the only conceivable way to avoid a Russian attack and to convince the Soviets that our aim was sincere neutrality.

I then went to Parliament, for Tildy and some other members of the cabinet were awaiting me. They wanted to appoint a political delegation with full authority to negotiate with the Soviet Union. This delegation would handle political affairs, such as leaving the Warsaw Pact and our neutrality. Tildy asked me to accept membership in this political delegation. Another delegation was appointed also, a group of military men to negotiate Soviet withdrawal.

Later, the radio announced the appointment of both these delegations. The military committee was headed by General Pal Maleter and was to start negotiations the next morning with the Soviet generals.

The other delegation which was fully authorized to carry on negotiations with the Soviet Union in connection with Hungary's new international political status, was headed by Geza Losonczy, a Communist cabinet member, and consisted of four other politicians, including myself.

That night I had to return to Parliament and could not go home till early morning. I had discussed the situation with party leaders and cabinet members. I shook hands with Maleter and wished him good luck in his negotiations, which were to take place the following day.

In between meetings, I joined a discussion in which Dobi, Erdei, a cabinet member, the Gray Eminence, Bognar, another cabinet member, and others took part. Some of these people's records were quite reprehensible, and they were shaken by the Revolution. The victory of the Revolution threatened their political existence.

Bognar, for instance, had a very bad reputation in the Smallholders Party. He had served the Communists all through the terror regime as a cabinet member, while in name he was still a Smallholder. The picture was characteristic of the Revolution. The generosity of the Revolution went so far that this type of person was not purged. They were given a chance to repent and expiate their sins. However, it was also true that they could not count on our sympathy.

They were talking about the expected Soviet attack and brought it up in connection with the Suez crisis. It is understandable that we, caught up by the fervor of the Revolution, could not pay enough attention to other happenings in world politics. We felt that the front page of newspapers excluded everything but Hungary.

A telephone call informed us that the first Soviet tank units had arrived at Szolnok, a Hungarian city 100 miles to the east-northeast of Budapest. Bognar was again more sure of himself that day than earlier. This struck me as peculiar. It was obvious that he was sure that Budapest would be attacked by Soviet troops. This would save his cabinet portfolio which was to be taken away by the Revolution. I followed his words, but I could also guess what was in his mind.

"It is obvious," he told me, "there is no other way for the Soviets but to take the same step in Hungary that the Western Powers took in Suez. That means an attack. Then both parties will be satisfied. I do not think it would mean a world war."

Bognar analyzed the situation keenly, without showing any feelings. The others were preoccupied with the fate of our country—or at least seemed to be. At last they asked for my view, too.

I glanced at my wristwatch and said sarcastically to Bognar: "Right now, it's 1:00 a.m. In a half hour I have to leave."

"Why?" somebody asked.

"Because I do not want to be taken in the same place together with Bognar."

There were malicious smiles to the detriment of Bognar.

"Be quick," he countered, "because there is a serious chance they will attack."

"Or that they will just move in to threaten and put the government under duress." I continued, "I am sure the West would not tolerate a new attack. By the way, did you hear that the U. N. sent observers?" I added, because there were such rumors and I thought that by mentioning this, I would weaken Bognar's self confidence.

"That would help," somebody interjected.

"If they really would come here—" Bognar said laughingly. "But they have a harder nut to crack—I mean the Suez, where I am not yet sure there is complete Western unity."

When I left, I still consoled myself with the thought that the Soviet troops would halt short of an attack, and that their primary task would be to threaten Tito and discourage him from showing any sympathy for the Hungarian Revolution.

That night was filled with anxiety and dismay. The country was overrun with Russians, and an attack could have started at any time. When I returned home the women still hadn't gone to bed. They were worried about the news of the Soviet troop movements.

"What do you think, Misi?" they inquired anxiously.

To reassure them I said. "The Western Powers will present an ultimatum to the Soviet Union and that will sober them up."

"Misi, dear, are you sure that Mr. Dulles knows this too?" Alicia inquired, laughing.

Lonci answered in a voice of gay sarcasm.

"Of course. Don't you know that Misi talks to him every day on the phone?"

"All right, all right," I grumbled. "Just wait till you see, when they convene the Security Council. Everything will be taken care of. There's no need to worry."

12 • ALL HELL BREAKS LOOSE

We awoke to beautiful sunshine on the morning of November 3rd. The city was relieved that no attack had taken place at night. Everyone knew of the Soviet troop movements, and the feeling was that if nothing had taken place at night the danger was past. We felt new hope again. The efforts of the government and responsible groups promised to bear fruit, and the working force of the country would resume its peaceful toil. Monday, November 5th. Volunteer units started to clean up the ruins left from the street fight, and the city almost reverted to normal life.

It was announced over the radio that Imre Nagy's government was reorganized and become a real coalition Government; the Smallholders, Social Democrat, and Communist Parties had three members each, the Petofi Party two members, while Pal Maleter was an independent cabinet member.

The Smallholders Party showed great self-restraint by accepting equal membership with other parties but this government still had far to go toward consolidation.

According to rumors, the West had already taken steps in connection with the Hungarian problem, and the Security Council of the U. N. was about to meet.

At last I had time to go to City Hall. With a few friends I mounted the old staircase. I was moved when we reached the corridor leading to my old office. When I entered what used to be the reception room, the secretaries welcomed me.

"Welcome, Mr. Mayor," they said.

We shook hands, and I went directly into my study. Temporarily Acting-Mayor Peter Bechtler was working there. We embraced each other emotionally. The last time we had seen each other was in the notorious Central Prison of Budapest, where both of us had been locked up. I explained why I couldn't spend full time in City Hall, and we discussed problems of the Hungarian capital.

We discussed a basic structural reorganization of the city government so that the traditional autonomous legislative body would control affairs instead of the City Council as introduced by the Communists. We felt that after this plan was put into practice, several self-governing provincial cities might adopt it. In fact, the government itself would be strengthened once it received the backing of independent city governments.

I concluded that, from Monday, November 5th on, I had to be on the job full time, devoting whatever ability and energy I might have to my beautiful city. I saw the press and explained the situation to them. As an explanation for the delay, I thought it advisable to give reasons of health rather than my activities in the Smallholders Party.

Thinking back on this visit to City Hall, it was one of the finest moments of my life. It was a great feeling to return to the place where I was awaited, and it was very hard to break away and leave them, even if it was only for two days.

I left City Hall in an optimistic mood. Although the difficulties were clear to me, I nevertheless felt that the work of reorganization had already started. If negotiations with the Russians were successful, we could create a normal state of affairs in the country within a reasonably short time. At long last, the Hungarian people would have a chance to live in a free country as befits free men. With our hard-working people and the richness of our land I felt that with good luck we might become one of the most flourishing countries in Europe.

That evening the leaders of the Smallholders Party visited Bela Kovacs in his home. We asked him to accept the chairmanship of the party. He thanked us warmly and accepted it. At his suggestion, we proceeded to elect a Secretary-General and two deputies. As a result of the secret ballot, I was elected Secretary-General. My two deputies were Ferenc Vidovits and Tivadar Partay. Vidovits, one of the most courageous members of our party, had recently been freed from prison. His election was a satisfaction to all of us.

We interrupted our proceedings to listen to the broadcast of Jozsef Mindszenty, Prince Primate of Hungary. He spoke with great dignity and a thorough understanding of the problems and unflinching loyalty of the Hungarians. His tone was one of forgiveness and it impressed all of us. After the speech we continued to discuss party affairs and prepared a press communique.

When the meeting adjourned Bela Kovacs suggested that we go to Parliament immediately, for Imre Nagy and Tildy wished to speak with us. We found a highly optimistic Tildy. He was convinced that the Russians would not attack. General Maleter and his associates had already held one conference with Russian military authorities and were about to start for another. Meanwhile, the government published the names of a five-member delegation with full authority to negotiate with the U.S.S.R. I was a member of the delegation. Tildy explained that our job would start in a day or two. He expected Soviet representatives to inform him within a day where the negotiations would take place. Tildy's guess was that it would be in Warsaw. I told him that I felt I would have been more useful at the United Nations meetings in New York. However, Tildy was convinced that my place was in the delegation, for we would be the ones to negotiate the most critical of all problems, and that was where the most able men were needed. He also mentioned the mysterious disappearance of Janos Kadar, a member of the Government, and of some of his associates. His interpretation was that they might have started direct negotiations with the Soviets, which, in the long run, might work out well for us. Imre Nagy was very busy and Kovacs could not stay any longer. Tildy suggested that we move into the Parliament building itself. This way it would be easier to call a cabinet meeting at any time. We left for home, but we indicated that we might move to Parliament the following evening. On our way out Tildy stopped me.

"Well, are you satisfied with the Government?" he wanted to know.

"Yes, Zoltan, I certainly am. You really became a government worthy of the Hungarian Revolution. May God bless you and help you."

"We'll certainly need that," someone in the room muttered. I turned towards the voice. It was the Gray Eminence. He looked pale and tired.

It was late when we started home with Bela Kovacs. The stars were shining, it was a clear night. For a while we drove, then we got out of the car and continued on foot. The city was asleep. Alone, in the privacy of the night, we discussed the future. We were elated by the fact that the Soviet Union was already negotiating with the military delegation, headed by General Maleter. This meant a *de facto* recognition of the Hungarian Revolution. We both expected difficulties in connection with details of troop withdrawals, but we agreed that every day meant progress toward reorganization. After the heroic sacrifice of our young people, which broke the chains imposed by the most powerful tyranny of our times, Hungary could look forward to a happier future.

When I reached home, Lonci was waiting up for me. I comforted her by giving her some of my optimistic views. I told her that, while I couldn't promise to be less busy in times to come, at least I would always be in a good mood. She would be happy, too, for we would bring Catherine up to Budapest.

"You are just like a child," she interrupted, speaking sharply.

"The whole country is full of Russians. The city is surrounded. We can't leave Budapest, and here you are talking about bringing Catherine here."

"Don't worry, dear, on account of the Russians," was my answer. "Once they were willing to start negotiations that automatically ruled out the possibility of an attack. The rest is up to the U. N. One day, you'll wake up and you won't see a Ruski anywhere. In fact, we'll have to go all the way to Warsaw or Moscow to see one."

My optimism made her feel a little better. We went to bed in a relaxed mood.

At early dawn we were awakened by sounds of heavy gunfire and artillery. As quickly as we could we put on some clothes and rushed to the next room to listen to the radio.

"This is Prime Minister Imre Nagy speaking," he began his broadcast in an emotion-charged voice. "Today, at daybreak, Soviet troops attacked our capital with the intent of overthrowing the legal democratic Hungarian government. Our troops are in combat. The government is still in control. I hereby inform the people of our country and the entire world of this act of aggression."

It was 5:20 a.m.

Nagy's announcement was followed by the national anthem. "Be faithful to your country always, oh Hungarian. . . ." All hell had broken loose. I glanced at Lonci. She was pale and quiet as she whispered, "It's just like the Russo-Finnish War." She couldn't continue, for the rest of her words were drowned in bitter tears.

13 • THE HORSEMEN OF THE APOCALYPSE

The women were packing feverishly and crying bitterly. The phone never stopped ringing. One after the other, my friends called. "Try to escape the Russians," was their one message. Alicia confessed that earlier Tildy had telephoned and asked that I go to the Parliament immediately. She had not awakened me but had told Tildy that he shouldn't bother me as early as that. Tildy answered that he had reason to telephone. I called Bela Kovacs. I told him that I was sorry I had been mistaken in my hopes and wished him all the best, asking for God's blessing.

The women were frantic. They had no doubts that the second intervention by the Soviet would be very powerful, and that the AVO would also be a party to it. "Let's get away as fast as we can," they begged me. We decided they should leave for a hospital, and I would try to save my life in some other way. I accompanied them down the street. After a while they stopped and asked me not to go with them. Lonci was on the verge of a hysterical breakdown. However, with amazing composure she controlled herself and begged me: "Flee! Try to escape to the West. Don't worry about me." I felt like dying.

Returning to the apartment I wandered around the rooms not knowing what to do. This was the end. The end of the Hungarian Revolution, the end of liberty. The windows were being shattered under the gunfire.

I decided to go to Parliament. It was my duty to declare Budapest an open city. On second thought I remembered that the radio was already under Soviet control. I bumped into two friends in the street, and when they saw me they yelled: "Are you crazy? Don't wander on the streets. Escape!" Across th square there was an old church. I went in and tried to pray. M mind was all confusion and desperation. Then I walked out in the street again. What should I do? I had no more country, n home. I had lost even my wife. Then I returned to the apartmer The phone kept ringing. I no longer answered. I shaved an dressed with meticulous care. I felt as though I was preparing for an important occasion, which required good grooming. I planned to go down to the street and ask the first young fighter to lend me his submachine gun for a few minutes. It had been many years since I had handled a weapon. During the war I decided that I would never be a soldier again. I had lost all my faith in weapons. They don't solve anything. I believed then that only reason, diplomacy, and politics could save humanity. Now, it seemed that ideas were powerless. One should die fighting, I thought. I was ready.

The phone rang again. I decided not to answer. Then, on second thought, I picked up the receiver. Maybe this will be the last person I will ever talk to, I thought gloomily. It was an old friend. I hadn't spoken to him for at least eleven years. He explained that he telephoned to invite us to hide in his place. I could stay there for days, weeks, or months. He had plenty of food, and his cellar was safe enough, no one would find me there.

"Why should I hide?" I queried.

"Because your life is in danger now, and we will need you later on when Western aid comes. Don't hesitate to come. Bring your family, too."

"Lonci has already left."

"Then come by yourself. Don't wait," he urged me. "As a good Hungarian I want to hide you, for we all need you. It's just for a few days and the West will send its help. I have just listened to the radio."

This seemed to me like the hand of God and I decided to

accept his offer. I started down the street walking toward his place which was in another part of the city. The street was empty except for a few frantic people. I heard the noise of gunfire and the stray bullets hitting the walls. I was too bitter to worry about personal safety. You are all alone. . . . Once again I realized this. You are all alone, and so is your country, I thought. Fate decided to change everything overnight. Yesterday all was hope, today everything is lost. My friend received me warmly and introduced me to his family. I was so depressed that I could hardly respond to their kindness. All I could think of was this pathetically brief spell of freedom. I tried to see what it meant in the light of history. From the rational point of view I knew that it made no sense, but at times heroism can do more than reason. Whatever historians think of these young heroes who dared battle the Soviet giant and fight Communist tyranny, they will always be heroic to me as David challenging Goliath. Probably the leaders of the world will be angry at these heroic children that they decided to take the initiative into their own hands instead of following the preplanned schedule, I thought. Maybe they will be angry at the Hungarians for causing all these complications. Whatever they may think, I felt that the saga of the Hungarian Revolution and the fight for freedom would become part of the human legend, like the Battle of Thermopylae.

In a world becoming more and more materialistic, these youngsters had written pages of superb heroism.

The telephone at my friend's place kept ringing. Barricades were erected all over the city, callers informed him. Freedom Fighters made last ditch stands against gigantic Soviet tanks. Then terrible news came. The hospital where Lonci and Alicia had sought shelter was surrounded by Soviet troops. The Freedom Fighters were inside defending the hospital, and a doctor, whom I knew, told me that the women were safe. Even through the receiver, however, I could hear gunfire and the sounds of battle from the hospital, which became a fortress.

"What's going on?" I inquired.

"Wait a minute . . . just a minute . . . I had to lie down on the floor," he continued, "these swine are shelling the hospital."

I heard a blast again and his voice died away. I called to him to talk. No answer. I called back but the number didn't answer any more. Almost automatically I took my coat and hat and said good-bye to my host.

"Have you gone mad?" he said. "Where are you going?"

"I am going to find Lonci."

"Are you crazy? You can't leave now. Look out in the street."

"I don't want to look out; I want to go," I said. "Good-bye and many thanks."

His wife came up, a beautiful, charming woman. I could tell by her voice that she was deeply moved.

"Please," she begged, "I also ask you not to go."

"You, too?" I said. "You are a woman. You should understand my position. After all, there are certain moments when a man cannot shrink from his duty."

"That's true," she replied, "but life can be cruel and create horrible situations. Please come with me," and she led me to the window. "Look out."

I saw three gigantic tanks in front of the gate and two other tanks with guns pointed on the corner. Two Russian guards were standing at the gate.

"It's impossible to leave this building," she said.

I realized that she was right. I felt impotent and desperate.

My friend tried to comfort me.

"Listen to the radio," he begged me. "There's no doubt whatever that Dag Hammerskjold will arrive here any hour. It's impossible that the United Nations won't move or hear all these desperate cries for help from the free Hungarian radio stations. The U. S., England, and France—they can't ignore these desperate cries."

"They are much too busy now with the Suez question," I said.

"That may be true," he said, "but they have sent an International Army there; they will surely do the same here."

Then he explained to me that, according to many opinions, the only reason the U. S. declared the British-French action in the Middle East to be an aggression was to be able to create a legal basis for declaring the Soviet interference an aggression too. The solution used in Egypt will be perfectly acceptable in the Hungarian case, too.

All this sounded very logical to me. "If only Lonci were safe," I said in frustration.

My friend and his wife tried to comfort me by telling me that the hospital was an old and strong building with good thick walls and a deep cellar. We listened to the radio, talked to people on the phone, and the evening passed. When I went to bed I couldn't sleep. I had nightmares that night, the beginning and the end seemed to have merged, time no longer had any meaning. It took quite an effort and some time to gain control over my nerves again. Finally, I succeeded and tried to put the mosaics of information together to get a more coherent picture.

The events of our situation seemed to fall into place. All over Budapest and throughout the country fighting was going on. Heroes were born and died by the minute. The armed youth, the workers, and the Hungarian Army were trying to fight back against the overwhelming power of Soviet troops and equipment. Although the Soviets occupied Budapest Radio, in a short time a number of free Hungarian radio stations all over the country were broadcasting news of the event to the whole world, asking the help of the free world. The government behaved in an exemplary fashion, and stayed in its place until the last minute. The radio broadcast the last message of Imre Nagy protesting against the brutal Soviet aggression and asking for help. I learned afterwards that he later fled to the Yugoslav Embassy. Tildy remained in the Parliament to face the Russians and earned the respect of everybody.

The night passed, and the following day in the same way. All of us waited near the radio and telephone to get more information. There was no question that the Soviet Union had used considerable power to annihilate the Hungarian Freedom Fighters. The gigantic tanks, however, did not succeed in crushing the heroism of these patriots for many days.

Late the next day, news came that General Bela Kiraly was gathering his mobilized tank units in the hills of Buda, preparing for a major counterattack. Another day of desperate waiting passed. The third day I could no longer bear the suspense and informed my host that I would have to leave, regardless of the consequences. Around eleven, the Soviet guard left the gate. I didn't want to embarrass my host and for his safety I carefully looked around before going down the staircase. He realized that I was determined to leave and no longer tried to dissuade me. I said good-bye, thanking them. They had been very nice to me, and I would never forget their hospitality. One of their daughters was the same age as mine, and she reminded me of my happy times with Catherine. I walked out the gate and started towards the street. When I passed a Soviet tank the soldiers yelled at me. I put my finger in my mouth, indicating that I was hungry and was going to eat. They let me pass.

I reached the wide boulevard which looked like a battlefield. Houses were in ruins, broken-down electric cables and torn-up car rails were everywhere. The only persons one could see on the street were standing in line in front of the food stores. Suddenly two Soviet tanks appeared. People tried to hide. I fled into a house. The Soviet tanks opened fire on the people standing in the food line. Then soldiers climbed out from one of them. Among them, rising from a Soviet tank, I saw a face which was ominously familiar. It was an AVO man I remembered from prison, gesticulating to the Russian soldiers, who climbed back into their tank. With loud rumbling the giant monster rolled on. I stood there, frozen with fear and disgust. So all the AVO rats who survived were leading the Soviet campaign of vengeance.

I had to find Lonci wherever she was. Then, maybe, I could escape with her to the West. I would have to go there to tell them our story; there was a great deal to tell. I would have to try to tell them how shameful and tragic it was that the Western World did not realize its unique opportunity to strike a blow for freedom. I would tell them that letting Hungary die would be their shame for all time.

A woman passed the house carrying a shopping bag. I glanced at her and for a minute our eyes met. It was the wife of an old friend of mine.

"Thank goodness, Misi. Friends are looking for you everywhere," she said. "Please come with me. I can't give you anything to eat for we are out of bread even, but I have a little rum left."

Once at their place she telephoned and in a quarter of an hour Peter had arrived.

"Thank God, old boy, I am glad you survived. Don't worry."

Like most other people, he had been convinced that the political delegation of which I was a member had left to negotiate with the Soviets and that, like the military delegation of General Maleter, we had been arrested when we arrived at the meeting place for negotiations. Soon a couple of other friends came in, all looking at me as if I had returned from the dead. I explained that I had to go find Lonci in the hospital. They fell silent, for the whole city knew that the hospital had been shelled by the Soviet tanks and there were many dead and wounded. Peter took his cap and said, "Let's go."

As fast as we could, we went through the battle-scarred streets. The whole city looked like a battlefield. Destruction and the dead were all over. It looked very much like it had when World War II ended, except that people had been frightened then when they saw a Russian soldier. Now they were determined and proud. Whenever Soviet soldiers tried to talk with them, they froze and turned their heads. Cold stares were all the Russians received from men, women, and children. The walls still bore the posters with the demands of the Revolution. I saw people stopping and adding one more to the demands printed. It was "A Neutral Hungary and Free Elections." Children distributed leaflets. "Ruskis, go home. The strike will go on until you leave."

When we reached the hospital the scene looked hopeless. The whole square was in ruins and the chapel of the hospital, centuries old, was a heap of rubble. We went inside the building and, after a search, we found Lonci and Alicia both alive, thank God. Lonci was feverish and hysterical. She embraced me, crying, "Please send those tanks away. I can't stand them anymore. I just can't bear to hear their gunfire."

For three solid days the hospital had been in a state of siege. More and more wounded had been brought in. Doctors and nurses were at a premium. When we were on our way out they brought in a stretcher. On it was a tall, dark-haired man with blood on his breast. He was shouting feverishly. His hair was bloody and his face was covered with sweat. "Fight! Forward . . . careful, they are coming . . . the Russians . . . the AVO. . . . That man was in the AVO, too. Be careful, I know them well . . . I want to fight, too, be careful, I know them all. I want to fight. Only blood can cleanse my crimes, blood. . . . Oh, God, oh, God . . . can you forgive . . ."

It was Daddy Longlegs, dying. I was deeply moved. I felt that when he passed on, He who forgives all sinners would judge not only deeds but intentions, and He would forgive the repentant.

We left the hospital. The streets were full of ruins, and the Soviet tanks rumbled by, shooting at random, killing without purpose. It seemed as if the Horsemen of the Apocalypse had been racing up and down the streets of Budapest.

We went into hiding with friends. Our next few days and nights were spent in going from place to place, hiding, and trying not to bring danger to those who helped us.

14 • SOVIET HESITATION

Following up the military action, the Soviet Union put into power a Quisling government, headed by Janos Kadar. As late as November 1st, Kadar had claimed to agree with every step Imre Nagy had taken. However, he claimed that he had organized his government as early as November 1st. In all probability, while Soviet statesman Mikoyan and his associate Suslov negotiated in Budapest on October 31st and November 1st they had held double dealings. While talking to Tildy, Mikoyan had accepted the most important conditions of the Hungarian Revolution. While talking to the Communists, he insisted that they continue in their loyalty toward Moscow. It was of paramount importance to the Soviets to win over Kadar, Secretary-General of the reorganized Communist Party. A rupture between Moscow and him would have been most embarrassing. To assure Kadar's backing, Mikoyan had probably pledged not only complete military and political support, but it appeared that he had promised that his regime might retain some of the achievements of the Revolution. Among these would be the continuation of the Workers Council, the multiparty system, use of the traditional Kossuth emblem, and a degree of autonomy in international affairs as well as in foreign relations. Furthermore, they may have promised Kadar that once the Soviet troops crushed the Revolution they would leave the country.

Kadar had spent many years in prison under the Rakosi regime, undergoing considerable torture. Thus, the combination of Soviet threats and promises may have weakened his resistance.

His later actions indicate that he must have asked immunity for the Imre Nagy regime, as well as an attitude of forgiveness toward those who had participated in the Revolution. Yet an important promise, which apparently the Soviets had decided to keep, was that Rakosi and his associates could not return to the country. My impression of Kadar always was that he had never given up his beliefs as a fanatic Communist. His feeling of patriotism for Hungary, if any, was limited. I knew him to be fanatic, cruel, and a Communist convinced of the eventual victory of Communist ideals.

On November 1st Mikoyan and his associates were far from sure about the Western attitude toward the Hungarian Revolution. They wanted to make certain that in case the Revolution was successful, they would still have a line of negotiation open with Imre Nagy and his regime. At the same time, however, they prepared for defeat of the Revolutionaries. They didn't want to be late with the organization of a Quisling regime, should the United Nations permit complete victory for the Soviets over the Hungarian Revolution. That is why Kadar and his associates were most important in Soviet calculations.

Soviet observers could not help seeing how, during the Hungarian Revolution and the fight for freedom, the Communist Party had fallen apart. It became clear that the majority of the one million members of the Party actually hated Communism and loathed the Soviet Union. The only way to put pieces together again was to try to find a Communist who openly opposed the era of terror created by Rakosi. Kadar was such a man, and a number of Communists looked upon him as the best person to continue Communist rule under healthier circumstances. In order to make this clear, I will have to go into the background of the development of the Communist Party in postwar Hungary.

When the Communist Party, backed by Soviet power, assumed control in 1947, it made every effort to increase membership. By cajoling and threatening people they tried to get everybody to join the Party. This era lasted until 1949. Then, another phase started. During that period the Party carefully filtered its membership. Persons who had obviously joined the Party under pressure, or for opportunistic reasons, were excluded. From that time on it became a special privilege to be a Party member. From an over-all total of approximately 1,200,000, the membership was reduced one-third to about 800,000. Approximately two to two and one-half million Hungarians were in direct contact with the Communist Party in one way or another. During the era of terror under Rakosi, the Communists proudly exclaimed that they were responsible for whatever progress happened in the country. As the years passed all Party members, including ex-Party members, started to realize that they would also be held responsible for the ugly deeds of their murderous leaders.

These were the men who had joined the Revolutionary youth in 1956 without hesitation. Many of them had participated enthusiastically in the actual fighting of the Revolution. Their consciences dictated this action. The origin of the Imre Nagy myth also goes back to the same source. They were anxious to find a leader who was a bona fide Communist, and who could still effect a break with Moscow, leading the country back into complete freedom. There was one reservation, namely, that no one be persecuted for former Party membership.

Even the idea of neutrality, the dream of the majority of Hungarians, had a special appeal to the segment of the population described above. The people felt that the country had always been destroyed as a result of its location between East and West, whenever East and West fought one of their historic battles. For obvious reasons, the mass of ex-Communists and minor Communist Party members were anxious that Hungary should not join any Western bloc. They feared that such an alignment would create an internal political situation where former Communists would be persecuted. Soviet political analysts apparently were aware of the attitudes of these men. That was why they had to find a Communist leader playing the role of a Quisling, who could counterbalance the Nagy legend with a reputation of his own. Only such a person should even try to take up the fragments of the Communist Party structure, shattered during the Revolution. This is why winning over Kadar was worth a few concessions to Soviet planners.

To characterize Soviet tactics it is worthwhile to note a few details concerning the second Soviet aggressions against the Hungarian Revolution on November 4th. This surprise attack was part of a carefully planned scheme. General Maleter, with most of the other top military leaders of the country, was invited to negotiate with the Soviets about their withdrawal. While in Soviet headquarters, he was arrested by the head of the Soviet Secret Police who had arrived in Hungary for that specific purpose. While this plan was put into operation, the Soviet representative at the United Nations, all innocence, suggested that discussion in the U. N. be postponed until the following week so that the international organization would have in its possession, "a more detailed and specific picture." I doubt if there were ever more treacherous, two-faced acts in the history of mankind.

When the Soviet troops poured in, many of them thought they had been taken to the Suez to protect the Arabs against Western aggression. It was hard for them to believe that the Danube was not the Canal. Some others were led to believe that they were in Berlin, they were anxious to find Fascist German generals.

Soviet officers were surprised to find that the Freedom Fighters were determined to take them on, even though their military superiority in equipment and men was obvious. Every house in Budapest became a battlefield, and the gigantic Soviet tanks shelled apartment houses and homes like fortresses. Once again, as in the earlier fights, the greatest source of strength to the Freedom Fighters was their lack of central organization or planning. It was the courage and initiative of the individual, fighting on his own, for his own belief, that made the fight possible. Probably the only organized resistance to the Soviet attack occurred at plants, which the workers defended as fortresses. Two factories should be mentioned as outstanding. The W. M. Works on Csepel Island in Budapest, which laborers defended like heroes. The other was the city in Trans-Danubia Dunapentele, where the Communists had built a major steel plant.

Fights raged all over the country. The backing the fighters received from ordinary citizens was again wholehearted. All homes were opened to the Freedom Fighters as bases of operations and millions of Hungarians demanded in voice and posters, "Ruskis, go home." All over the city this slogan was written on walls and on posters, in Russian as well as in English and German. The workers continued to send delegations to the Kadar government demanding that Imre Nagy be reinstated, that the Russian troops withdraw and that the neutrality of Hungary be respected as well. The unanimous nature of the nation's demands surprised the Kadar regime as well as the Soviet observers. When mass deportations were started, the anger it created made the Soviet military leaders deny that such events were taking place at all. Throughout the desperate days of fighting, the free Hungarian radio stations broadcast on a round-the-clock basis, pleas for assistance, like the following:

"Civilized people of the world, listen and come to our aid, not with declarations, but with force, with soldiers and arms. Do not forget that there is no stopping the wild onslaught of Bolshevism. Your turn will also come, once we perish. Save our souls! Save our souls!

"People of Europe whom we helped for centuries to withstand the barbaric attacks . . . listen to the tolling of Hungarian bells warning against disaster. . . . Civilized people of the world, we implore you to help us in the name of justice, of freedom, of the binding moral principle of active solidarity. Our ship is sinking. Light is failing, the shadows grow darker every hour over the soil of Hungary. Listen to the cry, civilized peoples of the world, and act; extend to us your fraternal hand.

"S-O-S! S-O-S!—May God be with you."

People were simply unwilling to lose their faith in the West. "The United Nations Secretary-General is arriving tomorrow," they told each other on the street. "A committee of U. N. observers is on its way. The U. S. has threatened the Soviet with military action unless they stop the Hungarian massacre."

Meanwhile tens of thousands of Hungarian refugees flooded the Hungarian border trying to escape to freedom. Men, women, and children, wounded, ragged, and dirty, all worn out, brought one message, "Please help." The outside world was generous to these refugees. Love, food, and homes were offered them. The warmheartedness of Austria endeared that little nation to the heart of every Hungarian. As the number of refugees swelled, coming closer and closer to 200,000, the Western world inclined more and more to regard the Hungarian problem as one of refugee care.

Meanwhile, in Hungary, the Kadar regime and the Soviet leaders had to stop their mass cruelty of punitive action. The conscience of the whole free world had been shaken. Kadar pleaded with the workers to go back to their jobs, and while he referred to the Revolution as a Fascist counter-revolution, he still promised general conciliation. Nevertheless, the workers continued their strike, and their armed detachments continued to guard the plants. In about a week a massive Soviet power thrust succeeded in crushing the military resistance. Passive resistance by the whole population continued, however. The Kadar regime was obviously afraid that the fight might flare up at any hour. They promised reforms to the workers and to opposition politicians as well. No one believed them. The mood of the country was one of general desperation, with occasional glimmers of hope. They still could not believe that Western diplomacy would fail to take advantage of Soviet hesitation and force the U.S.S.R. to make concessions through diplomatic pressure.

I am convinced, and so were most of us, that if the West had offered a meeting of heads of states or Foreign Ministers, or other diplomatic steps, they could have settled the fate of Hungary together with the fate of Eastern Europe in a satisfactory manner.

Days passed and we started to feel that possibly the Western world had no such plan ready. Even then, if there was no such plan ready, two weeks should have been ample time to shape a policy. After all, we had done considerable planning and had set up policies in the limited time available to us during the Revolution. It seemed to us that another logical hope was that the future fate of Hungary would influence developments in Poland, too. Meanwhile, the coalition parties of the Revolution started to establish contact with one another, in case the Kadar government resigned or displayed willingness to negotiate. I met Bela Kovacs again. He was somber and worn out, with very high blood pressure. He was a sick, bitter man once again.

"I told you that I have no hope. You don't know the Russians well enough and you don't know the West well enough," he told me. "Well, what's the point of talking about it now?"

The Gray Eminence showed up, too. He felt that the party should organize into one bloc and declare its willingness to accept basic social reforms effected under Soviet rule. Maybe such a sober compromise would salvage the multiparty system.

"Perhaps we should unite even more," he suggested. "Maybe we should accept the new government without an election for a predetermined period of time."

By that time we all knew the details of the plan for the solution advanced by Istvan Bibo, the heroic minister of the Petofi Party. According to this plan, all parties and social organizations should pledge cooperation for a ten-year-period and promise not to challenge or change any of the social reforms.

As late as November 15th, the non-Communist parties hoped that they could salvage most of the achievements the Revolution had fought for. We concluded agreements of cooperation during such negotiations.

As days passed, however, the trend seemed far from promising. The AVO was back, gaining power again, dragging away the leaders of the Workers Councils at night. Youth leaders and other men prominent in resistance became hounded persons. We realized that we were in mortal danger once more. Tildy was permitted to leave Parliament, and, after some time under house arrest, they permitted his wife and him to move to their son's home. He lived in the suburbs of Budapest. It was after great difficulty that I spoke with him on the phone. His voice sounded tired, but he still hoped that negotiations would be permitted. He still tried to believe that the Soviet action had been a fatal mistake, and he asked us to keep in contact with him.

I begged Bela Kovacs to return to the country. I explained to him that I would assume full responsibility for all that we did. After all, he had lent his name and good reputation to the government and the Parliament under pressure. He still hoped, however, that some compromises might salvage the situation and he wanted to use his name and reputation to stop the blood bath. He was ready to sacrifice his own reputation for the interests of the country. His health was rapidly deteriorating under these trials and pressures.

Imre Nagy and his associates, who had fled to the Yugoslav Embassy, receiving diplomatic asylum there, were lured out of their safety with a trick. The Kadar regime promised them immunity and freedom. When their group, including men, women, and children, left the embassy in a bus, Soviet armed units kidnapped them and took them away. We wondered what the role of Tito was in all this. One thing was certain, Imre Nagy, the patriot Communist who became disgusted with Communism and Soviet terror and who had become the courageous Prime Minister of the Revolution, was taken prisoner.

15 • THE SILENCE OF THE GRAVE

Everybody on the street, every friend, warned me to hide and escape. I still was reluctant to do so, for it seemed to me that if a person worked to bring back a multiparty system, he could not leave a sinking boat. I felt I should stay, for our continued efforts might bring about concessions and ease the suffering of the Hungarian people. Thus, days passed, and long difficult nights.

Lonci and I had to stay at the home of a different friend or acquaintance each night. By now, my wife absolutely refused to accept any of my optimistic suggestions. She saw the position of our country as dark and hopeless as it really was. She entertained no hopes concerning the political efforts of the parties or the heroic last stand taken by the workers and our youth. She longed to see her daughter and her mother again.

The Smallholders Party still met. Our meetings were hectic, the risk of attending them frightened the members; nevertheless, we were determined to do everything we could to salvage whatever could be salvaged of the achievements the Revolution had fought for.

We held a meeting on November 23rd. Our aim was to decide what the conditions of the Smallholders Party's participation in a possible new government coalition should be. I will never forget that day, for it was just a month since the Revolution had broken out. It was one of the great moments of history, I am sure, and it certainly was one of the greatest events I will ever live to see. It started the evening before, and early in the morning of the 23rd children were running all over the city with messages:

"Whoever identifies himself with Imre Nagy and the Revolution should stay indoors between one and two p.m. on the 23rd."

The plan caught the people like wildfire. Around noon, the number of persons on the street was smaller and smaller, by one o'clock Budapest became a ghost city. The streets were deserted, every sign of life had disappeared. Soviet tanks were rumbling up and down the avenues looking for the one and a half million persons who inhabited the capital. We checked with friends living in different parts of the city. Everywhere the streets were quiet. Imre Nagy and his government certainly received a unique mandate from the people. For all that we knew he was a prisoner somewhere under mysterious conditions. And still he received a vote of confidence which was virtually unanimous.

This was a silent city, a city of the dead, Budapest, with only the ghosts of the glorious, immediate past to be seen. It was a silent cry of protest against Soviet brutality and a last plea to the free world: "Why don't you come and help us, why don't you chase away the Horsemen of the Apocalypse, the rumbling Soviet tanks, from the streets of Budapest?"

To us, who had witnessed this unique demonstration it was unbelievable that after all the bloodshed, after the desperate fight by our workers and youth, after the mass deportation of our young people as well as the tens of thousands of refugees pouring into the West, the Western world still deliberated.

As the days passed, the Kadar government became more and more definite in its attitude toward the Revolution. Fascist Counter-Revolution became the official expression, and the AVO was reorganized. Even the Western route of escape became more difficult when the Red Army set up patrols near the Austrian border. Armed resistance was finally broken. There were no longer free Hungarian radio stations broadcasting. More and more people realized the terrible fact that we could not expect even political help from the West. The Hungarian people realized that they were left alone. "Poor Hungarian people. But after all what can we do? They are really heroic but they can't expect us to go to war for them." Thus, as had happened so many times in their thousand-year history, the Hungarians were all alone.

I met Bela Padanyi-Gulyas on the street. He looked ragged and torn, which surprised me for he was usually very well-groomed.

"What happened?" I inquired.

He told me that three days ago, he and his wife had started toward the border to Austria. The Russians had captured them. They had been held in prison for two days out in the country. Now they were free and would start for the West immediately.

"You mean after this ordeal you are ready to start again?"

"We certainly are. Even if it takes thirty-three more trips, we will try. Don't you realize that for us there is nothing here but prison? I told you so, I begged you, but you preferred to go on with your own optimistic dreams."

He realized the effect of his words for he embraced me.

"Look, Misi, I don't want to tell you unpleasant things. You behaved wonderfully, you are a good patriot, but for God's sake, don't hesitate any longer. Leave as fast as you can."

Wherever I went people I met put the same question to me. "You are still here? What are you doing here? Escape to the free world and tell them. Tell them all."

"One hundred and sixty thousand have already left," I said. "What is the use of one more?"

"You are more articulate. Perhaps they will believe you. Go ahead, don't hesitate. What are you waiting for? Do you insist on going back into prison?"

When I reached home that day my host was worried.

"The AVO has been searching the neighboring buildings."

"Don't worry," I said. "We are leaving right now. Where is Lonci?"

"She has gone and left this address," he said. "Oh, by the way," he added, "there is one more message, a lady called you and said that you should go to see her immediately, a friend of yours is there, dying."

I left with sad forebodings in my heart. Could it be Peter? I realized that I hadn't heard from him for two weeks. I telephoned Lonci from a public phone and left for the other address. When I rang the bell a woman came out, crying.

"The doctor has just come," she whispered. "A bullet hit his lungs."

We went into the bedroom. It was Peter. I could see he had a high fever.

"You must not talk," the doctor said.

Peter turned to the doctor. "Please . . . I must talk to him."

I shook his hand.

"Don't worry," I tried to say, cheerfully. "You will recover, you will recover in no time."

"You are an idiot, Misi," he answered. "It's all over."

"Don't say such silly things, Peter, life is long."

I realized that these were stupid banalities but I couldn't find any better words.

He answered slowly, and I could see that it was very difficult for him to speak.

"Misi, you are talking nonsense, but you know you still have another duty ahead of you."

"I did everything I could, there's nothing else for me to do anymore," I told him.

"Well then, take Lonci and the child and escape, all of you. Go to the outside world and tell them everything that happened."

He was obviously in pain, and the doctor asked that we stop talking immediately. He gripped my hand and I heard him whisper, "Go, I will watch you." I held his hand firmly, a warm, friendly hand, the best I had ever known or ever would know. His body shook, although he seemed to be dozing. I moved to the door and kept staring at him. By then he was in a coma. He kept shouting commands, garbled words and cries. Then, suddenly, there was silence. I knew that he was gone. I knew that I would never have another friend like him in this life.

When I returned home, Lonci was already crying. Our circle of friends had learned the sad news of his passing over the telephone. Many people were mourning in those weeks. Fathers, mothers, brothers, lovers, and friends died, leaving behind them bitter tears and mourning.

When I saw the Gray Eminence that day he kept me waiting. His handshake was light and I realized that the multiparty system was already a thing of the past. He soon put the fact into words.

"Those who accept Kadar and the leadership of the Communist Party can help to reconstruct the country as non-Party members," he said. "We are willing to sit down with Bela Kovacs and negotiate but," he said with his voice raised, for emphasis, "with Bela Kovacs, the individual, and not the Smallholders Party leader. As for Tildy, he committed grave mistakes, especially at dawn on the 4th," he added, whispering. "And as for the leadership of the Smallholders Party, well, you know yourself that it was organized illegally."

"That's enough," I said, and rose. "There's only one thing illegal in this country and that is the Quisling regime which sold us, body and soul, to Moscow. Its head as well as its members are looked down on in contempt by everyone in the nation."

"Anyone who is of this opinion," he answered, "might do well to leave, as long as it is still possible."

"The whole nation has this opinion, they can't all flee," I answered. "They have to live here—this is their country."

"Maybe some of the leaders could influence this regime," he added quietly.

"This regime," I said with anger and contempt in my voice. "These are the second-rate Quislings. Their actions can only be influenced by Moscow."

"But maybe Moscow can be influenced," he said, "if the right way is found."

"Do you plan to join this Quisling regime in order to influence Moscow?" I inquired. "Aren't you ashamed of yourself?"

"What matters in politics is not whether you are ashamed, but clear reason and purpose. Good heads are needed. And," he added, with a slight sarcasm in his voice, "of course those who will talk loudly in the safety of the outside world will have a wonderful chance to look down on those who stayed behind, to risk their lives with every word they utter."

I realized that there was nothing else for me to say or accomplish, and left. I still had to go and see Bela Kovacs.

When I visited him, I started out without any introduction.

"Bela, I'm leaving. I don't want to go back to prison."

"You do what you think is right," he answered.

"Bela," I said, "you must leave, too."

"Sure, I will leave," he answered. "I will leave for the country shortly. I am just staying here long enough for the negotiations with Kadar."

"Nothing will come of it, Bela. Leave everything and escape to the West."

"I will not leave," he said. "This is my country."

"Maybe you could serve your country better in the West than you can here."

He got up and nervously started to pace the room. Finally he spoke.

"You know what my fate would be if I would escape. Arriving at Vienna there would be scores of journalists surrounding me. They would start asking questions, squeezing me like a lemon for every drop of information. And then, when they had gotten everything, they would throw me away like a lemon which is no longer of any use. No, I won't leave, this is the place for me. I have no reason to feel guilty. What I stood for would have helped not only the Hungarian people, but the Russians and the Westerners as well."

"Bela," I said, "remember the West helps honest Hungarian politicians."

"Nonsense," he answered. "How would they know who is honest and who isn't? Not even we know for sure. Only at the end of life will we know the truth. Do what you want, but please leave me alone, I don't want to go. Do whatever you feel is best and always remain a good Hungarian."

"God bless you, Bela. We understand each other. We both happen to love our country and that's enough."

"Yes, that's enough," he said, quite happily, and he smiled. "It would be less dangerous to prefer fishing."

When I got home Lonci greeted me with the news that a friend from the country had arrived, bringing messages about her mother and our daughter. They were both well.

"Our friend also has a good way to escape."

"Are you ready?" I asked her.

"I am not sure," she said. "You go in any case. I don't know what I will do. You are a terrible man," she said, with a tired smile.

"Well, stay home with Catherine," I replied. "I will help you from abroad, and maybe in a year's time I will be back. After all, things are moving and the world may do something for Hungarians."

"Fairy tales," she said.

On the train I was worried, for if the AVO came along and asked for an identification card my name, with my prison identification, might seem quite a catch for these Reds. When we left, however, there was no slip-up. The train moved slowly in the snowy countryside, it was quiet and unheated. All over the windows there was still scrawled the warning: "Ruski, go home."

It was wonderful seeing Catherine again. She and the little dog Betyar knew very little about events in Budapest.

I went out to the garden once again. I still felt a pang of hesitation about leaving. Why not stay in the country? Why should I expose my wife and daughter to the dangers of the journey? The border guards already have a list with the names of those most wanted by the AVO. I am sure that my name was on the top of that list. If they captured me that would be it. They would hold a spectacular trial, blaming me for taking active part in the Imre Nagy regime. That would mean the gallows or Siberia. How about Lonci and my daughter in that case? These were thoughts which continued to torture me through the night.

In the morning we left for Budapest. When we arrived a friend was already waiting for us. He suggested that we should go to his place, and start from there in the morning. Lonci was still hesitating. "Let's just wait for a little, let's listen to the radio. Maybe some miracle, maybe something happened—"

"No miracles," our friend replied. "More and more Russian soldiers are on the Austrian border. It's getting more and more difficult."

He knew a comparatively safe way. We should start in the morning. The plan was that if he didn't hear from us through Radio Free Europe within two or three days, he and his friends would start searching the prison camps for us. Thousands of little details had to be handled. Lonci wanted to know if she should bring any jewelry. "No," was the reply. "If they capture you it means trouble."

"What will we have to live on?" she inquired.

"Live?" I answered. "I'm not going out there to live. I plan to shout as loud as I can, crying for help. I will visit all the cities of the West. I will try to rally their help and put pressure on their governments."

"A practical plan. A very practical plan indeed," Lonci said sarcastically. "You won't even have enough money for trainfare."

Late at night I called Tildy once again. He was glad that I called. He was no longer optimistic about the chances to negotiate. As for the Gray Eminence, he added, he had promised to visit him but he had never showed up."

"God bless you, Zoltan. You proved yourself to be a man of courage and a good patriot. God bless you for it."

"Thank you, thank you," he said warmly.

Bela Kovacs called me that same night. He had attended a conference with Kadar in Parliament. It was now obvious that there would be no chance to negotiate for possible participation in the government. Kadar, however, promised that his regime would not take any action of vengeance against the parties, the Workers Councils, and the youth, or against any other participants in the Revolution. He would leave for the country, Kovacs added, and planned to come back in about a month. If there was anything urgent we should keep in contact with Tildy. My reply was short.

"Bela, I just don't trust Kadar. I don't believe in all his promises. God bless you."

"God bless you too," he answered.

This was it. I made up my mind. With or without Lonci, I must leave. She said she would decide in the morning. As for Catherine, she liked the idea of traveling. We rose at dawn. I never realized that the Smallholders Party still was so well-organized. There was a car waiting for us, driven by an active member of the party.

"We learned about your decision to escape, it's just in time," he said.

Without saying a word Lonci, too, got into the car with

Catherine. A small knapsack held all our worldly possessions. I could not resist embracing my wife.

"Don't you worry, dear," I said. "Everything will be fine. We will get through. Besides," I added, "don't you remember when you visited me in prison, I promised you at the time that I would take you traveling?"

"You always keep your promises. But my country still stays behind," she answered.

"That's one thing I can't bring out," I answered. "But I can promise you that we will return into a happier and freer Hungary some day."

Early in the morning on November 30th we stood in the Eastern Railroad Station in Budapest. The train was so crowded that people were hanging on the steps. When we passed the mail car, hands reached out for us and pulled us up. There were still crowds there but we could at least stand. The train moved out slowly. As it was winding its way out of the city I couldn't help shedding a furtive tear. I was leaving behind the city I had known from top to bottom, from City Hall down to the underground dungeons of the prison.

The City of Heroes, Budapest: My City!

16 • FAREWELL TO DARKNESS

The crowded train rattled toward Austria; somehow people settled themselves, the women and children found places on the floor or on knapsacks. We didn't speak much, there was so little to talk about. We tried to guess about the future and wondered whether the AVO would search the train.

I overheard some railroad men talking at one station platform. A big, red-nosed man said, "This crowd will finally land in Siberia." His reference, of course, was to the possibility that we would be captured at the border. I glanced at Lonci; she was pale and frightened. The man continued to talk in a loud manner. I felt my face flush with anger. The railroad man must have noticed my expression, for he became embarrassed, not knowing what to do. The awkwardness of the situation was relieved by a man standing next to me who sensed the tension.

"Are we due to arrive in Gyor around noon?" he wanted to know.

The man on the platform started to explain in detail what the train schedule was. They realized the bad taste of their jokes in this situation. They also explained that the railroad men were looking out for the Russian patrols and the AVO men. They tried to time the arrival of the train so it wouldn't coincide with the presence of the dreaded authorities at the station.

"Don't worry," he added. "All the railroad men are with the refugees. They all want to help you."

Suddenly the tall man next to me, who had spoken before, turned to me.

"You don't know me. But I know who you are and that's enough. My task is to accompany you to the border. I will take care of all of you. Later on, we will move to the engine. You and your family will be hidden there. Even if the AVO men search the train, they won't find you."

"Thank you very much," I whispered.

"Don't mention it."

He was off, trying to get some water for Catherine.

In a whisper I explained all this to Lonci, trying to put her mind at rest. About an hour later, when we reached the station at Tata, I noticed our tall friend deeply engaged in conversation with some railroad men. First they talked in loud voices about the weather and similar unimportant subjects, then they spoke in whispers.

After a few minutes the tall man came up to me. He talked to me in a low voice. "The AVO plans to search the train at Gyor, asking everybody for identification. The train will go as fast as it can to get to the station before the patrol, if it's possible. The railroad men are keeping in touch with one another, trying to time the schedule accordingly." Should this scheme fail, however, I could always use his identification papers. He had a legal permit to go to the Austrian border to purchase some lumber, he told me.

"How about you?" I said. "What will happen to you?"

"Don't worry about me, I will just tell them about my relatives living nearby. Don't worry. All you have to look out for is getting through safely."

In a few minutes' time the train stopped. The tall man came up to me, pressed his identification card in my hand and took us up to the engine. There were two narrow pathways on the engine, that's where we were hidden. The engineer asked us not to talk and to lie down flat on our stomachs while we passed the station. It was far from being a deluxe trip. We squatted most of the way, every minute meant a minute nearer to freedom.

Nearing the Gyor station we were warned to lie flat on our stomachs and not to make a move. The engineer told us that according to rumors, an especially strong Russian patrol, combined with an AVO detachment, was going to search the train. The train stopped, and we felt the anxiety of every minute. They seemed like hours. Finally, the train started to move with a jerk. The engineer was happy. He said I could stand up, and he took me to the controls.

"Look out there," he said, pointing out through the window. "We sure pulled a fast one on them."

Approaching the station we saw two Russian tanks and an AVO detachment. The men were armed with submachine guns. There must have been about fifteen or twenty of them. They waved their arms, trying to halt the train. Our friend, the engineer, swore and put on full steam. The train started racing as never before. I saw Russian and AVO officers in uniform in the group.

"You filthy swine," the engineer swore, "you murderers. You killed my son. But your day of reckoning will come."

I was relieved. I knew that there was only one more thing to worry about, and that was crossing the border.

Around three o'clock in the afternoon the train slowed down on the open track and stopped. As if from nowhere my tall friend appeared, helping us with the knapsack and explaining, "We can't go on. The next station is full of AVO men and Ruskis. You'll have to start from here."

I shook his hand and tried to express our gratitude.

"Forget it," he said. "I hope God will help you to reach our friends abroad and shake up their consciences. I hope you will return to us soon."

With this we parted. The rest of the passengers, about two or three hundred people, also alighted from the train. Now we had to head for the fields. What followed was "operation mud". Going through the wet fields, our city shoes stuck deep in the mud at every step. They were certainly not made for this sort of excursion.

The crowd broke up into small groups. I would have liked to join one group which moved fast, their leader obviously knew the area. However, my friend's wife had come with us from Budapest, and I had to help her get through the tortuous path. We must have gone about a mile or so when we heard shots fired in front of us. In a few minutes we reached a railroad crossing. A railroad man was standing there with a bicycle.

"Turn around all of you, you are running into a trap," he shouted. "Don't you see that the forward group has been captured by the Russians? Lie down flat," he said, "the Ruskis will be here in a minute." I disregarded his warning, gripped Lonci and Catherine's hands and pulled them over the rails. Then I helped my friend's wife and daughter. We ran way ahead on the other side of the track at a distance from the rest of the group, hoping that we would not be conspicuous. We still heard the railroad man shouting, warning the others. Then he came over to us.

"Come along with me," he said, "you can hide at my house."

A few hundred yards ahead of us was a small house. It must have belonged to the railroad watchman. Several haystacks stood near the house. When we got there the place was crowded with refugees. The watchman and his wife gave us all hot tea and tried to make us comfortable. More and more people arrived. The watchman hid the newcomers in the haystacks. I struck up a conversation with him. I offered him money if he could get us someone to guide us across the border. "Stay here for the night," he said. "We'll see what happens tomorrow."

We took off our shoes and started eating some of the food from our knapsacks. Lonci had a terrible headache. I made her lie down on the bed. Catherine was excited and thoroughly enjoyed the situation.

"Look, Daddy," she exclaimed, "the stars are falling."

I glanced out the window. The Russians were firing rockets which lit up the whole area. Every time one went up its ghostlike color penetrated the room we sat in. From a distance we heard the rumbling of tanks. We felt tired and frightened.

Suddenly I heard men arriving in front and the clatter of guns. My military training immediately helped me to identify the noise. I could not be mistaken. "So that's it," I said. "The railroad man set a trap for us. It's the patrol arriving now."

I looked around the room, the watchman was gone.

"What is it?" Lonci asked in a frightened whisper.

"Just some guide, I guess, the one our host spoke about."

Lonci pressed her hand into mine and whispered. "These are soldiers. They've come to arrest us."

"Wait. We're not sure yet," I said. I grabbed my pocket knife and the big torchlight. It might be a hand-to-hand fight. I wouldn't sell myself cheaply. I hadn't fought for years, but if necessary I wouldn't hesitate to do my best. Everyone in the room was silent. There was a strong tension in the air. Then we heard the voice of the railroad man from the outside.

"Stay, friends, for a cup of tea. Don't bother about those unfortunate refugees. They are Hungarians too. We are all being punished by God. We have all these Ruskis on our necks."

"Well, that's true for sure," another voice answered. "In any case, nothing can happen at night. They can't start for the border now."

Slowly I walked to the door, opened it a little, and looked out. There were six soldiers sitting outside. I sighed, relieved. They were Hungarian regular soldiers whose sympathy was with the refugees. Refugee women were flirting with them and laughing gaily. Using the ancient weapons once again, I told myself. Apparently they were effective enough, because slowly the soldiers relaxed. They spoke about the reinforced Soviet units patrolling the whole border area. The Russians had sent up the rockets. They had also captured about a hundred and fifty refugees that afternoon and evening.

No, they didn't think we should start now. They would stay with us for a while, and then they would go on as if they hadn't seen us at all. Our host walked by and I grabbed him.

"What's going on?" I asked.

"The soldiers will leave," he whispered. "Then around nine o'clock two guides will come and take you to a farm. You will all go there and stay until it's safe to start for the border. Don't worry," he said, "everyone is keeping a watch on the Russians."

Around nine o'clock the soldiers said farewell. "Good luck," they told us before they left.

The first guide arrived a few minutes later and fifteen of us started out in the group.

It was an icy cold night. The mud froze on our shoes. We were bitter, tired, and desperate. The one exception was Catherine. She enjoyed every minute of this strange excursion. To her it was a game. The man in the front lay down and the others followed suit. No one would scold her for muddying her coat. It was a splendid game, she thought. Lonci was less enthusiastic. She was worried lest Catherine catch cold. Whenever we lay down in the mud she tried to pull the child to herself, so she wouldn't get too wet.

Finally, we spied some lights in the distance. After another weary walk we arrived at the farm. It was a wonderful feeling to be in a warm room once again. The place was full of people, most of them refugees. Two farm girls were sleeping in beds, the rest of us lay down on the floor using our overcoats as a bed.

The guide told us that we could start after midnight. He suggested that we try to sleep and get some energy. Then he turned on the radio. Radio Free Europe broadcasts throughout the night. Our guide listened to it for it provided good information about the Soviet troops which guarded the border.

I tried to comfort Lonci and Catherine. I did my best to tell them some jokes, rubbing their limbs to warm them. Catherine was impatient, she wanted to start right away.

"Where are we going, Daddy?" she asked.

"We are going to Austria, dear," I answered.

"There are no Ruskis there, are there?" she inquired. "And no one wants to put you in prison there. Right?" she persisted.

"That's right, my dear. Austria is in the free world."

"Why can't Hungary be free too?" she said. "I wish she were."

I didn't quite know how to answer that question.

After midnight we started out on the most difficult part of our journey. We had ten miles ahead of us, through cornfields, half-frozen mud, woods, and irrigation ditches. The icy wind chilled us to the bone. It seemed to be an endless journey in the darkness. Every step meant an effort to disengage our feet from the heavy clay and put them falteringly forward. The whole world disappeared in the darkness. We were a small piece of isolated humanity trying to find its way from the known terror into the unknown wilderness. We were tired beyond feeling. Our legs were numb. The knapsack straps bit into our shoulders. I never knew that a small sack could be that heavy. The darkness was broken occasionally by searchlights. This meant that we were pursued and gave us added impetus to move again. Every time the light came near, we lay down in the mud, and listened to our pounding hearts. It took a superhuman effort to get up again. The journey went on endlessly.

The light gray shadow of a road caused our guides to stop. They motioned us to be quiet and listened to the sounds in the night.

I heard them whispering: "Maybe we will make it in time," one of them said.

"Don't you think it better to wait?" the other one inquired.

"The Russian patrol will come the same way. If we stay

they'll get us," the first one said. "If we start and run fast we have a chance."

"Let's go," he said.

We crossed the highway. About two hundred yards beyond it we heard the rumble of tanks.

"Lie down flat," our guide ordered us.

A rocket streaked skyward, lighting up the whole countryside. We hugged the ground trying to melt into the freezing mud. The tanks rumbled by close to us and fired shots at random along the road. The searchlight swung round and round, barely missing our little group. Lonci grabbed Catherine and buried her head under her coat. We waited, terror-stricken, but the tank kept on going, and soon its rumble died in the distance. We jumped up and started to run, gathering all our strength for this final spurt. The guide kept saying:

"Keep on . . . we are very close now. . . ."

In minutes we reached a bare, open area like a half-completed highway. The grass was cut on a strip of land about six yards wide. The ground was smooth. The guides stopped us and told us that this was the border. Here they said good-bye, and told us to head straight for the dim lights in the distance. That was the first Austrian village. We should be very careful to go straight on with no wavering, for the border line zigzagged here, and if we were not careful we might yet land in the arms of a Russian patrol.

"Good luck to you in the free world," they said, and disappeared in the night.

Almost instinctively I crouched down and picked up a piece of earth—the earth of the Motherland. Then I threw it away. There was plenty on my shoes, I thought, and besides my heart was filled with it, filled with the strange mixture of smiles, tears, friends, houses, rivers, hills, birds, trees, and even prisons, all of which combined to make up one's Motherland. I looked back for a final view of this land I loved so much and had suffered so much for, trying to find in this last glimpse a symbol to carry away with me. There was nothing but darkness. Then suddenly I saw a shimmering light in the distance. I do not know what it was, but it gave me the symbol I was searching for. In the oppressive darkness the flickering of a spark which can not be extinguished, and burns for ever like the torch of freedom and eternal hope.

PART THREE · SEARCHING FOR HELP

"Shall I weep if a Poland fall? shall I shriek if a Hungary fail?"

—Tennyson

1 • IN THE IMPERIAL CITY

It turned out that walking in clay and mud did not become easier after the Free World's wet fields were reached. There were still exhausting hours ahead of us. The sun was already rising when we reached a sleeping little Austrian village. Hot coffee, cookies, and above all, warm words and friendly smiles awaited us in the building of the Austrian Red Cross. Our tense nerves relaxed. It was time to stretch our trembling legs for a while. However, I was impelled by my mission. I wanted to meet the leaders of Austria as soon as possible.

Mayoı Theodor Korner of Vienna had given me a book eleven years prior to that, when he was my guest in Budapest. Before starting, I had cut out the front page on which he had written a few words of friendship. These few words had a magic effect, for he was at the time President of the Austrian Republic.

After a few excited and confused telephone calls, we escaped the fate of having to board a refugee train and enter a refugee camp. In a few hours' time we started for Vienna in a car. We were so worn out that we hardly remembered the trip. The next thing I recall was that we were in the room of the Chief of Police of Vienna, where we were given hot tea. A few more questions made it clear that our story was not a hoax, and that I was the legitimate owner of the President's dedication. Soon warm clothing and blankets were given us, and two jovial Austrian gentlemen arrived. They were to be our hosts. A car took us out to a villa near Schonbrunn. Never did I find the prospect of bed so tempting as then. We were all worn out, both

Lonci and Catherine could hardly stand on their sore feet, exhausted by our forced march through the mud. Our hosts were tactful and left us alone.

We did nothing for two solid days but rest.

Lonci was in a very sad mood. She had been crying continuously and felt lonely and dispirited.

I was worried about my own problems. How would I carry out my mission? How would I start? The whole free world seemed incredibly big and unapproachable. I was overwhelmed by the feeling that all efforts were in vain. Certainly, other Hungarians, former refugees, who once played an important role in our country's history, and who were now living in the free world, had already done their best, but had failed. How could I move the free world? How could I start it? I had an idea but I felt it was too bold and unconventional.

"And now," Lonci asked, "what do you intend to do now?"

"To carry out my mission," I answered firmly.

"You are a hopeless dreamer," she answered in a tired voice.

"Maybe I am, but I am still determined that the world can and should help Hungary. It is not too late, the flame of Hungarian freedom has not died out yet."

Lonci sighed. She did not answer. I had to encourage myself and her, too. I told her in a few broken sentences about my idea which I believed would work—which must work, because it was a very simple and a completely new approach—I would get the help of the free governments in an indirect way and would appeal to the great capital cities of the free world, asking them to issue a solemn declaration for Budapest.

As I discussed it with her I became enthusiastic. I felt that I had really found the key to the problem.

"Listen," I continued, "after the capital cities have issued a solemn declaration, public opinion will be electrified again, as it was during the revolution. As a result of this, the governments will have to act—to protest—to come forward with new ideas in connection with Hungary's freedom. The United Nations will have an extraordinary meeting."

"And Hammerskjold will go to Hungary with sword in hand and challenge Khrushchev to a duel," she interjected in a sarcastic voice.

I was slightly offended, and accused her of lacking faith in my projects, which, however, generally turned out successfully.

"Good luck to you," she told me. "There is no one who wishes more than I that you will be able to enlist the help of the free world.

"No one wishes to see her country free more than I do," she added, with a catch in her voice.

I pondered over my plan for hours and hours. I felt that it would work.

After two days rest, I decided to fall back upon my rusty German and explained to my hosts that I had not come there to rest. I had a mission, and that was to arouse the world to help Hungary. They expressed their sympathy, but explained that Austria's position was precarious. She was a neutral country and the Soviet Union was already attacking the Austrians for helping the Hungarian refugees. They had to confine their help to humanitarian assistance, but they couldn't permit any political action. When I explained to them the details of my project, rallying the help of the great cities of the West, they were more at ease. Apparently they preferred this type of plan to party politics.

Vienna seemed almost a Hungarian city by then. We heard Hungarian spoken all over the place. I hadn't been there for ten years and at that time, part of the city was still under Soviet occupation. This seemed to have dampened the enthusiasm of the people for clearing away the rubble of war. Now, however, Vienna was free, with splendid shop windows, traffic, and a spirit of optimism and welfare characteristic of that city. Now Austria's great magnanimity in helping the Hungarian refugees was really touching.

In the good clothes we had received from our hosts we enjoyed the feeling of belonging again to well-dressed, decent society. A few days later I met Anna Kethly, the only cabinet member of the Imre Nagy regime who was here in Vienna. I was delighted to see the beautiful elderly lady who had spent a lifetime fighting for her political beliefs. In the process she had come to know the Nazi, as well as the Communist prisons. She, too, was determined to do everything possible to mobilize the free world for Hungary. When I told her about my plan concerning the free cities she was excited, and made arrangements to introduce me to the Mayor of Vienna, Mr. Jonas, who, like Miss Kethly, was a Social Democrat.

Mayor Jonas was helpful and offered to bring me into contact with the International Union of Local Authorities at The Hague. At this point two problems appeared for the first time. One was a legal one: Could official organizations deal with me as Mayor of Budapest? My answer was that I was a former Mayor of Budapest, who had been reelected during the Revolution. While this meant a great moral endorsement for me, I never considered presenting myself, after fleeing, as actual Mayor of Budapest. The free world, however, was worrying which regime should be formally recognized, that of the Revolution, or the Quisling regime which had taken over. It was hard for me to understand that, seeing a small nation bleeding itself white, the free world would concern itself with legal formalities. Anna Kethly helped me. She declared that if they didn't accept Kovago as the Mayor of Budapest then she would not be regarded as a cabinet member of the last free Hungarian regime. After all, she explained, our mandate originated from the same source, the Hungarian people.

Mayor Jonas gave his backing and got in touch with The Hague in connection with my project.

The second problem was the matter of travel expenses. I had no money whatever, and although I had written to some friends in America, I doubted that they could supply me with funds for such purposes. I knew no organization. During many years in prison I had lost contact with everyday life, and with everybody inside and outside of my country. I had no rich relatives anywhere. Furthermore, I learned that the International Union of Local Authorities was rather limited in its finances. Although my hosts hinted that, if the worse came to the worst, they would try to raise the money, I was anxious to avoid accepting such additional magnanimity. Meanwhile Lonci was feeling ill and Catherine had a high fever. Life looked far from rosy.

Many Hungarian refugees wanted to see me. I respected the request of my hosts and did not invite any of them to their place. However, I came across quite a few people on the street and was delighted to meet some Smallholders Party leaders, too.

It did not take long to find out that unfortunately the unity of all Hungarians, which was so striking during the Revolution, did not exist among the refugees.

I did not want to get into factional disputes, and I was happy to have my own project. I had come to the free world to continue our common fight against the Soviets and Communism.

I heard stories about nonpolitical American organizations giving relief to refugees. To me all this seemed remote. Europe was close and real. The United States seemed far away and vague. I met a young Hungarian priest who had lived in Vienna for many years. He helped me by putting my petitions into good German. However, he had no financial means, either. I met another Hungarian who had lived in Vienna for many years. This man was somewhat skeptical when I told him about my plan. I decided not to give in, and told him the details with all the enthusiasm I could muster. This was after lunch in his house. He listened to me patiently and then said:

"There's only one person and one organization who can help you. The person's name is Dr. Marcel Faust, and the organization is the International Rescue Committee."

I had heard Dr. Faust's name quite a few times before; he helped numerous Hungarians without regard for their religious or political beliefs. The organization's name was new to me. My Hungarian friend said that we should go to their offices without delay, for one of the vice-presidents of the organization was in Vienna just then and it might be a good idea for me to meet him.

"Do you speak any English?" he inquired.

"I speak some," I answered. "For four years I learned English from the *Encyclopaedia Britannica*," I told him, jokingly.

I could see the surprise on my friend's face.

That same day he took me to meet Dr. Faust and the vice-president of the International Rescue Committee, Mr. Joseph Buttinger. I tried to use my best Padanyi-Gulyas and Encyclopaedia Britannica-style English in explaining my project. Apparently I succeeded in explaining what I wanted, for Mr. Buttinger answered that the plan sounded interesting, and that the International Rescue Committee would consider it. He would discuss further details with me later on. We agreed that I would need an interpreter to accompany me to The Hague, someone fluent in two or three languages. I was quite impressed by Mr. Buttinger. I realized that he was a man of lofty intelligence and qualities of heart, too.

The next day I met him again. In simple words he explained to me that the International Rescue Committee, which is not a political organization but an organization maintained by free American citizens to help refugees everywhere, wanted to make my trip to The Hague possible. They were convinced that, through my plan, they would be able to help the Hungarian people, too. I was completely taken by his magnanimity. In Hungary we sometimes used to think that Americans were cold businessmen who had no use for sentiment.

My plan evolved in the following form: I would ask the cities for a solemn declaration of their solidarity with Budapest. If in addition they should raise funds for the rebuilding of Budapest, they could deposit the money in their own banks or in an international bank. When Budapest was free again, they could then erect new buildings with the funds. I cherished the hope that all the large cities of the free world would come forward with offers to build a new school, a hospital, a nursery, or some other structure. All the buildings designed in the varied architectural styles of the donors would be erected in a certain part of Budapest, and would proclaim to future generations the magnanimity of free men throughout the world.

It was not easy to find the right person to be my assistant. The new refugees were out, for none of them had the fluency with the languages which was a "must." The old refugees were skeptical and some were cynical. They did not have the enthusiasm we needed. Finally, of all people, it was a young poet whom I selected. Lonci's parents had known his parents.

When I met the young man in a coffee house I inquired if he was the same person, J. C., whose parents had been good friends of my wife's parents. In a cold tone he inquired whether I wanted to meet him or his parents. His understanding was that I wanted to interview him to be my secretary, not his father, who is dead. I liked his answer, for I don't believe in judging people through the merits or faults of their parents. When I finished explaining my project, he inquired what my interest was in pursuing this project.

I became red with anger and he said, "Please don't be angry. We agreed to speak frankly."

"Well," I answered more calmly, "I want this to benefit my

country and not myself. I don't want to collect money but I want them to reconstruct Budapest."

"When?"

"When Budapest is free again," I answered. "I am convinced that a solemn declaration by the cities will prompt the governments into action."

"A nice plan," he answered. "I am glad to meet an unselfish man."

"This is not a matter of unselfishness," I answered. "To live according to one's own code of honor is, in the final analysis, the greatest selfishness. In this interpretation I am selfish. I would be the happiest man in the world, however, if I could help my country to be free again."

He liked my answer and explained that he spoke and wrote English, French, and German. Translation was his hobby. He had no permanent job, for he was a poet. After all, he added, this damn world needs poets more than businessmen with bulging pockets. He would be glad to come with me to The Hague and to do his best.

"And, by the way," he asked, "who supplied the money?"

"An American organization," I answered.

"And what do they want for it?"

"Nothing. They just want to help the Hungarian cause."

"That's hard to believe," he muttered. "Did they pat your shoulder when they took out their checkbooks?"

"No," I answered. "In fact, they were very tactful."

"That's new," he said. "Here in Europe, Americans have a different reputation. They think they can buy everything with money. They brag, they are loud, and they put their feet on the table."

"I agree with you that that's their reputation," I said. "But I haven't seen any of this."

The next few days were spent in preparation for the trip. Memorandums were written and translated into three languages.

I saw Anna Kethly once again. She was to leave for the United States. Her intention was to appeal to the people of the U. S. and to the government for aid to Hungary. She asked me to come with her. I explained to her that all the preparations had been made to pay a visit to The Hague, and I felt that reaching the European governments was important, also. I had to decline her invitation.

She told me she would try to arrange it so that we would have an opportunity to appeal to the U. N. in the name of Hungary.

Our hearts went with her as she carried our hopes to the greatest nation in the world.

Christmas was getting near. After eight years, this was the first Christmas I would spend with my family. Vienna took up the Christmas spirit; all the shop windows and streets were decorated. Catherine recovered and she enjoyed window-shopping in the city. Lonci was still a pessimist and worried considerably.

"Let's get away from here," she said.

For days she had been worrying about some suspicious characters who were hanging around the house. One day I received a threatening letter. Apparently, the arms of the rats were long.

"Let's get away from here," Lonci repeated.

"Where to?" I asked.

"To the States," she said. "It's no good to stay here. We have lost our country, but we did not lose our fear."

"We can't go to America yet," I said. "We have important tasks in Europe."

"It's no use," she said. "Europe is weak. Our only hope is in America."

Soon the city was full of rumors about the pending visit of Vice-President Nixon. He was to arrive to examine the question of refugees and the Hungarian problem generally. Many people in Vienna were anxious to see him. I would have liked to have met him, but I realized that, with all the top politicians and leaders of large organizations, who had excellent connections, my chances were very slim. In any case, how could the Vice-President of the U. S. receive a refugee politician?

I mentioned my desire to Mr. Buttinger. He said that he would use his own connections as well as those of the I.R.C., and perhaps I would have a chance to meet Mr. Nixon. In any case, he suggested I should have a memorandum ready.

Just before Christmas, Mr. Nixon arrived. He did not believe in protocol. The first night after his arrival he went out to the Austrian-Hungarian border.

On December 20th, the U. S. ambassador called me. He informed me that the following evening Mr. Nixon would receive me. That would also be the occasion for me to present my memorandum.

The next evening I was there in the ambassador's study where many people surrounded a dark-haired young man. His informal behavior impressed me immediately. When I was introduced to him, in a few English sentences I expressed my thanks to him for receiving me. I then suggested that we continue our discussion through an interpreter. Mr. Nixon, however, told me that he understood me quite well, and we could continue in English without an interpreter. He started by asking me a few questions.

He wanted to know if I understood the moral dilemma that the U. S. was facing. If they gave special help to the Hungarian refugees, then more and more people would leave Hungary. That would mean a very serious loss to my country. If they didn't give the refugees their support, they would be in an impossible moral position. I was quite surprised by this question, for I never saw the facts in this light. My answer may have sounded naïve, for it was along the following lines:

The U. S. was strong enough to solve the whole Hungarian

question. If the primary problem, that of the fate of the country, was solved, the refugee question, which was only a secondary problem, would take care of itself.

Then I handed my memorandum to the Vice-President and he ended the interview with a friendly smile.

After Mr. Nixon left, Vienna relief organizations handling Hungarian affairs received help from the U. S. Government. He became a champion for raising the Hungarian refugee quota.

The day before Christmas I accepted an invitation to address five hundred refugee Hungarian students. I felt touched when I rose to address these young heroes. I spoke from my heart, informally, and concluded by saying, "Wherever life takes you, remain Hungarian in your hearts. Be good and hard-working citizens in your new countries, but don't forget your motherland, and do everything in your power to help her regain her freedom. From now on, what you have to give is not armed fight or heroism, but study with perseverance and diligence. God bless you all."

Christmas Eve was spent with our hosts. There was a tree, a real Christmas tree, and we lost control of our emotions. I had to speak in my broken German in that emotionally charged atmosphere. I doubt if my grammar did justice to Goethe. I think it was one of the worst yet, and one of the most effective speeches I ever gave. Tears were in everyone's eyes.

Christmas Day we went to church and felt very sad. We prayed to the Lord to return freedom to our small nation. That's what we did, and that's what Hungarians did all over the world.

2 • THE HAGUE, PARIS, LONDON

On the second day of Christmas, accompanied by J. C., I started for The Hague. There they put us up in a small jewel of a hotel behind the Royal Palace. I soon learned to like the Dutch national character which is level-headed and kind with a keen sense of humor. Both Mr. Arkema, Secretary-General of the International Union of Local Authorities, and his deputy, Mrs. Revers, liked my project, but emphasized the fact that the Union was anxious to avoid introducing politics into its agenda. On the other hand, they were anxious to do everything they could for Budapest. They promised to present my project, with their recommendations and a favorable opinion to the Board. The Board would meet in the Spring. Mr. Arkema explained that my project was closely connected with international politics. Should the great Western Powers take a positive stand, then the International Union would probably follow suit. By the same token, if the Western attitude was negative, the project itself would meet with considerable difficulty. I spent two days as a guest of the Union, visiting nearby cities.

One night we were invited for dinner at an old windmill, the inside of which had been made into a modern restaurant. Suddenly the telephone rang. It was a long-distance call for me from the United States. An old friend who had been one of my commissioners in Budapest when I was mayor, was calling from the States.

"Leave everything there and come to the United States," he told me.

I explained my project as briefly as I could, and told him that I couldn't consider leaving before that was finished.

"You should come," he answered. "You will be too late if you delay. New headline news will occupy the interest of the public, and the Hungarian problem will not be so pressing later on. The Special Committee of the U. N. is scheduled to meet very soon. You should arrive in time and be among the first to testify."

I could sense the importance of this news, but I could not believe that the Hungarian cause would soon be forgotten.

When I returned to the table my Dutch hosts were anxious to know why I had been called from the United States. They all agreed with my secretary, that I should finish my task in Europe, and offered their help in every way they could. They promised to arrange a visit to Paris and London.

Returning to Vienna, I arrived just in time to wish Lonci a happy New Year. Full of optimism, I tried to talk to her about a free Budapest and the success of my plan.

"You are a hopeless dreamer," she answered. "Besides, I think I agree with your friend in America that your place is there where they direct the destiny of world politics."

The invitation arrived from Paris, indicating that another invitation to London was on the way. The same evening another message reached us from the States, inquiring about the date of my arrival and asking me to go to the United States Consulate to arrange for my travel documents. My secretary, who was always faithful and helpful, seemed reluctant to help me with the trip to the U. S.

"You will leave," he said, "and never return to Europe. All the talented people leave this continent," he said bitterly.

My Austrian friends also reached me, offering the hospitality of their country. They were sure that, as an engineer, I could find a suitable position there, and I would still be close enough to Hungary. Lonci once again brought up the mysterious characters who loitered around the house. They seemed to have been there all the time.

"Let's go to America," she said. "As long as we fled to get away from prison or the firing squad, why not choose the freest and happiest country of all?"

I stopped over in Munich and visited Radio Free Europe. I met several old friends, and we discussed the role Radio Free Europe had played during and after the Revolution. I expressed my appreciation for their accurate news coverage and for all the assistance they had given to the cause of freedom.

After a few days we left for Paris. I had been a great admirer of French culture all my life and always felt moved when I arrived in the City of Light. The reception I got this time flabbergasted me. A special reception committee waited for us when we arrived in the beautiful suite of one of the great hotels, flowers from the Mayor of Paris and city officials awaited Lonci. The environment was royal, with flowers all over the place. I couldn't help but muse upon how life changes. Six months ago I was in prison in Budapest and now all this. Lonci's reaction was even simpler.

"It's a shame to say so, but I would exchange all these gorgeous flowers for the simplest one from our own garden at home."

No doubt homesickness is a serious challenge to all of us. I learned in prison that one carries his own country in his heart. Even so, it was not easy. I did not try to comfort Lonci, for I knew I couldn't.

Soon Mr. Buttinger arrived and informed me that the U. N. would give the floor to Anna Kethly, General Kiraly, and to me. We fixed a date for my trip to the States. Mr. Buttinger offered his own home in New York for my two months' stay. I was deeply moved by all this kindness.

We left for our official reception in a motorcade with motorcycle policemen accompanying us. It was a glorious parade for a poor exile down the Champs Elysees. Traffic was stopped everywhere and I hope the proud Parisians forgave me for the inconvenience. All pomp and circumstance was ours. The French have a noble tradition in giving the best of these. I was slightly nervous about my speech in French. I knew how sensitive the French were about their beautiful language.

The reception itself was full style with numerous representatives of French public life present. I received a beautiful engraved bronze plaque. On the back of it the history of Paris was engraved in beautiful miniature. The inscription said, "To Jozsef Kovago from Paris." I felt deeply moved by this honor.

That evening there was a dinner in our honor. Lonci looked beautiful in her new dress from Vienna. Suddenly, during the dinner, she rose and started to leave the room. Her face was deadly pale, and she looked at me apologetically. We were all surprised and puzzled. When she reached the door, out in the corridor, she collapsed and fainted.

Everyone went to her assistance and, in a few minutes, she revived. The evening, however, was ended, for it was obvious that she needed a real rest. Our hostess warned me that I should give Lonci a chance to rest and suggested we spend a few days in Paris. I had to refuse, explaining my commitments, and telling her regretfully that as much as I would like to, I couldn't stay. Before leaving Paris, we received an official answer that the city would introduce my project at the coming meeting of the Board of the International Union of Local Authorities.

We arrived in London by air. I had to face my first press conference in English and a television interview.

We were guests of the London County Council. Mrs. Helen C. Bentwich, a charming lady, was the chairman of the L.C.C., and the whole reception was far more than I dared to expect. I was received in the study of the building of the L.C.C. The same day we were invited for lunch at the home of Sir Cullum Welch, the Lord Mayor of London, whose efforts to help Hungarian refugees were well-known.

The next few days in London were unforgettable. I met many leading public personalities and quite a few old friends. I was once again impressed by the British, their patience, and their sense of humor.

Catherine insisted on making friends with the elevator man and traveled up and down at least fifty times a day.

During the five days I spent in London, we never mentioned the Suez incident but often thought about it. Many Westerners presumed that we Hungarians blamed the British-French-Israel action for the suppression of our Revolution. This sounds logical to persons who don't live in Eastern Europe. To those of us brought up in that particular corner of the world, the whole action seemed like part of an over-all strategic plan. After it was over, we felt that if those who decided international policies had more imagination, then neither Hungarian freedom nor the prestige of Westerners in the Near East would have been lost. In our eyes this loss of prestige had helped a semi-Communist dictator to gain power.

A few days later we said good-bye to our British hosts. We shook hands warmly with my poet secretary, who said:

"Tell the U. N. everything. Don't try to be nice. Don't forget our little Hungary."

In a few minutes we were on the plane starting for the New World.

I felt very strange. This plane would take me to a big, strange land, which I did not know much about and expected so much of. I was crossing another big border. After seven years in prison, it was strange to cross so many borders. From prison to freedom in my own country, from Hungary to Europe with all its friendly compassion, were big steps, but they were familiar to me. Now I was leaving my Motherland in a broad sense, the whole European community. Previously I had never strayed, nor even tried to think beyond its frame. My whole upbringing, schooling and discipline were so typically European that it was very difficult to realize that I would be living outside of this world of my father, my teachers, and my culture. Still I felt that I must take this step to find the answers to the burning problems of my country. I felt as if I was taking the bleeding heart of Hungary with me.

We had failed in our effort. The diplomacy of the free nations, the resolutions of the U. N. did not achieve anything, but if I could just describe to the U. N. firsthand experiences, what really happened in Hungary—if we, the few remaining representatives of the only legal government of Hungary, the government of the Revolution, could testify and acquaint the world with the brutal injustice and cynical defiance that had taken place, the conscience of the U. N. would be so aroused that even the Soviet government would have to retreat.

This was the most important task. For this I was willing to leave home, country, and continent. This task dwarfed in importance all the previous plans for helping free Budapest. Without success in this present endeavor there would be no Free Budapest for a long, long time.

I turned to Lonci.

"Well, this will be quite a trip. Are you happy that we are going to America at last?" I asked her.

"You know well that's hard to be happy anywhere but at home. At least in America we will live without fear," she answered.

3 • THE CHAMBER WAS EMPTY . . .

We were flying over the Atlantic in a fast, modern plane. It was a rather rough flight and I showed Catherine what to do in case of airsickness. She was annoyed, exclaimed that she loved the flight. Lonci, on the other hand, felt extremely ill.

Meanwhile, my neighbor, a well-dressed American lady, was sleeping happily. Obviously a seasoned traveler, she had put on slippers for the evening and had a black kerchief over her eyes. While she slept, one of her arms fell over my shoulder. Soon her head followed. Very carefully, to avoid awakening her, I turned back to Lonci. She was awake and smiled, which by the way, was the only time she smiled on the long Atlantic crossing. Whispering, she said, "This is a good omen."

Soon, however, the plane dipped jerkily into an air pocket, and the young lady stirred and turned in the other direction. We spoke to her later during the flight. She was Inez Robb, a well-known columnist on her way back from the Austrian border. I had the pleasure of reading her articles later on and appreciated her good words for the Hungarian cause.

Before long we were arriving. The gigantic city of New York unfolded for us and in a few minutes we landed at Idlewild.

The reception was heart-warming. The smiling faces of old friends dissolved any feeling of strangeness in those first minutes in America. Anna Kethly greeted me warmly, and I was especially happy to see the faces of former city colleagues in the welcoming party. I was introduced to several distinguished people including a former ambassador, Angier Biddle Duke, President of the IRC and Leo Cherne, Chairman of the IRC. There were also newsmen and photographers, and flashbulbs were popped but the over-all tone was one of extreme friendliness.

I hardly had time to shake hands with most of the people before I was ushered into a limousine dispatched by New York's Mayor Wagner. We drove to Mr. Buttinger's apartment which was to be our first home in America.

Lonci and Catherine, both tired and worn out, soon fell asleep. I was too excited to sleep. It was hard to believe that I was in New York. I tried to rest, but when the moon came out I felt myself drawn to the window. Below me was Central Park, radiant in the light of a full moon. In the background were the contours of the skyscrapers, like huge building blocks set up by playful giants.

I can not remember distinctly the days that followed. I was overwhelmed by this great country and virtually besieged by my compatriots.

The day that stands out in bold relief, however, was the one when I was received by Mayor Wagner of New York in the City Hall of the greatest city of the world. The mayor of the city apparently wielded greater power than rulers of several small countries.

I had many discussions with leaders of different exiled Hungarian groups and was particularly interested in the opinions of the former political leaders of my country, who had lived for several years in the U. S. I also met several old friends who, though they were not politicians, could give me a picture of how this part of the world felt. The picture was not very encouraging. They said that while we had the sympathy of the entire free world, we could not expect much beyond that. They thought that we were already late. The Hungarian Revolution had been written off as a current political asset, and had become a case for charity.

I did not believe this. In the past I often resented the fact that the political leaders who had been forced to flee earlier had never achieved much in the free world for the cause of our country. I was convinced that I had to do better. After all, we who escaped after the Revolution were representing not only the parties which opposed the present Russian-backed regime but the entire nation. Our country, in its greatest spontaneous ballot—the Hungarian Revolution—had voted Communism out of existence, sealed its will with the blood of its youth and was trusting us to deliver this forceful message to the free world. It was beyond the scope of responsibility of any free nation to assume this problem. It was up to the conscience and guiding principle of the whole world—the U. N. This body comprises all nations, large and small, and it is the duty of each to see that justice is done. The collective responsibility involves shouldering responsibility rather than shying away from it!

I was burning with anticipation, preparing my speech day and night; putting my whole heart into it, and also the heart of the ten million Hungarians languishing in the new Communist dungeon.

The day finally came, when our delegation, Anna Kethly, General Bela Kiraly, and myself were to present testimony to the Special Committee of the U. N. in the great chamber. Anna Kethly gave her testimony on the first day while I was still working feverishly on mine, making last-minute changes, to bring out important points so that it would convey everything I felt I had to say.

January 28th was a bright winter day, but I could not see much of the streets or of the people. Finally I stood in the Chamber to deliver my message to the entire world. It was very quiet when I started. I was so impressed by the tremendous importance of the moment that I could hardly find my voice and did not dare to look away from the prepared text of my speech. It took a superhuman effort to start to speak:

"Mr. Chairman, members of the Committee," I began.

"I was deeply moved when I crossed the threshold of this imposing building which houses the most prominent political body of the world, the activities of which are followed hopefully by hundreds of millions.

"We Hungarians feel that mankind looks to the United Nations for the answer to the burning question: do the governments, whether they represent a small or large nation, have to submit to maxims, based on moral principles, or may the jungle law of the stronger be permitted to reign uncurbed? The answer to this problem hinges on the case of the numerically small but spiritually great nation to which I belong.

"I have come to give testimony . . ."

I paused for a moment, and glanced up to note the reaction to my introduction.

The chamber was almost empty. The delegates and spectators must have gone to witness the arrival of King Ibn Saud of Saudi Arabia.

My poor, tortured little country. . . . You are all alone!

EPILOGUE

Obviously, neither the Hungarian problem nor my story ended with my testimony before the U. N.'s Special Committee. By the time I had concluded my speech, the visitors and delegates had returned, and this attentive audience was visibly impressed by the tragic facts I had to present to them.

It is a matter of historical record that the U. N.'s Special Committee and the General Assembly tried valiantly, but without success, to intervene in the brutal oppression of Hungary. It is also a matter of historical record that the Hungarian puppet government continues to follow the Moscow line and has added to its ignominious behavior the executions of Imre Nagy, of General Pal Maleter, and of a large number of Hungarian patriots.

In the months that followed, I travelled extensively throughout the United States with the help of the IRC. Wherever I went I was received with friendship and understanding by the warmhearted people of this country, by mayors of cities, governors of states, and other distinguished personalities. I felt honored by these receptions and by the keys of various cities that were given to me; but what really attracted me to this country was its sincere sympathy toward my nation and its cause.

I felt that the friendship of the American people and of its government would be a great asset in the endeavor which I intended to carry on in behalf of my nation. I met old friends, made new ones, and was able to establish a home for my family.

My original plan to seek world-wide assistance for the rebuilding of a future Free Budapest had to be shelved, for practical plans must await the solution of political problems. Still, I hope that when the appropriate time comes, the many friends of Budapest will help me to realize my dreams.

In 1958 I was sent by the Hungarian Committee on a goodwill tour to South America. I visited Brazil, Argentina, Uruguay, Chile, and Peru. The purpose of our delegation was to present the Hungarian cause and to discuss the threat posed by Communism. The declaration of Lima, the capital of Peru, as the sister city of Budapest was one of the memorable highlights of this tour. I will never forget the touching sympathy and deep understanding on the part of the South American people and their leaders for Hungary. It made me feel that this growing continent will always be a staunch supporter of our common cause.*

In 1959 I took part in another goodwill trip as a member of a delegation of the Assembly of Captive European Nations.† We visited most of the countries of the Far East, the free nations of Asia, and Australia. During this tour we offered testimony to those countries which are prime targets of Communist imperialism, that small nations will be ruthlessly swallowed up unless they gird themselves with the spirit of true democracy. Space does not permit me to enumerate all the places we visited, nor the warm receptions we were accorded during this trip of more than 40,000 miles. It is difficult to describe what my feelings were while visiting these places, or while receiving the keys to the cities of Tokyo and of Manila, or while seeing the mani-

* The Hungarian Committee is an organization consisting of former democratic political leaders of Hungary, now in exile. It is the spokesman for Free Hungary. Its chairman is Mngr. Bela Varga; its vice-chairman is Jozsef Kovago.

† The Assembly of Captive European Nations is composed of free representatives of nine Eastern and Central European nations now under Communist domination. Member nations are: Albania, Bulgaria, Czechoslovakia, Estonia, Hungary, Latvia, Lithuania, Poland, and Romania.

festations of the oriental culture which, a few years ago, were just part of a faraway dreamland.

In India I had the honor of meeting the great leaders of the country and the privilege of a private interview with Prime Minister Javarhalal Nehru. I have often wondered whether he recalled our conversations during the brutal suppression of the Tibetan revolt, which came a few weeks after my visit.

A momentous event occurred at the end of our trip when, in Rome, the Holy Father, Pope John XXIII, gave us and our nation his benediction.

Now I am back again in this quiet suburban community in Delaware, where, among friends and neighbors, I hope to find peace and inspiration. The joy of being home again has been marred by the tragic news that Bela Kovacs, one of the greatest Hungarian patriots of our time, was hounded to death by the Communists. His spirit will guide us Hungarians, at home and abroad, to continue our quest for freedom.

CPSIA information can be obtained
at www.ICGtesting.com
Printed in the USA
BVOW10s0759290517
485402BV00021B/927/P

9 781314 784299